W9-DAV-959

UNDERSTANDING THE CHINESE PERSONALITY

UNDERSTANDING THE CHINESE PERSONALITY
Parenting, Schooling, Values, Morality, Relations, and Personality

William J.F. Lew

Chinese Studies
Volume 6

The Edwin Mellen Press
Lewiston•Queenston•Lampeter

3-14-99
120

20

Library of Congress Cataloging-in-Publication Data

This book has been registered with the Library of Congress.

ISBN 0-7734-8298-9   (hard)

This is volume 6 in the continuing series
Chinese Studies
Volume 6 ISBN 0-7734-8298-9
ChS Series 0-88946-076-0

A CIP catalog record for this book is available from the British Library.

Copyright © 1998   William J.F. Lew

All rights reserved. For information contact

The Edwin Mellen Press   The Edwin Mellen Press
Box 450   Box 67
Lewiston, New York   Queenston, Ontario
USA 14092-0450   CANADA L0S 1L0

The Edwin Mellen Press, Ltd.
Lampeter, Ceredigion, Wales
UNITED KINGDOM SA48 8LT

Printed in the United States of America

In memory of

my beloved brother Tien Shin, a selfless intellectual

TABLE OF CONTENTS

✦   ✦   ✦

TABLES

Page

Page

✦ ✦ ✦

FOREWORD

People throughout the world seem to share an instinctive belief that the Chinese as a people have some distinct and unique characteristics. This is understandable in part because the Chinese are the products of one of the world's great civilizations. This also, however, means that there are well entrenched stereotypes and myths about the Chinese, which are not based on evidence, but are being perpetuated by people who have never met a Chinese. Americans, for example, have long had two contradictory images of the Chinese: the one is the good and wise Chinese, the Charlie Chan, and the other is the bad and threatening Chinese, the Fu Manchu. Which image dominates at any particular time usually depends upon the state of political relations with China. Thus, during the Pacific War Americans developed a very positive view of the heroic Chinese nation resisting their Japanese invaders. Then came the Cold War era and the view of the Chinese Reds as implacable enemies. After the Nixon opening, Americans instantly reverted to the image of the good Chinese, which was, of course, dampened by Tiananmen.

Behind the shifting images of the Chinese there was also an enduring view of a sophisticated Chinese culture, based on the wisdom of Confucianism. That is until Mao Zedong inspired the Chinese people to turn themselves into fanatical revolutionaries. China was then cut off from the rest of the world by the Bamboo Curtain. The picture of shouting Red Guards waving their Little Red Books, of masses of drably dressed people mindlessly repeating slogans, and of single-minded cadres compulsively introducing politics into every aspect of life, all suggested that the Chinese people had somehow been transformed into a new breed of people. Then came the opening and the sudden surge of visiting delegations, who all came back to report that the Chinese were still "Chinese" even though they had adopted some novel practices. The world was left puzzled, as it had been before, as to what to make of the Chinese. What are they really like?

The Chinese themselves have not been all that helpful, for as a people they have not in modern times engaged in much detailed self-analysis or collective introspection. When Chinese have written about themselves they have advanced dual images that are not so different from the contradictory ones held by Americans. There has been the good and wise Chinese as described, for example, by Lin Yutang in his gracious essays honoring of a wonderfully sophisticated, relaxed, and humane culture. But there has also been those who seem only able, to find fault with Chinese national character; as for example, China's most famous modern novelist, Lu Hsun, who ruthlessly depicted Chinese national character in scathingly negative terms. A similar harsh judgment of the personality of the Chinese was advanced in the 1980s by Bo Yang in his *The Ugly Chinamen* tirade. It seems almost as though the Chinese, if they cannot idealize their culture and their ways of behavior, feel compelled to denounce themselves in the most extreme fashion.

Bluntly put, foreigners have not had many reliable places to turn in order to get a trustworthy reading of the Chinese national character. Now, however, Professor William J. F. Lew has come up with a solid, data rich analysis of Chinese in China, Taiwan, Hong Kong and the United States.

His analysis is framed in the context of his years of research and teaching in the four site areas, and more particularly it is based on 21 qualitative and quantitative studies, involving standardized questionnaires and interview schedules with statistically significant numbers of respondents. His work thus combines the qualitative skills of a sensitive and keen-eyed participant observer with the methods of rigorous, quantitative social science.

Lew's approach means that he is able to dissect Chinese character from a wide range of angles and perspectives, and thereby identify key personality traits, basic predispositions, and fundamental value orientations. His study probes Chinese socialization practices, particularly family patterns and school experiences. Although some slight differences were found in the responses of the Chinese living in the different places,, the results on the whole provide solid ground for making some significant generalizations about all the Chinese studied. A small but paradoxically interesting finding was that in spite of the efforts of the government in Taiwan to preserve Chinese traditional culture and of the authorities in Mainland China to destroy that culture, it turns out that the mainland respondents, on some of the scales, revealed attitudes about authority that were closer to the presumed Chinese traditional view of authority than those of the Taiwan respondents. However, more significant was the general finding that the generational differences were greater than the geographic, thus giving support to the idea that modernization has had an effect on Chinese character.

Not surprising was Lew's finding that the most dominant Chinese trait is a strong sense of authority-directedness. Chinese seem greatly concerned with authority, looking to it for support and guidance, but also being quick to complain if it fails to perform properly—or to reward those who have behaved properly. Lew is concerned with the durability of democracy in Taiwan because of this authority-centered characteristic. A second major characteristic which is also not surprising is that the Chinese manifest a high degree of achievement motivation. Indeed, intense concern about getting ahead, both academically and commercially, is a major theme that appears at numerous points in his various studies.

More surprising was his discovery that narcissism is a dominant trait of the Chinese he studied. Their socialization experiences seems to make them not just determined to get ahead, but also to be acutely aware of their virtues, and thus to feel that they deserve to be recognized and praised for how good they believe they are. The intense socialization pressures both in the family and at school seem to have the dual effect of making the Chinese both authority-directed and narcissistic, and thus somewhat thin-skinned about criticisms and quick to point blame toward others. Indeed, it seems that the dominant Chinese family pattern of a demanding father and a supportive mother contributes to this combination of traits. Lew, however, also found that there are other complex patterns of mixing hard and soft treatment by fathers and mothers, but the general results are a blend of disciplined behavior and self-assurance.

Some of the lesser but still significant traits that were identified include: perseverance, dependency, dominance, emotionality, aggressiveness, double-facedness, and snobbery. He also found that the Chinese tend to place a high value on power (in such forms as status, prestige, authority, wealth and dominance over others), followed by security, conformity, benevolence, and respect for tradition. Although Lew is totally disciplined and objective in his research, he is not afraid to make judgments. On the whole he is respectful of the Chinese, but he also does not hold back in criticizing many of the traits he found. He is particularly critical of the Chinese educational system with its heavy emphasis upon examinations and rigorous screening, and its lack of concern for the development of the whole person. Some Chinese may want to reject his personal criticisms but they cannot ignore the bulk of his findings.

The strength of William Lew's book does not lie solely in his empirically based generalizations about Chinese character traits, or in his personal judgments; it is also to be found in the mass of data that came out of each of the separate studies he conducted. Readers can examine the reported responses for themselves and draw further conclusions. In this respect, the book has the quality of being almost a reference work. Such a perusal can stimulate questions about how the respondents might have reacted to different queries and to further probings. Hopefully this will inspire further studies, and thus this pioneering book will encourage the growth of solid social science studies of national character along the lines that Alex Inkles called for in the 1960s, but which then seemed so daunting that it killed interest in national character as a subject of systematic study. Professor Lew has set appropriate standards for such work.

Lucian W. Pye
Massachusetts Institute of Technology

✦ ✦ ✦

PREFACE

Understanding the Chinese people in the context of culture is instrumental in studying and/or understanding any aspect of Chinese society, such as Chinese politics. Perhaps Professor Pye(1988) was right when he criticized the Chinese for their lack of a willingness to engage in critical self-analysis. This is the first book based on empirical study to present a detailed and in-depth analysis of the Chinese people in general and the educated Chinese in particular. This book differs in contents, methods, and style of presentation from Lin Yutang's *My Country and My People* (1939), Francis Hsu's *Americans and Chinese* (1981), and Michael Bond's *The Psychology of the Chinese People* (1986).

I was born and raised in mainland China. I have also lived and worked in Taiwan and Hong Kong. Few Chinese or non-Chinese have had such an opportunity to observe the Chinese people and their culture. My experiences in the three Chinese societies have contributed to my insight into the Chinese people and to my interest in studying them empirically. I began to notice the differences between Chinese and Americans when I first visited the United States as a student in 1954. Then in 1972 when I accepted an invitation from the East-West Center in Honolulu to spend a year there as research fellow, I had a notion that to study the Chinese people might be a significant thing to do for two reasons. First, the Chinese make up one-fifth of the world's population; there are Chinese everywhere who may be the reader's neighbors or colleagues. Second, China is emerging as a world power whose influence no one can afford to ignore.

In the academic year 1977-1978 when I had a sabbatical leave from the Chinese University of Hong Kong where I had been teaching since 1973 until I returned to Taipei in 1987, I developed a dream to study Chinese personality at Harvard University. I was then an Honorary Research Associate at Fairbank Center for East Asian Research. This dream gradually materialized over the years after I returned to Hong Kong and later to Taipei. Starting in 1983 till 1995, I collected data in mainland China, Taiwan, Hong Kong, and the United States with a questionnaire I devised and through biographical interviewing, participant observation, and personal communication.

The Chinese people are often misunderstood or wrongly stereotyped by people in other lands. As a matter of fact, there are all kinds of people in Chinese society as in other societies. Yet I must admit that the Chinese, in comparison with Americans whom I have been observing since 1954, seem to possess some negative or undesirable traits in greater degree. I more or less share the view of Lu Hsun (Lu Xun), the author of *The Story of Ah Q*, a widely translated Chinese satire. Lu Hsun quit his medical training to become a writer in order to save his country by remedying through literature the weaknesses he saw in Chinese national character. I, too, have observed that there has been something wrong with the personality of many Chinese people, including the dignitaries and commons, the educated and less educated, which, along with other factors, seems to have been accountable in some measure for centuries of poverty, ignorance, corruption, dictatorship, civil wars, and power struggles. On the positive side, the Chinese are a highly intelligent and achieving people. Their intelligence and achievement motivation have promoted economic growth first in Hong Kong, then in Taiwan, and now in mainland China. It follows that my research project on which this book is based has a two-fold aim:

to help people in other countries to understand the Chinese and to call attention of my compatriots to the necessity of preserving the positive traits and preventing the negative traits in personality development of future generations through proper parenting and schooling. It is hoped that this book will be a token of my service to the intellectual world in general and to my beloved country in particular. By my country, I mean the *whole* China, including Taiwan, Hong Kong, and the mainland.

The whole research project on which this book is based consists of 21 component studies as shown in the table of contents. The book has eight chapters. The introductory chapter describes the whole project including purpose, sampling, instrumentation, data collection, and data analysis plan. Chapter Two through Chapter Seven report the 21 studies in detail. The last chapter presents conclusions of the project and an overall discussion of the major findings and their implications. The book is intended for nonacademics as well as academics, for nonspecialists as well as specialists. The research was more qualitative than quantitative. The statistical analyses used in some quantitative studies were relatively simple so that most readers can comprehend them. Some of the research designs and data analysis plans were original and indigenous. The approach of the present project was anthropological and sociological as well as psychological. In case the reader is not interested in every chapter of the book, I am sure that he or she will find at least several chapters interesting.

I am most grateful to my late elder brother Tien-shin and his wife without whose arrangements I would not have left the Chinese mainland and, therefore, would not have the opportunity to write this book. In writing this book I have been given much emotional support by my wife Hannah and my three grown-up children David, Catherine, and Henry, and my nephew David. Henry also bought me a computer and taught me how to use it, which facilitated the writing of this book.

Catherine and Henry both assisted me in the publication process. My long-time mainland friend Chou Yi-bai, after separation for 34 years, escorted me during my three research trips in China. Lucian Pye of MIT wrote the foreword for this book. Thomas Berndt of Purdue University and Ovid Tzeng of Yang Ming University reviewed my manuscript. Kuo-shu Yang and Kwang-kuo Hwang of Taiwan University, Alan Liu of the University of California at Santa Barbara, Michael Bond, Leslie Lo, Kit-tai Hau and Ping Chung Cheung of the Chinese University of Hong Kong (CUHK), Harry Triandis of the University of Illinois, Shalom Schwartz of the Hebrew University of Jerusalem, and John Feldhusen of Purdue University read portions of the manuscript and offered valuable comments. Alan Liu and Thomas Berndt also gave me much moral support. Dean M. Chin of Chengchi University game me much encouragement. Kit-tai Hau, my friend and former student, did most of the computer analyses for me. Yale University Press, Norton, Sage, Caslon, Jossey-Bass and Associated University Presses have considered my work and made useful comments or suggestions that led to subsequent revisions of my manuscript and eventual offer by the Edwin Mellen Press to publish it. I am grateful to them.

I am also grateful to the National Science Council of the Republic of China, the CUHK's Center for Contemporary Asian Studies and New Asia Ming Yu Foundation for their research grant. Finally, I am indebted beyond my capacity to repay to all the friends and students who have helped me in data collection and all the persons who have participated in the research as interviewees, informants, and respondents to my questionnaire.

William J. F. Lew (known in Chinese as Lui Juin-fu)
Taipei, Taiwan, March 1998

✦ ✦ ✦

CHAPTER ONE

INTRODUCTION

To understand China is essential in studying or doing business with China and its people. The 21st century will witness increasingly close interchange between China and other nations. No sensible person can afford to ignore China's growing influence in the world community. China's influence is further enhanced with the emergence of *Da Chung-hua* or "Greater China" (Harding, 1993). Greater China in a cultural sense or cultural China consists of mainland China, Taiwan, Hong Kong, and Chinese communities throughout the world (Tu, 1991). As Shambaugh (1993) points out,

> The post-Cold War world is witnessing the reconfiguration of international relations with the emergence of new actors and relationships on the world stage. These new actors and patterns of relations are reshaping familiarities of the post-war era. ... Among the new realities of our era is the emergence of "Greater China."
> ... Greater China comprises various actors, dimensions and processes. Together they pose a potential challenge to the regional and international order. Some already speak of Greater China as the world's next superpower. If the political obstacles can be overcome and China reunified under a single sovereign authority, it is likely that superpower status will become a reality.(p. 653)

To understand China, or rather, Greater China, we must understand its people and culture. This is the first book about the people and culture of Greater China with cases and samples drawn from mainland China, Taiwan, Hong Kong, and the

1

Chinese community in the United States. In this book the Chinese people are seen through their personality types and traits in the context of culture, the Chinese culture is seen through its major components---family, school, values, morality, and interpersonal relationships. This book reports, as Purdue University psychologist Thomas Berndt says, "the broadest and most in-depth investigation of Chinese personality to date" (personal communication, December 13, 1995). The University of California-Santa Barbara political scientist Alan Liu predicted in a letter (February 21, 1995) that this book "will definitely have an impact."

Chinese culture is authoritarian and Chinese society is hierarchical. Rather than situation-centered (Hsu, 1981), social-oriented (Yang, 1981), tradition-, inner-, or other-directed (Riesman, 1961), Chinese culture and society may be more properly described as authority-directed (see Study 3 in Chapter 4). Whoever possesses authority or greater authority has the power to control, influence, or dominate people without authority or with lesser authority. When people fail to agree among themselves, it usually takes the authority figure to settle the differences. The authority figure may be the parent, teacher, boss, judge, policeman, government official, or the person in a higher political or social position. As a rule, Chinese people seldom take the initiative to act for common good beyond routine duties unless required by the authority figure. The higher ones authority, the greater power he or she has. Of all types of authority (intellectual, moral, social, etc.), political authority is the most influential and powerful. News coverage on TV or in the newspaper in Taiwan, for example, is often dominated by the activities of the high-ranking government officials, particularly the president. Even though the first popularly elected president Lee Teng-hui of the Republic of China on Taiwan repeatedly claims that the sovereignty is vested in the masses and people are his bosses, he is still the highest authority without whose sanction no crucial controversy (e.g., education reform or constitutional amendment) can be settled although he does not possess the absolute authority of an emperor in ancient China.

"Personality develops in the context of culture, just as culture only exists through the thoughts, feelings, and behaviors of concrete people" (Westen, 1985, p. 299). Culture refers to all man-made things, such as art, law, belief, custom, and institution (Fernandez, 1975). Personality is primarily shaped by culture although heredity affects it to some extent. As the items in various personality measuring instruments indicate, personality encompasses behaviors, cognitions, feelings, attitudes, beliefs, and preferences (Werner & Pervin, 1986). A personality trait is defined "as a person's average level of response over a given range of situations" (Zuroff, 1986, p. 997). A trait often occurs in a group of individuals within a culture. Traits are useful in describing, evaluating, explaining, and/or predicting behavior. Personality types are categories of personality. A type is useful in describing persons with identical or similar traits.

Chinese personality or national character has both positive and negative traits (see Study 3 in Chapter 4). This book is a research report of a large project which was broken down into 21 component studies as covered in Chapter 2 through Chapter 7. It is intended for any person who seeks a correct understanding of the Chinese people, a people with both strengths and defects in character that are hypothesized to have a tremendous impact on China's national development. For efficient reading, I invite the reader to start with this first (introductory) chapter and the last (concluding) chapter before reading other chapters. These two chapters can serve as a guide to read the rest of the book. The reader may read for life enrichment or career advancement the whole book or only those chapters/studies that interest him or her.

Sample and Method

To let the reader know how I drew my samples and how I collected and analyzed my data, a brief account of my research methods is in order. During the

12-year period (1983-1995) of my research, the methods I used included questionnaire survey, biographical interviewing, and participant observation, similar to those used by many behavioral scientists. I also collected data through correspondence with my informants, and through case reports and discussion reports as assignments for the students in human development classes I taught at the universities in mainland China, Taiwan, and Hong Kong. Content analysis and simple statistical analyses were applied to my data. The diverse methods and statistical analyses used are explained in the report of each of the project's 21 component studies covered in the chapters. Further explanation is provided in the appendixes.

More than 3000 educated men and women of various ages were administered the questionnaire by myself or by my friends and students in the four Chinese societies, which produced four regional samples somewhat randomly drawn. The biographical interviewing and participant observation were all done by myself. Of the 2640 who completed and returned the questionnaire, 925 (662 males, 263 females) were from 22 provinces in mainland China, 651 (398, 253) from Taiwan, 787 (442, 345) in Hong Kong, and 277 (178, 99) in the United States. There were more men than women in the total sample because more men than women, especially those from rural areas, received higher education in Chinese society.

The age of my subjects ranged from 19 to 91 (mostly from 20 to 65). They had at least two years of college education. Most of them had four or more years of higher education and were working as teachers, engineers, researchers, administrators, and civil servants. Some of them were graduate and college students. Those in the United States were Chinese studying at major American universities or working in various parts of the country, most of them came from Taiwan and the rest from Hong Kong and mainland China. Some of my Taiwan and Hong Kong subjects had been abroad to study or travel. Almost all my mainland subjects had never left their homeland; they were "pure" mainlanders.

The reason I chose educated persons or "intellectuals" (in the broad Chinese sense) as subjects is two-fold: First, they are more knowledgeable and influential than the less educated people. Second, they play a decisive role in determining the destiny of China. Although my subjects were primarily educated people, I acknowledge that the less educated Chinese also exert their influence on national development as Nathan and Shi (1993) inferred from their findings of a survey. My data on less educated or uneducated Chinese were collected from two sources: (1)through my own observation as participant in the daily activities of my compatriots regardless of educational level and (2) through the reports of my educated subjects by analyzing the relevant information they provided in interview as interviewees or in assignments as students in the class I taught.

Most prior works on Chinese personality used American or English instruments with high school or college students as subjects (Yang, 1986). The instrument I used was the questionnaire I devised, namely, the Multi-Trait Personality Inventory (MTPI). The issue of importing measuring tools versus developing indigenous instruments is related to the emic-etic (culture specific-universal) issue (Berry, 1969; Yang & Bond, 1990). The need for a Chinese language instrument may be accounted for by the fact that (1) there is no recognized personality measuring tool designed for the Chinese people; (2) the Chinese language versions of Western instruments fail to fully convey the exact meanings of the original language as a result of translation; and (3) some expressions are found in English but not in Chinese, and vice versa. So I began the work of devising an indigenous tool during the academic year 1972-73 when I was a Fellow at the East-West Center in Honolulu.

I revised the preliminary instrument and constructed in 1980 the Multi-Trait Personality Inventory (MTPI) with 122 bipolar items in the Chinese language.

Assisted by Michael Bond, social and personality psychologist at the Chinese
University of Hong Kong, the English version of the MTPI (see Appendix 1) was
produced by back translation (Brislin, 1980).

The MTPI is both emic and etic as it includes both culture-specific (emic)
Chinese trait names and the universal (etic) trait items found also in Western
cultures. It has three parts. The 122 bipolar items constitute the bulk (Part II) of the
questionnaire, which also has a part (Part I) securing information on the subject's
identity, family and childhood experiences including his or her father's and mother's
child-rearing attitudes and behaviors. Part III of the questionnaire has an open-ended
question asking the respondent to describe the types of personality of educated
Chinese he or she has observed. The MTPI has two responses for each of the 122
items measured on a 6-point scale. The first response is self-perception and the
second response is the subject's perception of other educated Chinese, thus yielding
a "self" score and an " other" score respectively. In most analyses with the MTPI
data, only the self score was used. The other score was only used for comparison
when necessary.

In order to find what is common in all educated Chinese, wherever they are,
all subjects in the four samples were placed in the same factor analysis. We tried 4,
5, 8, 9, 10, 11 factors and finally settled at nine factors because as determined by the
scree test (Cattell, 1966) the 9-factor structure seems to be the most adequate for the
Chinese personality so far as our four samples are concerned. Although the Big Five
has been claimed to be the universal model (McCrae & Costa, Jr., 1987), we agree
with some researchers (McAdams, 1992; Mershon & Gorsuch, 1988; Noller, Law,
& Comrey, 1987) that the 5-factor theory has limited usefulness and further research
is called for to use more specific and more informative factors to cover the
ever-enlarging personality sphere. Some statistical information concerning the MTPI
is provided in Appendix 2.

Our nine factors are Introversion--Extraversion (E), Negligence--Self-Discipline (D), Democratism--Authoritarianism (A), Dominance--Submission (S), Adventurism--Cautiousness (C), Self-Orientation--Other-Orientation (O), Dependency--Independency (I), Traditionalism--Modernism (M), and Healthiness--Neuroticism (N). Conceptually, our E, D, M, and N are similar to Extraversion, Conscientiousness, Openness to experience, and Neuroticism respectively in the Big Five. Our A, S, and O are conceptually related to Agreeableness in the Big Five. And our C is a specific Chinese factor while tangential to both Agreeableness and Openness to experience. Yet our Independency (I) seems to be a specific independent dimension of Chinese personality. Our nine factors were also validated against Cattell's 16 PF with a Hong Kong sample (238 graduate students including 118 men and 120 women) and we found the MTPI's convergent validity satisfactory (see Appendix 3).

In addition to questionnaire survey, I spent much time in biographical interviewing (Levinson et al, 1978). I personally interviewed more than 200 of the 2640 MTPI respondents including 120 in mainland China and the rest in Taiwan, Hong Kong, and the United States, each for an average of two hours. Some of them were interviewed two or three times because they had more to tell. I also observed as participant in various activities of my compatriots in the four societies. I corresponded with some of my mainland subjects whenever I needed further information.

Additional data were gathered from case reports written by graduate students and group discussion reports submitted by graduate and undergraduate students attending my classes at universities in mainland China, Taiwan, and Hong Kong. Michael Bond once told me in person that I have "a gold mine of data." In order not to waste my data, I have presented them in rather great detail although I have cut down my original ten chapters of some 150,000 words to the present eight chapters of about 100,000 words. All the raw data. including completed questionnaires, students reports, interview and observation protocols, are available for scrutiny or further analyses by interested colleagues.

Structure of Presentation

There are eight chapters in this book. This introductory chapter gives a brief account of the book's contents, its purposes, and research methods used for the project on which this book is based. The research project comprises 21 small studies, more qualitative than quantitative, reported in Chapter 2 through Chapter 7. Chapter 2 consists of three studies on parenting patterns as related to the child's personality development. It provides evidence concerning various parenting patterns and their impact on the child's personality development that has never been reported before. The emphasis is on the effect of socialization by both mother and father in a joint manner instead of one parent only, usually the mother.

Chapter 3 reports three studies on family, school, and personality, from which the reader can gain further insight into Chinese personality and culture. One study concerns family harmony as related to parenting and the child's personality. The other two studies concern educational practices and educational reform, which provide evidence to contradict Stevenson's (1992) argument that Americans should learn from Chinese education. Chapter 4 comprises four studies on personality types and traits of mainland, Taiwan, and overseas Chinese (Chinese in Hong Kong and the United States) and of Chinese in general. It gives a whole picture of Chinese personality or national character with data drawn from diverse Chinese populations at home and abroad. One of the studies dealt with the differences in Chinese personality due to differences in geography, gender, and perception.

Chapter 5 provides two studies on life span personality development, one with Hong Kong cases and the other with mainland cases. The two studies tested the validity of Erikson's theory of eight stages of personality development. The results supplemented as well as supported Erikson's theory. Six studies make up Chapter 6 which explores relationships between values and personality. This chapter also looks at values and personality from various angles including mate preferences, ambitions and aspirations. It demonstrates that Chinese culture is neither predominantly collectivist nor generally individualist, it is about 60% collectivist and 40% individualist. It also reveals 69 Chinese values which may be categorized into eight of Schwartz's (1992) ten universal value types with social power as the most dominant type of Chinese values.

Morality and interpersonal relationships are the two themes treated in Chapter 7 which contains three studies. The two themes are closely related because morality is both the outcome and process of reciprocity between the individual and others in the social environment. This chapter identifies the stages of moral judgment and moral behavior of the Chinese in terms of Kohlberg's theory. It also explicates the nature of ten interpersonal relationships (e.g., parent-child, teacher-student, heterosexual relationship) in Chinese culture.

In the concluding chapter, a summary of the major findings is provided and the implications of the findings are discussed. The findings have a wide range of implications, particularly for international understanding, cultural ideology, national development, social change, child-rearing and educational practices, and future research on personality and culture. One important implication is that power struggle in Chinese politics will continue between the mainland and Taiwan as well as within the two Chinas. The reunification of the two sides of the Taiwan Strait is unlikely in the foreseeable future. Another important implication is that China or "Greater China" can never be optimally developed or modernized unless proper reforms are made in her authoritarian parenting and inflexible schooling.

I have tried my utmost to let the evidence talk in this book and not to let my patriotism bias my investigation. I suspect that my compatriots might challenge me for having not painted a brighter picture of the Chinese people and their way of life as reflected in parenting, schooling, values, morality, and interpersonal relationships. But I am optimistic about China's future development because the Chinese are exceptional people of unrealized potential (Pye, 1985) and China's potential for optimal development is tremendous.

✦   ✦   ✦

CHAPTER TWO

PARENTING PATTERNS AND
THE CHILD'S PERSONALITY

The importance of family influence on the child's behavior and development is evidenced by the fact that as much as 30% to 100% of the environmental variance and 15% to 70% of the phenotypic variance in personality, cognition, and psychopathology lie within families (Daniels & Plomin, 1985; Rowe & Plomin, 1981). Measures of family environment in fact typically assess behavior of parents (Plomin, McClearn, Pedersen, Nesselroade & Bergeman, 1988). While research in family influence, especially in socialization or child-rearing practices, has been widely conducted by psychologists, anthropologists, sociologists, educators, psychiatrists, and political scientists in the West, notably in the United States, similar internationally published work by researchers in Chinese societies is relatively scarce (Ho, 1986, 1989).

The direction of effect in almost all early studies of socialization was considered to be from parents to child (Walters & Walters, 1980). Since Bell (1968) marshaled evidence and argued that parents both influenced and were influenced by their children, research in socialization and parent-child relations has shifted more or less from a unidirectional model to a bidirectional perspective that emphasizes the reciprocal nature of human interactions (Brunk & Henggeler, 1984; Mink & Nihira, 1986). No matter which model or perspective is prevailing, the influence of parents or caregivers cannot be discounted. Although the child is born with a need to engage the environment, the nature and consequences of the initial transactions depend on

11

the responsiveness of the parent or caregiver (Estrada, Arsenio, Hess & Holloway, 1987).

Furthermore, the direction of influence may be different in different types of family. In a study of direction of effect Mink and Nihira (1986) found different directions of influence between the family and the child in different family types. Their analyses resulted in three family types; namely, the learning-oriented, the achievement-oriented, and the outer-directed. A cross-lagged panel analysis (Kenny, 1975) revealed that with the learning-oriented families, the child influenced the family. With outer-directed families, the child's self-help skills influenced parents, but parents influenced the child in higher level skills such as social adjustment, motivation, and competency in community living. With achievement-oriented families. however, the family or parental behavior influenced the child's behavior in all significant panels. In other words, Mink and Nihira (1986, p. 614) found that

> the general direction of effect was different in each family type and that only
> in the achievement-oriented family was the flow of effect in one direction
> only: from family to child. In other two family types, the flow of effect
> varied and depended on the variables involved.

I am particularly interested in the achievement-oriented family because it happens to resemble the average Chinese family. Even in mainland China where the one-child family policy has been implemented since 1979, most parents hit their children. The reasons given are that the child does not do home work, plays too much, is disobedient, or, most commonly of all, gets low grades at school (Davin, 1990). This sounds like the modal family in the achievement-oriented type which values control (Mink & Nihira, 1986), as control or discipline is a distinct feature of child-rearing practices in the authoritarian Chinese culture. Mink and Nihira (1986, p. 612) described the achievement-oriented family as follows:

In the achievement-oriented families, parents defined many different types of activities (e.g., school, work, play) in terms of competition. These families were organized in a hierarchical manner and family rules were enforced and tended to be rigid.

The intent of the present chapter is to report a research comprising three separate but related studies, two being qualitative and the other quantitative. It aims to provide empirical data for ascertaining the influence of parental behavior on the child's personality. Two features make the present investigation different from most prior studies: (1) Instead of studying one parent as socializer, this research explored the influence of both parents socializing at the same time in a joint manner. (2) Instead of using children, adolescents, or college students as subjects, the present work had educated Chinese men and women of various ages as informants in the small discussion groups (Study 1) and in the retrospective interview (Study 2) for the two qualitative studies, and as respondents in the questionnaire survey (Study 3) for the quantitative study.

Study 1 was based on the personal experiences and observations of the participants in small discussion groups at two Chinese universities. From it we will get an overview of the parenting styles in mainland China and their effect on the child's personality. Study 2 provided information derived from case study of the interviewees in mainland China and Taiwan to illustrate the major socialization patterns of both parents and their influences on the child's personality development. The purpose of Study 3 was to supply some simple quantitative data on joint parenting and related variables to supplement the two qualitative studies.

Since children's perceptions of parenting are highly predictive of personality and adjustment (Plomin et al, 1988; Rowe, 1981) and retrospective perceptions of childhood family environments are important in investigating long-term effects on personality and adjustment (Plomin et al, 1988), the present research used the subject's retrospective perceptions of parenting along with contemporary perceptions of their own behavior and personality in examining the relationship between parenting and the child's personality. We might think that one's personality is related to his or her perceptions of family environment, but this is not the case. As Plomin et al (1988) point out, correlations are low between the Family Environment Scale (FES) measures and major dimensions of self-reported personality questionnaires. It was expected, therefore, that the present research would yield some meaningful results.

STUDY 1

PARENTAL BEHAVIOR AND THE CHILD'S PERSONALITY

In this study we had 159 informants. They were 75 men and women (juniors, seniors, graduate students, and teaching assistants) in two departments (Education and Psychology) at one university in Chekiang province and 84 men and women (sophomores, juniors, graduate students, and instructors) in one department (Education) at another university in Fukien province. Both provinces are in southeastern China.

The informants were given a series of questions concerning parenting in mainland China for discussion. The questions included (1)What are the discipline techniques used--induction, love withdrawal, power assertion, positive reinforcement, and/or just ignoring or neglecting? Which is the most common? Which is the most effective? (2)Give any new model and/or cite an observed case to verify the existence of any of the eight parental behavior models--overprotective or overcaring, overpermissive or overindulgent, hostile or repulsive, restrictive or controlling, hostile and restrictive, hostile and permissive, loving and restrictive, and loving and democratic. How many models do you find? Which model is the most common? Which is the least common? (3)Does parental behavior varies with the child's sex, age, birth order, number of siblings, and other factors? (4)Does parental behavior varies with the parent's age, personality, level of education, and socioeconomic status? What are the differences, if any, between father's and mother's behaviors? (5)What are the child's personality traits commonly found under each of the eight parental behavior models? For the last question the subjects were referred to Lew (1982) for some hypothesized traits derived from Conger (1973) of children socialized under each of the eight models.

While I taught as visiting professor of developmental psychology the two classes of students (informants) at the two universities in mainland China, Lew (1982) was used as a textbook. A major assignment of the course was a group discussion report on Chinese parental behavior. The students as informants discussed in small groups the questions mentioned above in class under my supervision. Each group had at least five but not more than ten members, and was required to turn in a report recording the discussion. Content analysis of the reports was performed. All responses, opinions, or observations as contents of the reports relevant to the above questions were taken into account. Only those that found consensus in two or more reports were singled out for presentation as follows.

Seventeen group discussion reports were collected, seven from the university in Chekiang and ten from the university in Fukien. According to the reports, the following observations were made in at least two discussion groups, most of them appearing in more than one-third (six) of the reports, which indicates a consensus of quite a few participants in the group discussions.

1.   All the common discipline techniques found in other cultures are observed in mainland China, notably induction, love withdrawal, and power assertion. Scolding and physical punishment are very common. Negative reinforcement, especially rebuke, is used much more often than positive reinforcement, especially praise. A parent may employ one or more techniques, but one of them is generally used more often than others.

2.   The most effective discipline technique is induction coupled with

principled power assertion when necessary.

3.   All the eight parental behavior models or patterns are found in Chinese families. The most prevailing pattern in the one-child families, especially after 1979 (Croll, Davin, & Kane, 1985; Jiao, JI, & Jing, 1986), is that of overindulgence or overpermissiveness. The most common model in other families (with two or more children) is that of love and restriction. The one-child family policy is more effectively enforced in the city than in the countryside.

4.   In large families with four or more children, parents may be either permissive or restrictive; one or two of the children may be favored. In small families with one or two children, indulgence and/or overprotection are common practices. Hostile or repulsive parents are rare in China, except in some families of discord.

5.   The parental behavior model considered best for the child's optimal development is the democratic or authoritative type.

6.   Parental behavior changes as a function of the child's age (Ho & Kang, 1984; Roberts, Block, & Block, 1984). Chinese parents are usually overprotective, overcaring, restrictive, and authoritarian during early and middle childhood of the offspring. When the child approaches adolescence, parents gradually allow him or her more autonomy, freedom, and independence. They gradually decrease the frequency of hitting, scolding, or frightening the child when he or she is about twelve years old, especially when realizing the ineffectiveness of such practices.

7.   Chinese parents demand the first-born more strictly and expect of them more highly, requiring them to set an example for the later-born. They are more permissive or neglectful to the middle child and more indulgent to the youngest child. As a result, the eldest child tends to be introverted and sophisticated, the middle child extraverted and adventurous, and the youngest child naughty and willful.

8.   In general, a male child is preferred to a female one, who will sooner

or later be married off to become a member of a different family. Thus a son is also expected of more than a daughter.

9.   High-achieving, good-looking, intelligent, obedient, and/or cheerful children are favored by most parents.

10.   Socialization patterns and techniques vary with parental age and personality. Older parents are generally less strict and controlling than younger ones. The impulsive and emotionally unstable parent is usually more authoritarian and uses power assertion more often than the patient and emotionally stable parent. The latter is generally more democratic and rational than the former.

11.   The under-educated parents (those who have never reached secondary school level) treat children more extremely; they are either too punitive or too permissive. They tend to use material reward when reinforcing children. The well-educated parents (those who have attended college) are more democratic and rational. They employ verbal and moral reinforcement as well as material reward. Almost all the well-educated people live in the city.

12.   Although socioeconomic status (SES) is deemphasized in Communist China and it is not so differentiated as in a capitalist society, it does exist and exert its influence on people's lives. As a rule, the higher SES parents have higher expectations for but are more permissive to their children than lower SES parents. The middle-class parents treat their children more properly than both higher and lower SES parents.

13.   Although "strict father , tender (or kind) mother" is the prevailing joint parenting pattern when both parents are considered, the situation is made easier for the child by three factors: (1)father has less time to spend with the child; (2)mother shields the child from father's intervention; and (3)the rising feminism reduces the father's authority.

14.   Fathers are more controlling and punitive to sons while mothers are

more demanding and restrictive to daughters. Aggression (verbal or physical) is more common among boys and is strongly forbidden. Sex training, on the other hand, is more severe for girls than for boys. Girls must be kept safe from any potential sex assault or possible indecent contact with the opposite sex.

15.   Many parents, especially the less educated ones, still hold the traditional notion that the child is a part of "bones and flesh" of the parent, and therefore to be owned, valued, and protected as the parent's own body or property.

16.   Physical punishment is common. Fathers generally strike more heavily and painfully than mothers do although in some cases mothers may hit children more often. Many people still believe that a filial son grows under the rod. On the whole, the rural family is more traditional than the urban family in child-rearing beliefs, attitudes, and practices.

17.   Both parents in most urban families have full-time jobs. They have less time and energy to socialize children than the rural parents.

18.   Many grandparents serve as parent surrogates. They are more lenient than parents. The only child may be spoiled or pampered by both parents and four grandparents.

19.   The current trend is for parents to become less traditional in child-rearing practices; they tend to be less strict and authoritarian, and more lenient and democratic.

20.   The parents emotional state or mood affects parental behavior. In case parents quarrel, or a parent confronts career or financial difficulties, the child is most likely to experience irrationality in parental behavior or attitudes that may result in unpleasant treatment by one or both parents.

21.   A parent who has not spent enough time with a child for some reason (such as being too busy with work or having the child in grandmother's care) will not love that child as much as the one with whom the parent has spent sufficient time

together.

22.   A parent, especially the father, may have two faces. For example, the father may be strict, aloof,and taciturn to his children but tolerant, amiable,and talkative to his friends. Or he may be cold to other people but overconcerned about his children's well-being.

23.   Many parents overemphasize children's academic achievement to the neglect of their social, emotional, moral, and physical development for a healthy personality.

24.   A major cause of conflict in parent-child relations involves the parent's overdiscipline and/or overconcern on the one hand and the child's struggle for autonomy and independence on the other hand. While demanding autonomy and independence, the child, even if having passed adolescence or early adulthood, may still depend on the parents to meet his or her financial and/or emotional needs.

25.   Parental interference with the child's social activities is another source of generation conflict. Many parents permit no association with peers without parental consent lest the child be led astray by "bad" friends.

26.   Parental behavior has an everlasting effect on the child's personality development. Possible personality traits of the child reared under each of the eight parenting models are shown in Table 1. The models apply to both parents. For example, both parents may be overprotective or overcaring (Model 1), or one parent may be loving and restrictive (Model 7) and the other parent loving and democratic (Model 8). It is also possible that a parent is democratic or authoritative on some occasions but restrictive or authoritarian on other occasions. It is assumed that if the mother and the father adopt different behavior models or if any one parent is inconsistent in his/her behavior toward the child, the child may develop a combination of pertinent personality traits shown in Table 1.

Table 1
The Child's Possible Personality Traits Developed under Eight Parenting Models

Parenting model	Possible personality traits of the child
1. Overprotective or overcaring	Introverted, egocentric, dependent, sometimes rebellious
2. Overindulgent or overpermissive	Unable to face challenge and tolerate frustration, finds social adjustment difficult, defies authority
3. Hostile or repulsive	Low in self-esteem and self-confidence, has social and academic difficulties, neurotic, hostile to people
4. Restrictive or controlling	Passive, rigid, and inhibited in social and cognitive behavior, low in curiosity and creativity
5. Hostile and restrictive	Ill-tempered, neurotic, indulges in fantasies, dissatisfied with reality, rebellious
6. Hostile and permissive	Tends to act out resentment, rebellious, prone to be delinquent or criminal
7. Loving and restrictive	Introverted, reserved, passive, docile, polite, dependent, compliant, conforming
8. Loving and democratic	Extraverted, independent, assertive, creative, emotionally stable, sometimes disobedient and rebellious

Note: The eight parenting models are derived from Schaefer's (1959) circumplex model for maternal behavior. They are applied to the behavior of both parents here. The first four models or patterns are unidimensional while the last four are bidimensional (Lew, 1982).

STUDY 2

THE CHILD'S PERSONALITY UNDER SEVEN JOINT PARENTING PATTERNS

Sixty-two people (45 men and 17 women) in mainland China (ML) and 47 people (34 men and 13 women) in Taiwan (TW) served as informants (interviewees). Their age ranged from 19 to 69. They had at least two years of college education; most of them had completed higher education and were working as teachers, engineers, researchers, administrators, or other professionals.

In a semi-structured retrospective interview, each interviewee as informant was asked about (1) his or her family structure and constellation; (2) father's and mother's education, occupation, personality, and child-rearing practices; and (3) his or her own life history and personality traits. The interview lasted two hours on the average. Some informants were interviewed two or three times for more than ten hours.

Throughout the interview I, as the interviewer, recorded and observed the responses and reactions of the interviewee. The direct and close observation of the subject during the interactions enabled me to gain deeper insight into the personality of the subject beyond his or her self-description. Additional data were collected through subsequent correspondence with some ML subjects and personal contact with some TW subjects.

The content of each recorded interview was analyzed (Brislin, 1980) and categorized in terms of the Chinese conceptions of parenting *yan* (strict, severe, and controlling), which is similar to the Western conception of control (Lau, Lew, Hau, Cheung, & Berndt, 1990), and *chi* (tender, loving, and permissive), which is analogous to the Western conception of warmth (Lau et al, 1990). The content analysis also considered the amount and manner of contact and discipline, each parent's and child's behavior and personality traits, and the quality of parent-child relationships (e,g., friendly, intimate vs. remote, cold). Any personality trait or behavior of either parent associated with *yan* and *chi* (pronounced like voiced *ts*) as listed in Table 2 is counted as one point except physical punishment for *yan* or lack (seldom or never) of it for *chi* which is counted as two points. To qualify for *yan* or *chi*, five or more relevant points are needed for either parent.

In order to examine the combined influence of both parents, the joint patterns of socialization were depicted in terms of the two adjectives commonly used in the Chinese language to describe or highlight parental behavior and attitudes toward the child--*yan* and *chi*. As such four patterns were derived; namely, father *yan* and mother *chi* (FYMC), father *chi* and mother *yan* (FCMY), both *yan* (FYMY), and both *chi* (FCMC). In addition, three more categories were used: both parents just about right or in proper complementarity (FRMR), father as principal socializer (FAPS), and mother as principal socializer (MAPS). The number and percentage of cases analyzed for each of the seven patterns or categories are presented in Table 1.

While most cases could be categorized in accordance with the seven patterns described above, some cases were left uncategorized for two reasons: (1) Some cases involved extended families or parent surrogates (e.g., grandparents, elder siblings, nurses, step-parents), and/or they, chiefly some ML cases, were entangled with sociopolitical factors, wherein influences on the child came from many sources, which made it impossible to discern the relationship between parental behavior and the child's personality. (2) In a few cases the behaviors and attitudes of at least one parent were very unstable or inconsistent, which made it impossible to categorize them.

Unexpectedly, as Table 1 shows, there were only one ML case and two TW cases in FCMC category because most cases in this joint parenting model were categorized as FRMR, which seems to be a more suitable term for them. There were more ML cases uncategorized. Some of them, if not for the two reasons given above, could be categorized as FYMC, the traditional modal pattern of joint parenting in Chinese society, to which 31.9% of TW cases belonged. Another common category was FRMR under which 27.4% of ML cases and 19.1% of TW cases fell.

Table 1
Number and Percentage of Cases Categorized under Seven Patterns of Joint Parenting in Taiwan and Mainland China

Joint parenting pattern	Mainland		Taiwan	
	n	%	n	%
Father *yan* and mother *chi* (FYMC)	4 (1)	6.45	15 (3)	31.9
Father *chi* and mother *yan* (FCMY)	8	12.9	2	4.3
Both parents *yan* (FYMY)	4 (1)	6.45	4 (2)	8.5
Both parents *chi* (FCMC)	1	1.6	2	4.3
Both parents just about right (FRMR)	17 (7)	27.4	9 (3)	19.1
Father as principal socializer (FAPS)	2	3.2	4 (1)	8.5
Mother as principal socializer (MAPS)	6 (2)	9.7	6 (1)	12.8

Table 1 (Continued)
Number and Percentage of Cases Categorized under Seven Patterns of Joint
Parenting in Taiwan and Mainland China

Joint parenting pattern	Mainland		Taiwan	
	n	%	n	%
Uncategorized	20 (6)	32.3	5 (2)	10.6
Total	62 (17)	100	47 (12)	100

Note: The figures in parentheses indicate the number of female cases included.

To grasp the meaning of *yan* and *chi* in joint parenting patterns and its implications for the child's behavior and personality, the behavior and personality of both parents and the child in each of the seven types of joint parenting family are briefly presented below.

1.   *Father yan and mother chi (FYMC)*

In the FYMC family, the father tends to be impulsive, ill-tempered, aloof, authoritarian, and strict. He is inclined to demand obedience, resort to physical punishment, value traditional virtues (e.g., conformity, filial duty, moderation), and have high expectations for sons than for daughters. The mother tends to be affectionate, tender, good-tempered, tolerant, rational, and protective or overprotective. She seldom or never uses physical punishment. The male subject is generally ambitious, self-confident, and, with the exception of one male case, straightforward, critical, idealistic, impulsive, and tender-hearted. The man in the exceptional case, though ambitious and self-confident, is not impulsive, critical, and idealistic. It is probably because his father, though strict and authoritarian, seldom hits or beats him, that seems to have made him different from other male subjects as children of the FYMC families. The female child in this type of family is also different from most male children. She is docile, submissive, agreeable, cooperative, and realistic. The reason for this may be that the father in the FYMC family does not hit or spank his daughters as severely as his sons. Frequent physical punishment, especially when it is severe, would make a significant difference.

2.   *Father chi and mother yan (FCMY)*

In the FCMY pattern of socialization, the father seldom moralizes or scolds children. He never or seldom administers physical punishment. He is generally rational, patient, kind, and even-tempered. The mother, on the other hand, usually hits and scolds children. She may be able and smart, but tends to be strict, demanding, impulsive, bad-tempered, and irrational. With such parents, the child is more extraverted than introverted and usually has a high need for achievement. He or she is inclined to cherish traditional values and/or have a strong superego. He or she is in general tender-hearted, altruistic, and sometimes neurotic (nervous, anxious, or compulsive).

3.   *Both parents yan (FYMY)*

FYMY families are relatively scarce. In such a family, the mother is usually not as *yan* as the father. The father in the FYMY family is generally traditional or conservative, strict, authoritarian, and impulsive or hot-tempered. He scolds and physically punishes children. The mother in such a family tends to be introverted, traditional, hardworking, strict, and impulsive. She also scolds and physically punishes children in most cases. The child, regardless of sex, is often introverted, anxious, and/or emotionally unstable. The male subject is usually critical, intolerant, and/or authoritarian.   One case (a ML woman) is somewhat different. It is categorized as FYMY because the father is strict, restrictive, stern, authoritarian, and awe-inspiring, and the mother is stern, impatient, naggy, angry, and seldom smiles, which gives the impression of a family with both parents considered *yan.* This case differs from other FYMY cases in that the father is also calm, even-tempered, gentle-hearted, and self-disciplined; and, more important, that both parents seldom resorts to physical punishment. These differences may account for the fact that the subject, a girl student in a ML college, is rational and tolerant, though anxious and hypochondriacal.

Another case worth special mention is a male TW college student with polio. We might wrongly think that his timidity and feeling of inferiority are related more to his physical handicap than to the behavior and personality of his parents. For the sake of comparison, I have a polio-stricken ML subject of the same sex , similar age and similar level of education, whose personality is very different from that of the TW subject here. That ML case can be found under the category of FAPS (father as principal socializer), which will be presented later. The comparison will illuminate the fact that parental behavior or parenting has a greater and deeper impact on the child's personality than the child's own variables (a physical disadvantage in this case).

4. *Both parents chi (FCMC)*

As a matter of fact, the number of families with both parents satisfying the criterion of *chi* set in the present study (i.e., either parent has a *chi* score of 5 or more) is much smaller than expected. Therefore, this category may well be merged with FRMR (both parents just about right), which seems to be a better term for the combined parental behavior characterized by both parents "*chi*" in the general sense of the word. By "just about right" I mean that there is a kind of balance, complementarity, or mutual compensation in the amount and manner of *yan* and *chi* between the two parents. The FRMR category will be presented next. I will give one example in FCMC, or rather, FRMR as follows.

The subject is a 61-year-old financial cadre (municipal government official), a native of Hunan province on the Chinese mainland. He secretly joined the Chinese Communist Party in 1948, four years after graduation from a prestigious university and one year before the mainland turned Communist. He has a younger stepbrother by his father's concubine. His father was a self-educated businessman before 1949, who was sociable, generous, charitable, gentle-hearted, and good-tempered. He valued traditional virtues and guided children with reason. The subject's mother was an uneducated housewife. She was kind, generous, tolerant, and even-tempered. Both parents kept good relations with people and seldom punished the subject. Like his parents, the subject is agreeable, sociable, generous, charitable, patient, tolerant, gentle-hearted, and good-tempered. I already knew him quite well before 1949 when I left the mainland. After more than forty years, he remains to be the same person I used to know except being older and having no spare money to help the needy. He confirms that his personality has not changed since teenage although his thoughts have undergone some fluctuations since college years.

5.   *Both parents just about right (FRMR)*

The definition of this pattern of joint parental behavior (FRMR) was already given in the last section . There are proportionally more women in the FRMR category than in other categories. In both ML and TW FRMR group for either sex, the fathers and mothers in general are good-tempered or emotionally stable, seldom or never scold or hit children, and have reasonable demands or expectations for children. Both male and female subjects as sons and daughters are all even-tempered or emotionally stable, agreeable, independent, and realistic or moderately ambitious. Most of them have leadership abilities and are already leaders in various capacities (student leaders, department heads, school or foundation administrator). By coincidence or naturally, most female subjects in my case study of FRMR are charming or attractive ladies.

6.   *Father as principal socializer (FAPS)*

Although most mothers spend more time with children than fathers do, some fathers, as principal socializers, exert greater influence on children than mothers. They guide and discipline children much more than mothers. In this category, the mother as a rule supports the father's role and authority or takes a somewhat hands-off attitude toward the child. The father as such is the central authority figure of the family. He is in general affectionate as well as authoritarian. He is strict and demanding. He has high expectations for the child's achievement. The children grown up in such families, with some exceptions, are generally emotionally stable and well developed in personality.

One case in this category matches another case under FYMY in that both subjects have suffered from polio and both are male and the youngest children about the same age. These two cases, one ML and one TW, have demonstrated that parenting style exerts greater influence on the child's personality development than biological and sociopolitical factors. A TW female case also deserves elaboration. I interviewed the subject three times in 1979, 1982, and 1990. In the last interview, I checked some important points in the first two interviews to see if her remembrances were consistent and found that they were. For instance, she remembered clearly that the last occasional spanking she received from her father occurred at the age of twelve. In the 1990 interview she said that her father still angered at age 72 when she disagreed with him in something her father insisted on. She said that she is in many ways like her father except that she has a better temper. She admires him as the best father in the world. She said she dislikes her mother because her mother has never liked her. She admitted that her mother is a beautiful woman and she does not look like her mother but resembles her father. I gather that this last point might have something to do with her variant relationships with parents.

In a family with father as the principal socializer, the father's influence is evidently greater than the mother's in many ways such as personality and career development. The mother's influence, however, cannot be disregarded. As one TW male subject (a Cabinet minister) pointed out, "Mother's influence is incorporeal." He said that he has some personality traits more like his mother's than father's, such as self-controlled and emotionally stable. Whether this is due to mother's early influence during preschool years or due to heredity, or both, is not easy to tell. To get a more complete picture of his life and development, I also had an opportunity to interview his father.

7.   *Mother as principal socializer (MAPS)*

This category can be illustrated by two cases: a 22-year-old ML woman (graduate student) and a 40-year-old TW man (publisher). The graduate student is extraverted, active, playful, emotionally stable, sweet, attractive, chased by boys since high school, has good human relations, enthusiastic in helping people, disinclined to hurt people, sometimes weak-minded like father and sometimes strong-minded like mother. Her father is a clerk and has received only one year's schooling. He works and lives away from home, comes home for a day or two every other month. He is thrifty, good-tempered, weak-minded, submissive, resigns authority to wife, enthusiastic in helping people, and seldom scolds or punishes children. Her mother attended school for five years and also works as a clerk. She is not as good-tempered as husband, but able and smart, makes every decision for the family. She is stubborn, strong-minded, helps people, avoids hurting people, often scolds and occasionally hits children.

The publisher is introverted and somewhat shy, but emotionally stable, easygoing, tender-hearted, optimistic, thoughtful, credulous, sympathetic, fair and just in dealing with people. He desires to influence people, is liberal in thoughts but conservative in deeds. He is enterprising and has leadership and management abilities. His father is a farmer and had two-year schooling. He is hardworking, even-tempered, easy-going, permissive to children, henpecked, gullible, weak-minded, and indulged in gambling. The publisher's mother is a housewife without formal education. She is hardworking, austere, independent, self-confident, resolute, ambitious, optimistic, shrewd, able in domestic and financial management. She favors sons, seldom scolds or punishes children, and has authority over husband.

Although most mothers spend more time with children than fathers do, most fathers take a reasonable amount of time and interest in sharing the responsibility of child rearing. In the MAPS family, however, the father either has no time or takes no interest in socializing the child. In such a family, if the mother were not the principal socializer strong in character or strong in will power, the child would develop a personality different from what has been demonstrated in the two cases presented above. In most MAPS cases the mother is strict but not harsh.

In general, the mothers in the MAPS families exert greater influence on the children than fathers do. Some mother's influence seems to emerge more from modeling than from direct discipline. Some traditional mothers have received little or no formal education, yet they possess the traditional virtues befitting a Chinese woman, such as being hardworking, thrifty, self-sacrificing, and devoted to family. The father's influence in the MAPS family cannot be totally disregarded, however. Either through modeling or through heredity, or both, the child in most cases still develop some, though not many, personality traits resembling his or her father's. The father's laissez faire attitude in child rearing also puts the mother's influence in fuller swing than would otherwise be possible.

Characteristics of *yan* and *chi*

From case data provided by 109 men and women I interviewed in Taiwan and mainland China, we may conclude by presenting Table 2 showing the Chinese conceptions of *yan* and *chi* in terms of parental behavior and personality.

Table 2
Attributes of *Yan* and *Chi* Characterizing Chinese Parents

Yan	Chi
Strict	Tender
Controlling, restrictive, forbids	Warm, loving, affectionate, approachable
Stern, aloof, awe-inspiring	Indulgent, lenient, permissive
Severe, harsh	Kind, mild, gentle-hearted, tender-hearted
Authoritarian, egocentric	Concerned, self-sacrificing
Overprotective, interferes	Accepts, protects, takes good care of child
Impatient	Patient
Impulsive	Calm
Intolerant	Tolerant
Emotionally unstable	Emotionally stable
Bad- (ill-, quick-, hot-)tempered	Good- (even-)tempered
Angers, yells	Seldom or never angers or loses temper
Nags, warns, moralizes, seldom smiles	Agreeable, humorous, jokes, plays with child
Disciplines	Spoils, pampers, makes no demand, has no expectation
Punishes (physically or in other manners)	Seldom or never punishes
Scolds, rebukes, reprimands	Seldom or never scolds
Demands (especially obedience or compliance)	Democratic, lets child have autonomy, treats child as friend
Requires, orders, commands	Authoritative, rational, reasons, discusses with child
Has high expectations of child	Guides, teaches, explains
Values traditional virtues (e.g., toleration, filial piety, conformity, good manners)	Spends time with child
	Understands child's needs
Hostile, rejects or dislikes child	Has intimate relationship with child

Differences and similarities in sibling's personality

The influence of family environment, particularly the parental influence, on personality of the child is important in accounting for sibling differences and similarities (Hoffman, 1991). Due to joint or sometimes single parental influence, we found both differences and similarities in sibling's personality. Three cases are selected for illustration as follows.

1.   *Department head* (ML man, age 52): He was born as a quiet child with an easy temperament while his first younger brother was born noisy with a difficult temperament. Parents loved him more than his brother. Perhaps due to parental treatment interacted with their temperament, he is emotionally stable and normal in weight while his brother is impulsive and underweight. His brother, though three years younger, looks older than he.

2.   *College junior* (ML woman, age 22): Father favored younger brother and mother favored her. Father beat both but beat brother more harshly although not often. Now she and brother are both extraverted, but brother is disobedient in school and at home whereas she is agreeable at school although willful at home. Besides, brother is shy before girls while she is at ease with boys.

3.   *Doctoral student* (TW man, age 27): Father favored the first younger sister and mother favored the second one. Yet he and elder sister were favored by neither parent. Father was stricter to him than three girls, scolding him often and knocking him on the head sometimes. As a result probably, he has the worst temper of all children. His youngest sister has never been hit by parents and has the best temper of all. The first younger sister, favored by father and defying mother, is more extraverted and lively than other siblings. He and elder sister are both intellectual and idealistic, sharing a strong character.

Most cases demonstrated environmental influence within the family, primarily the effect of parental treatment or child-rearing practices. Most subjects mentioned physical punishment, which, if severe or harsh, obviously has a detrimental effect on children's personality development, especially on its emotional aspect. The above cases testify that siblings in the same family have differential as well as similar experiences, including parental treatment, which influence their psychological development (Daniels & Plomin, 1985).

Resemblance between the child's and the parent's personalities

The evidence of joint parental influence on the child's personality development can also be found in the child's personality resembling that of the parent. Whether the resemblance is due to observational learning, genetic influence, or child-rearing practices, however, cannot be easily pinpointed. Some of the similarities between the child's and the parent's personalities were already demonstrated in various cases presented in the preceding sections. The evidence was further confirmed by the answers given by the interviewees when I asked 45 men and 17 women in mainland China whether their personality is like that of either parent in any way. Most of them said that it is like that of their father or mother, or both, in some way or in some traits. The result is shown in Table 3. As can be seen from the table, the percentages for both sexes in the four categories (like father, like mother, like both, and like none) are very similar. The largest percentage for both sexes falls in the "like both (parents)" category--38% for sons and 41% for daughters.

Table 3
Resembling Parent's Personality as Reported by
62 Interviewees in Mainland China

Interviewee	Like father		Like mother		Like both		Like none		Total	
	n	%	n	%	n	%	n	%	n	%
Male	14	31	11	24	17	38	3	7	45	100
Female	5	29	4	24	7	41	1	6	17	100

STUDY 3

FOUR JOINT PARENTING STYLES AND RELATED VARIABLES

The subjects were 2640 educated Chinese men and women of various ages in mainland China (ML, n=925), Taiwan (TW, n=651), Hong Kong (HK, n=787), and the United States (US, n=277) as described in Chapter One. They were administered a questionnaire.

Besides demographic items, Part I of the questionnaire (MTPI) asks a series of questions in Chinese about the subject's childhood experience in the family and the behavior and parenting practices of his or her father and mother. The questions such as the following are asked: who was the person with the greatest authority in your family; who loved you most; who disciplined you most; what was the combined or joint pattern of your parent's behavior and attitudes toward you (the subject is asked to choose from the four patterns--FYMC, FCMY, FYMY, FCMC--as described in Study 2); was your father's (mother's) control or discipline too strict, rather strict, too lenient, rather lenient, or just about right (to choose one). In addition, there are eleven items on a 4-point scale concerning either parent's child-rearing practices or attitudes, such as permissive, restrictive, loves me, overprotects me, talks to me, allows me autonomy, moralizes to me, discusses with me.

In Part II of the questionnaire, there are 122 items in bipolar form. Each item comprises two trait descriptors in opposite direction, one at the right end and the other at the left end, measured by a 6-point scale. Some items are short, such as bold--shy, optimistic--pessimistic, while other items are longer, such as often blames others--often blames self, tolerant of different opinions--intolerant of different opinions.

The questionnaire was administered personally or through students and friends in mainland China, Taiwan, Hong Kong , and the United States as described in Chapter One.

In addition to the attributes of parental attitudes *yan* and *chi* derived from interview data in Study 2, we found the behavioral correlates of *yan* and *chi* from questionnaire data as shown in Table 1 here.

Table 1
Behavioral Correlates of Parental Attitudes *Yan* and *chi*

Correlates of *yan*	Correlates of *chi*
Control or discipline (70% of fathers and 74% of mothers were perceived to be restrictive and strict in control or discipline in FYMC and FCMY families respectively)	Love (47%, 24%, and 8% of subjects perceived their mother, father, and grandmother love them most respectively)
Authority (52% of fathers and 46% of mothers were perceived to have the greatest authority in FYMC and FCMY families respectively)	Contact (47%, 13%, and 6% of subjects had most contact with mother, father, and grandmother respectively)
Anger (about 50% of either parent became angry sometimes or frequently; anger reflects a bad temper and often leads to punishment of the child)	Approachability, autonomy, communication, indulgence, and overprotection (more *chi* than *yan* parents were perceived to be approachable to subjects, allow them autonomy, talk to and discuss with them, indulge and overprotect them)

As Table 1 indicates, *yan* implies control or discipline because 70% of fathers and 74% of mothers were perceived by the subjects to be restrictive and strict in control or discipline in FYMC (where the father is *yan*) and FCMY (where the mother is *yan*) families respectively. *yan* also suggests authority and anger. Anger reflects a bad temper or emotional instability, which often leads to scolding and/or physical punishment of the child. On the other hand, *chi* implies, as the table explains, love, contact, approachability, autonomy, communication, indulgence, and/or overprotection.

Table 2 gives the number and percentage of male and female subjects brought up in the four types of family of joint parenting. As the table shows, far more (49%) male subjects perceived their families in the predominant traditional pattern of FYMC than in other patterns. About equal percentages of female subjects perceived their families in the two common patterns--FYMC (32%) and FCMC (33%).

Proportionally, more fathers were *yan* to sons (49% in FYMC + 12% in FYMY) than

to daughters (32% in FYMC + 13% in FYMY) and more mothers were *yan* to

daughters (22% in FCMY +13% in FYMY) than to sons (14% in FCMY + 12% in

FYMY). The figures in this table should be more representative of reality than the

similar figures in Table 1 of Study 2 where about one-third of the ML cases were left

uncategorized.

Table 2
Number and Percentage of Male and Female Subjects in Four Patterns of
Joint Parental Behavior

Subject	Pattern of joint parenting								Total	
	FYMC		FCMY		FYMY		FCMC			
	n	%	n	%	n	%	n	%	n	%
Male (sons)	787	49	237	14	190	12	403	25	1617	100
Female (daughters)	297	32	199	22	114	13	303	33	913	100
Total	1084	43	436	17	304	12	706	28	2530	100

Table 3 displays the number, percentage, and birth order of subjects in the

four joint parenting patterns of family. While there are relatively few FYMY families

(ranging from 10% to 13%) for subjects of any birth order, there are more FCMC

families for youngest children (32%) than only (26%), middle (27%), and eldest

(28%) children. When compared to subjects of other ordinal positions, we find

proportionately fewer only children (37% vs. 41% youngest, 44% middle, and 43%

eldest) in FYMC families and more of them (27% vs. 16% youngest, 17% middle,

and 16% eldest) in FCMY families. The table also shows interestingly that

proportionately more fathers (27% in FCMY + 26% in FCMC) were *chi* to the only

child while more mothers (27% in FCMY + 10% in FYMY) were *yan* to him or her in comparison with children of other ordinal positions.

Table 3
Number and Percentage of Subjects in Four Types of
Joint Parenting Families by Birth Order

| | Family of joint parenting | | | | | | | | | |
| Birth order | FYMC | | FCMY | | FYMY | | FCMC | | Total | |
	n	%	n	%	n	%	n	%	n	%
Only Child	50	37	36	27	14	10	35	26	135	100
Youngest child	202	41	80	16	54	11	158	32	494	100
Middle child	564	44	219	17	154	12	341	27	1278	100
Eldest child	278	43	104	16	85	13	177	28	644	100

Table 4 lists the number and percentage of young (age 30 or under) and older (above 30) subjects with various number of siblings in the four types of families. We detect from this table two important trends: (1)The percentage of children in the traditional FYMC family is decreasing regardless of number of siblings, especially that of the only child (20% in the young generation vs. 45% in the older generation). (2)The percentage of children with less than five siblings in the FCMY families, on the other hand, is increasing, especially that of the only child (44% and 18% in the young and the older generations respectively). While the percentage of subjects in FYMY families is small regardless of the number of siblings, the percentage of subjects with less than three siblings in the young generation appears to be on the increase in the FCMC relative to the traditional FYMC families (25% vs. 20% for the subjects with no sibling and 35% vs. 32% for the subjects with one or two siblings).

Table 4
Number and Percentage of Subjects in Four Types of Joint Parenting Families by Number of Siblings and Generation

Number of siblings	Generation	FYMC n	FYMC %	FCMY n	FCMY %	FYMY n	FYMY %	FCMC n	FCMC %	Total n	Total %
0 (only child)	Young	9	20	20	44	5	11	11	25	45	100
	Older	41	45	16	18	9	10	24	27	90	100
1 or 2	Young	124	32	69	18	56	15	137	35	386	100
	Older	113	45	40	16	29	12	69	27	251	100
3 or 4	Young	230	40	121	21	72	13	152	26	575	100
	Older	210	48	63	14	52	12	116	26	441	100
5 or 6	Young	107	43	39	15	30	12	75	30	251	100
	Older	154	52	43	15	22	7	78	26	297	100
7 or more	Young	32	48	5	8	10	15	19	29	66	100
	Older	74	50	23	15	22	15	30	20	149	100

Note: Young generation = age 30 or under, Older generation = above 30.

Table 5 further demonstrates the age difference indicating a decrease in the percentage of families in the traditionally predominant pattern of FYMC. The youngest (19-30) age group perceived only 38% of families in this category of joint parenting style while a greater percentage (47% to 52%) was perceived by the older age groups. Since the older groups above age 30 are similar in distribution of the four parenting patterns, I merge them into one age cohort to compare with the youngest group in the three Chinese societies or regions of residence for both sexes (see Table 6).

Table 5
Number and Percentage of Families in Four Patterns of Joint Parenting as Perceived by Four Age Groups

	Family of joint parenting									
	FYMC		FCMY		FYMY		FCMC		Total	
Age group	n	%	n	%	n	%	n	%	n	%
19 - 30	503	38	254	19	173	13	394	30	1324	100
31 - 40	287	47	96	16	78	13	150	24	611	100
41 - 50	191	52	54	14	32	9	93	25	370	100
51 - 69	90	47	29	15	17	9	56	29	192	100

From the cell percentage in Table 6, we note, as suggested by the difference in percentage between the older and the young group, that an obvious trend is toward a decrease in FYMC (see the cells of HK females, and ML and TW of both sexes), but an increase in FCMY (ML and HK females) and in FCMC (ML and TW of both sexes). Greater change occurs in the increasing tenderness and permissiveness of the parents, especially the father, toward daughters. The percentage of FYMY families, however, remains the lowest of the four types in most cases and little change is discerned.

Table 7 is a reorganization of Table 6. For reader's convenience, we will for the time being equate *strict* for *yan* and *kind* for *chi* although the two Chinese words are richer in meaning than the two English substitutes. As Table 7 shows, a larger percentage of male than female subjects as adult children, young and old, perceived father strict in all three Chinese societies, which suggests that more fathers are strict to sons than to daughters. The table also shows that except for older Hong Kong (HK) subjects a larger percentage of female than male subjects considered mother strict, which suggests that more mothers are strict to daughters than to sons. On the other hand, Table 7 reveals that a higher percentage of daughters than sons, regardless of age, saw their fathers kind while a higher percentage of sons than daughters saw their mothers kind, which suggests that more fathers than mothers are kind to daughters while more mothers than fathers are kind to sons. For HK subjects of the older group, their mothers did not differentiate much between sons and daughters, more mothers were perceived as kind by them (71% of sons and 72% of daughters) than those perceived as strict by them (29% of sons and 28% of daughters).

Table 6
Distribution of the Four Joint Parenting Patterns
in Three Chinese Societies by Age and Sex

Sex	Age	n & %	Mainland				Taiwan				Hong Kong			
			FY MC	FC MY	FY MY	FC MC	FY MC	FC MY	FY MY	FC MC	FY MC	FC MY	FY MY	FC MC
Male	Young	n	101	22	32	65	50	14	10	26	142	61	41	68
		%	46	10	15	29	50	14	10	26	45	20	13	22
	Older	n	187	46	44	101	151	37	24	59	47	18	12	27
		%	49	12	12	27	55	14	9	22	45	17	12	26
Female	Young	n	23	27	16	52	37	29	14	67	90	66	44	71
		%	19	23	14	44	25	20	10	45	33	25	16	26
	Older	n	41	18	13	38	33	16	7	23	19	6	8	18
		%	37	16	12	35	42	20	9	29	37	12	16	35

Note: Young = age 30 or under, Older = over 30. The U.S. sample is not included due to its relatively small size.

The sex means (percentage) in Table 7 further suggest that in all three Chinese societies more fathers are kind to daughters than to sons and strict to sons than to daughters. The mean percentages also suggest that mainland China (ML) and Taiwan (TW) subjects were similar to each other while somewhat different from HK subjects in their perceptions of parenting. For example, the mean percentages of ML, TW, and HK daughters who perceived their fathers as kind were 59%, 57% and 49% respectively. The difference between ML (59%) and TW (57%) is much smaller than that between either ML or TW and HK (49%). Far more HK (34.5%) than either ML (24.5%) or TW (23.5%) daughters perceived their mothers as strict. Meanwhile, a greater percentage of HK (51%) than ML (41%) and TW (43%) women saw their father strict although the percentage is smaller than that of men in any of the three societies who saw their father strict. Another distinctive feature of HK subjects perceptions of parenting is that the difference in mean percentage of, for example, those perceiving their mother strict between HK men (31%) and women (34.5%) is smaller than that between ML (24.5%) or TW (23.5%) men and ML (32.5%) or TW (29.5%) women. All these may suggest that ML and TW parents treat their sons and daughters more differently or less equally than HK parents and that HK daughters receive more or earlier independence training by parents, especially by mothers, than their ML and TW counterparts.

Table 7
Frequency (%) of Behavior (*Yan* and *chi*) of Each Parent as Perceived by Male and Female Adult Children of Two Age Groups

| Parental Behavior | Mainland | | | | Taiwan | | | | Hong Kong | | | |
| | Male | | Female | | Male | | Female | | Male | | Female | |
	Y	O	Y	O	Y	O	Y	O	Y	O	Y	O
Father *yan*												
FYMC	46	49	19	37	50	55	25	42	45	45	33	37
FYMY	15	12	14	12	10	9	10	9	13	12	16	16
Total	61	61	33	49	60	64	35	51	58	57	49	53
Mean	61		41		62		43		57.5		51	
Mother *yan*												
FCMY	10	12	23	16	14	14	20	20	20	17	25	12
FYMY	15	12	14	12	10	9	10	9	13	12	16	16
Total	25	24	37	28	24	23	30	29	33	29	41	28
Mean	24.5		32.5		23.5		29.5		31		34.5	

Table 7 (Continued)
Frequency (%) of Behavior (*Yan* and *chi*) of Each Parent as Perceived by
Male and Female Adult Children of Two Age Groups

Parental Behavior	Mainland				Taiwan				Hong Kong			
	Male		Female		Male		Female		Male		Female	
	Y	O	Y	O	Y	O	Y	O	Y	O	Y	O
Father *chi*												
FCMY	10	12	23	16	14	14	20	20	20	17	25	12
FCMC	29	27	44	35	26	22	45	29	22	26	26	35
Total	39	39	67	51	40	36	65	49	42	43	51	47
Mean	39		59		38		57		42.5		49	
Mother *chi*												
FYMC	46	49	19	37	50	55	25	42	45	45	33	37
FCMC	29	27	44	35	26	22	45	29	22	26	26	35
Total	75	76	63	72	76	77	70	71	67	71	59	72
Mean	75.5		67.5		76.5		70.5		69	65.5		

Note: Y=young group (aged 19 to 30), O=older group (age>30). Mean is the mean percentage for either sex= (Y + O)/2. All the figures in the table are percentages.

Yan is not necessarily bad. Although there are relatively few families with both parents perceived as *yan*, 23% and 22% of my subjects in the FYMY families thought respectively their father's and mother's control or discipline to be "just about right." *chi* apparently does not mean no control or no discipline at all in the eyes of the respondents to my questionnaire. In the FCMC families 51% of the respondents perceived both parent's control or discipline "just about right." This finding justifies the merging of the FCMC and FRMR categories in Study 2.

When asked who disciplined him or her most in the family during childhood, most (1432 or 54%) subjects reported that it was the mother, 835 or 32% of my subjects mentioned the father, and the rest said grandparents and elder siblings. It thus becomes clear that in Chinese society mother is the principal socializer in more than half of the families and father is the main disciplinarian in about one-third of the families. Discipline in the Chinese family usually involves physical punishment.

Both the parent and the child take it for granted. Even in mainland China where the one-child family policy has been implemented since 1979, most parents seem to believe that they have to hit their children (Davin, 1990).

In the traditional extended family, usually of three generations, the grandparents had greater power or authority than the parents. This is no longer true. Although 42% of my subjects lived in families of three generations during childhood, only 9% and 6% of them reported that their grandfathers and grandmothers respectively had the greatest authority in the household. On the other hand, 65% and 18% of the respondents recalled that their father and mother respectively were the person with the highest authority in the family.

As to the relative effect of the four joint parenting patterns on the child's personality development, I compared the personality traits of the adult children (the subjects) reared in the four types of families by sex and age, using F (ANOVA) and Scheffe test. In order to see the results in detailed actuality, the 122-item responses were used in calculation instead of personality factors or dimensions because the 122 trait items describe the actual personality characterisitics of Chinese people more exactly than personality factors or dimensions do. The personality traits of men and women in two age cohorts or generations of the four parenting patterns in the four societies or regions of residence (including the U.S.) are shown in Table 8. Only the positive and negative traits of a group (e.g., ML female of the young generation) with statistically significant difference from the same group in any other pattern are listed. A few neutral (neither positive nor negative) trait items are not listed, such as strict - lenient, interested in money - uninterested in money, easily moved to tears by touching stories - never moved to tears.

From Table 8 we note that the ratios of positive to negative traits in the four patterns are as follows: (1) FYMC-- 2 : 5 for male and 5 : 16 for female; (2) FCMY-- 5 : 2 for male and 5 : 1 for female; (3) FYMY -- 0 : 5 for male and 6 : 7 for female; (4) FCMC -- 9 : 2 for male and 8 : 4 for female. These ratios indicate the following facts: (1) FYMC is the most undesirable joint parenting pattern, especially for daughters. (2) FYMY is the second worst pattern, especially for sons. (3) FCMY is fairly good for children of both sexes. (4) FCMC is the most desirable pattern, especially for sons. These findings are consistent with the results in Study 2 in that the FCMC (or FRMR as defined in Study 2) is the best pattern of joint parenting for personality development of the child and that FYMC and FYMY are both undesirable for the child's personality development.

If we look at sex and generation differences in Table 8, we further find these results: (1) FYMC's effect on personality development of the young male generation is unclear; it is, however, generally undesirable for the young generation of women and the older generation of men. (2) FYMC is not too bad for the older generation of daughters, but very undesirable for the young generation of daughters as demonstrated by the 13 out of 16 negative traits for young women in this pattern. (3) FCMY is fairly good for both young and older generations of both sexes; the sex and generation differences in this pattern are negligible. (4) Although FYMY has obvious negative effect for the older generation of both sexes, it has some positive effect greater than expected for the young female generation.The reason may be that due to social change parents are not so *yan* to daughters as they used to be. (5) FCMC is good for both generations of both sexes, especially for men of the older generation as demonstrated by six out of nine positive traits for older men with no negative traits for them.

Table 8

Personality Traits of Children Reared in Four Types of Joint Parenting Families

Type of Family	The Child's Positive and Negative Personality Traits			
	Son		Daughter	
	Positive	Negative	Positive	Negative
FYMC	Quiet(MLo)*** Adaptable(HKy)**	Talks without working(MLo)* Egocentric(TWo)* Dominant(HKo)* Inclined to moralize(HKo)* Inconsistent in word and deed(USo)*	Humble(MLo)*** Patient(MLo)** Is a person of deed (TWo)** Helpful to colleagues(TWo)* Eloquent(HKo)*	Hypocritical(MLy)** Snobbish(MLy)* Often blames others(MLy)* Clumsy in speech(MLo)* Despises others(MLo)* Uneasy with authority figure(MLo)** Jealous of colleagues(TWy)** Demanding(TWy)** Materialistic(TWy)* Unwilling to be led by a leader(TWy)* Egocentric(TWy)* Low in need for achievement(HKy)** Irresponsible(HKy)**, (HKo)* Easily tempted(HKy)**, (USy)*** Never self-examining(HKy)* Often forgets(HKy)*

Table 8 (Continued)
Personality Traits of Children Reared in Four Types of Joint Parenting Families

Type of Family	The Child's Positive and Negative Personality Traits			
	Son		Daughter	
	Positive	Negative	Positive	Negative
FCMY	Tolerant of different opinions(TWy)**, Adaptable(HKy)***, Works quietly(HKo)*, Concentrates on work(USo)*, Consistent in word and deed (USo)*	Overconcerned about "face"(MLo)*, Pessimistic(TWy)*	Sincer(MLy)**, Often blames self (MLy)*, (HKy)**, Humble(MLo)**, High in need for achievement(HKy)**, Responsible(HKy)**, (HKo)*	Dictatorial(MLo)***
FYMY		Talkative(MLo)***, Jealous of colleagues(TWo)*, Ill-tempered(HKy)*, Talks without working (HKo)*, Unable to concentrate on work(USo)*	Unsnobbish(MLy)*, Willing to be led by a leader(TWy)*, Responsible(HKy)*, Self-controlled(HKy)**, (USy)***, Often self-examining (HKy)*, Has a good memory (HKy)*	Dictatorial(MLo)***, Arrogant(MLo)***, Inpatient(MLo)**, Is a person of word(TWo)*, Jealous of colleagues(TWo)*, Clumsy in speech(HKo)*, Interested in self only(HKo)**

Table 8 (Continued)

Personality Traits of Children Reared in Four Types of Joint Parenting Families

Type of Family	The Child's Positive and Negative Personality Traits			
	Son		Daughter	
	Positive	Negative	Positive	Negative
FCMC	Quiet (MLo)*** Works quietly(MLo)* Optimistic(TWy)* Cooperative(TWy)* Helpful to colleagues (TWo)* Unegocentric(TWo)* Good-tempered(HKy)* Democratic(HKo)** Is a good listener (HKo)*	Intolerant of different opinions(TWy)** Unadaptable(HKy)**	Sincere(MLy)** Democratic(MLo)*** Humble(MLo)*** Helpful to colleagues (TWy)**, (TWo)* Forgiving (TWy)** Spiritual (TWy)** Unegocentric (TWy)* Thoughtful to others (Hko)**	Snobbish (MLy)* Often blames others (HKy)** Low in need for achievement (HKy)** Easily tempted (USy)***

Note: This table shows differences in personality traits of subjects between patterns of joint parenting by age (o = older generation aged 31-69, y = young generation aged 19-30), sex, and region or population (ML = mainland China, TW = Taiwan, HK =Hong Kong, US = ML, TW, and HK Chinese studying or working in the United States). The abbreviations in parentheses indicate the population and age group to which the subjects belong and that in those subjects the difference was found (e.g, MLy = the young subjects sampled in mainland China). The alpha level for significance (*$p<.05$, **$p<.01$, ***$p<.001$) indicates statistically significant difference from at least one of the other three patterns of joint parenting.

From the above results we may infer that the effect of the four parenting styles varies somewhat with the age and sex of the child and with the society and culture in which the child is reared. It is probable that the quality and quantity of *chi* and *yan* vary with the age and sex of the individual child. That may explain why FYMC is undesirable for the older generation of men and young generation of women, but not too bad for the older generation of women; and why FYMY is generally undesirable for all except that it also has some positive effect for the young generation of daughters.

One of the reasons why FCMC is good for the child's personality development is probably its contribution to family harmony. My questionnaire data indicate that most FCMC families (88%) are either fairly harmonious (56%) or very harmonious (32%). We may, therefore, infer that FCMC is more conducive to family harmony than any of the other three types of family. From the simple statistics in Table 9, we can probably say that FYMY is the least conducive to family harmony. A study of family harmony as it is related to the child's personality development will be reported in Chapter Three of this book.

No matter what is the joint parenting style, there exists a generation gap between the parents and the child, especially between the father and his child. Table 10 reveals the responses to the question with whom the subject as adolescent often discussed his or her problems. More subjects (n =623) during adolescence (aged 12 - 19) discussed their problems with schoolmates than with either father (n = 196) or mother (n = 378). There were, however, nearly as many subjects (n = 613) who discussed with nobody as those who discussed with schoolmates. Another fact worth noting is that a greater percentage (35%) of subjects in FYMY families discussed with nobody than those in other three types of family.

Table 9
Joint Parenting Types and Family Harmony

Joint Parenting	Family Harmony								Total	
	Inharmonious				Harmonious					
	Very		Fairly		Fairly		Very			
	n	%	n	%	n	%	n	%	n	%
FYMC	40	3	192	18	648	60	204	19	1084	100
FCMY	17	4	89	20	258	59	73	17	437	100
FYMY	13	4	80	26	172	57	39	13	304	100
FCMC	11	2	73	10	393	56	229	32	706	100
Total	81	3	434	17	1471	58	545	22	2531	100

Table 10
Persons with Whom the Subjects in Four Types of Family Discussed Their Problems during Adolescence

| Type of family | Nobody | | Father | | Mother | | Brother | | Sister | | Teacher | | School-mate | | Friend | | Total | |
	n	%	n	%	n	%	n	%	n	%	n	%	n	%	n	%	n	%
FYMC	250	24	74	7	185	18	44	4	60	6	35	4	282	27	108	10	1038	100
FCMY	112	27	38	9	60	15	8	2	21	5	8	2	116	28	49	12	412	100
FYMY	99	35	18	6	26	9	6	2	10	4	3	1	75	27	46	16	283	100
FCMC	152	23	66	10	107	16	30	4	41	6	11	2	150	23	103	16	660	100
Total	613	25	196	8	378	16	88	4	132	6	57	2	623	26	306	13	2393	100

An imbalance exists in research efforts devoted to rural versus urban settings. Considering the fact that the majority of China's population is rural, Ho (1989) suggests that more research in rural settings should be done. In my MTPI there is a question asking where the respondent lived before the age of 12 -- in a village (or on a farm), a small town, or a city. Table 11 presents the frequency of family types in terms of the three geographical localities where the respondent lived during childhood.

Table 11
Frequency of Joint Parenting patterns in Three Childhood Life Settings:
Village, Town, and City

Life setting	Joint parenting pattern									
	FYMC		FCMY		FYMY		FCMC		Total	
	n	%	n	%	n	%	n	%	n	%
Village	296	47	82	13	77	12	178	28	633	100
Town	225	44	92	18	52	10	143	28	512	100
City	563	42	265	19	176	13	388	28	1392	100

In the distribution of the four joint parenting patterns in the three childhood life settings as revealed by Table 11, we discern a trend of decrease of FYMC in the city (42%) versus the town (44%) and the village (47%). We may say that this trend is negatively associated with urbanization -- the greater the urbanization, the fewer the families of FYMC. On the other hand, the percentage of FCMY families increases with urbanization -- from 13% in the village to 18% in the town and 19% in the city. The other two types of family remains unaffected by urbanization.

General Discussion

When looking for a family environment effect on the child's personality, developmental psychologists often study child-rearing patterns, or parent-child interaction, or parental attitudes toward children (Baumrind, 1971; Hoffman, 1991; Siegel, 1985). To explain dependency in a child, for example, one would expect to find an overprotective parent (Hoffman, 1991). In spite of the fact that some theorists argue for a bidirectional perspective, the childhood years in the family are still seen by environmental researchers as particularly important to personality development (Lamb & Bornstein, 1986).

This chapter comprises three related studies on Chinese parenting and the child's personality. The focus is on the effect of parenting on the child's personality development. One feature that makes the present studies different from prior work is their emphasis on combined or joint socialization by both the father and the mother rather than by a single parent, usually the mother. Study 2 and 3 presented seven and four types of joint socialization respectively. They were the first attempts ever to examine in depth the meaning and significance of the two central constructs of Chinese parenting *yan* and *chi*. Another feature distinguishes the present research from most previous studies. In view of the fact that much of the internationally published work on parenting and personality has been done in other countries and research on Chinese subjects in Chinese societies is very much in need, the three studies here were all carried out in Chinese society with Chinese subjects. Study 1 was conducted in mainland China (ML), Study 2 in ML and Taiwan (TW), and Study 3 in ML, TW, Hong Kong (HK), and the United States Chinese community (US).

Research in Western societies has largely confirmed the assumption that mothers are warmer than fathers and fathers are more controlling than mothers (Block, 1984; Lamb, 1981; Maccoby & Martin, 1983). A similar assumption existed in traditional Chinese culture (Berndt, Cheung, Lau, Hau, & Lew, 1993; Ho, 1981; Hsu, 1985). Chinese fathers were described as *yan* (strict); Chinese mothers were described as *chi* (tender or kind). It may be hypothesized, however, that four combinations of parental roles or attitudes exist in Chinese culture rather than the traditionally assumed one of a *yan* father and a *chi* mother (FYMC), the other three combinations being a *chi* father plus a *yan* mother (FCMY), both parents *yan* (FYMY), and both parents *chi* (FCMC). This hypothesis was tested in Study 3 by questionnaire data with simple statistical analyses of related variables pertaining to the child (age, sex, birth order, number of siblings, personality traits, childhood life settings, etc.). The hypothesis was also explored in Study 1 along with parental behavior models borrowed from Western theorists, using data provided by mainland Chinese informants. Study 2, based on data collected from biographical interviewing, found three more joint parenting patterns in addition to the four patterns just mentioned.

Although Chinese children generally prefer a *chi* to a *yan* parent, the former is not always good and the latter is not always bad for the child's development. As Table 2 of Study 2 and Table 1 of Study 3 indicate, a *yan* parent may value traditional virtues while a *chi* parent may indulge or spoil the child. A certain parental behavior may be interpreted as *yan* on one occasion and *chi* on another occasion. Overprotection, for example, is perceived as *yan* when it implies control and interference but as *chi* when it reflects love and care. Generally speaking, the two Chinese constructs or factors of parenting are similar to the two major parenting dimensions Control and Warmth identified in Western literature. Parental control, like *yan*, may convey both care and interference (Lau & Cheung, 1987). It may mean both authoritative parenting and authoritarian parenting (Baumrind, 1971). The authoritative parent guides the child in a rational and democratic manner whereas the authoritarian parent trains the child in a dominating and egocentric way.

Yan or *chi*, probably most Chinese parents exert some kind of control or discipline. Study 2 found nearly a quarter (22% or 23%) of my subjects in the FYMY families perceiving both parent's control or discipline as "just about right" and a half (51%) of my subjects in the FCMC families considering both parent's control or discipline "just about right" as well. It may be inferred that the chance of a *chi* parent to use the right kind and degree of control or discipline is more than double that of a *yan* parent (the ratio=51% : 22% or 23%). Contrary to expectation, Study 2 found that more of my subjects as adult children recalled their mother (54%) than their father (32%) as the chief disciplinarian during childhood, the rest referring to their grandparent or elder sibling. It is probably because some kind of discipline is necessary and the mother usually has more contact with the child than the father and other elder members of the family. Regardless of the sex of the parent, the right kind and degree of control or discipline, one that does not resort to severe physical punishment, is definitely salutary to the healthy development of the child. This was suggested by the three studies reported in the present chapter.

An important trend was that the number of the traditional FYMC families is decreasing whereas that of the FCMC families is on the increase in both mainland China and Taiwan (see Table 5 and 6 of Study 3). This trend reflects increasing tenderness and permissiveness of the parents (especially the father) toward children (especially daughters) in the two major Chinese societies. As Study 3 suggested (see Table 6 and 7), TW and ML subjects were more similar than HK subjects in their perceptions of parenting and TW and ML parents treated sons and daughters more differently or less equally than HK parents. Fathers were perceived as *yan* by more TW (62%) and ML (61%) men and as *chi* by fewer TW (38%) and ML (39%) men than their HK counterparts (57.5&% perceiving father *yan* and 42.5% perceiving father *chi*). Besides, more often than their ML and TW counterparts HK parents (especially mothers) were perceived as stricter and less tender toward their daughters. This may be attributed to the fact that Hong Kong is more Westernized and thus HK parents treat their sons and daughters more equally or less differentially. In addition, HK daughters seem to receive more and earlier independence training than their ML and TW counterparts. That Taiwan is more like mainland China than Hong Kong in their adult's perceptions of parenting may be accounted for by the fact that Taiwan and the mainland are more deep-rooted than Hong Kong in the same traditional culture of China.

Table 7 of Study 3 reveals an interesting result that more HK men (31%) and women (34.5%) and more ML women (32.5%) than their counterparts in other subsamples named their mothers as *yan*, which may at least partially explain why they are more independent than their counterparts in other Chinese societies as I observed them. As to why in general fathers are perceived by sons as more *yan* and less *chi* than mothers and mothers are perceived by daughters as more *yan* and less *chi* than fathers, it may be due to two reasons. First, there is greater and more frequent conflict between the same-sex parent and child (between father and son and between mother and daughter). Second, the father expects more highly of a son than a daughter and thus puts greater pressure on him for achievement while the mother values a son to a greater extent than a daughter and thus loves him more.

Most researchers have studied the behavior of mothers and not fathers, or they have used measures of parenting that do not distinguish between mothers and fathers (Berndt et al, 1993; Lytton & Romney, 1991). This also leads to the dearth of information on the features of same-sex parent-child relationships. The present studies would help bridge the gap between earlier studies of parental socialization and more recent studies of parent-child relationships (e.g., Maccoby & Martin, 1983; Youniss & Smollar, 1985). The present research also offered an opportunity to compare parenting patterns and parent-child relationships in the three largest Chinese societies. While it replicated some findings in Berndt et al (1993) using my ML, TW, and HK data but with different data analysis plans, the present research extended our previous analyses (Berndt et al, 1993) with a greater variety of information, including joint parenting patterns, the child's personality, sibling differences, and more.

Nevertheless, the sample and method used in the present research may be questioned by other researchers because my sample was restricted to educated adults and the method relied on retrospective and contemporary reports which might be influenced by the subject's implicit theories about the world. Besides, the first two studies were qualitative and the third one used relatively simple statistical analyses, the results of the three studies may not be very convincing. Yet my sample was large and included persons of both sexes and various ages from different societies, which made age, sex, and societal comparisons possible although the U.S. subsample was relatively small (n=277) and therefore not included in some analyses.

As for methodology, different methods have yielded similar findings in the past. For example, data from retrospective reports by adults, contemporary reports by adolescents, and direct observations of parent-child interactions have suggested the same conclusions about genetic and environmental influences on parent's warmth and control (Plomin, McClearn, Pedersen, Nesselroade, & Bergeman,1988; Rowe, 1981). Future researchers may, however, use other samples and other methods with more rigorous designs and sophisticated statistical analyses to test the results of the present studies.

✦   ✦   ✦

CHAPTER THREE

FAMILY HARMONY, EDUCATION,
AND PERSONALITY

This chapter will report three studies, one quantitative and two qualitative. Study 1 dealt with the relations among parenting, family harmony, and the child's personality. Although family climate has received some attention in research (e.g., Kleinman,Handal, & Enos, 1989; Kurdek & Fine,1993; Shulman &Prechter,1989; Tolson & Wilson, 1990), family harmony as a related construct has rarely been studied. A recent study by my colleagues and me (Lau, Lew, Hau, Cheung, & Berndt, 1990) and Study 1 of the present chapter attempted to fill this gap in research. The subjects of Study 1 in this chapter were over 2600 educated men and women from the four Chinese societies (mainland China, Taiwan, Hong Kong, and the the U. S. Chinese community) and the instrument used was the questionnaire MTPI as described in Chapter One of this book. Statistical analyses were applied to the data collected by the questionnaire.

The last two studies were qualitative. Study 2 reported Chinese education as experienced and observed by college students in mainland China. The data were collected through student's written reports of small group discussions in the class while I was teaching as visiting professor at two universities in two different provinces. From this study we may get a close look at Chinese education witnessed, discussed and reported by college students, mostly juniors and seniors in the department of education. It is interesting to note that what was found in mainland

China was similar to what was observed in two other Chinese societies---Taiwan and Hong Kong. I did studies with the same method in Taiwan and Hong Kong when I taught there at the university and found nothing basically different.

Study 3 examined a case of educational reform in Taiwan. As participant, I observed, recorded, and critically reviewed the whole case. I also watched and analyzed the attitudes and behaviors of the people (parents, teachers, professors, journalists, government officials, etc.) involved in the case with a view to understanding their personality. This study, therefore, revealed not only the process of the reform but also the underlying personality of the people involved. It supplemented Study 2 by presenting a specific case in Chinese education in a society parallel to that on the other side of the Taiwan Strait. From Study 2 we know that Chinese students are dissatisfied with their education. From Study 3 we realize that educational reform is not easy in Chinese society.

STUDY 1
PARENTING, FAMILY HARMONY, AND THE CHILD'S PERSONALITY

Family harmony is a central value in Chinese culture. "Family prospers in harmony," so goes the Chinese proverb. Family harmony reflects good family relations and agreeable family climate. A family lacking harmony is characterized by conflict and tension among its members. Yet family harmony as an important condition for healthy family functioning has rarely been empirically studied in Chinese or Western societies. Its relation to parenting was only recently investigated by my colleagues and me using my mainland Chinese data (Lau, Lew, Hau, Cheung, & Berndt, 1990). The study found that family harmony is positively related to parental warmth and negatively related to parental control. This is consistent with the finding of Study 3 in Chapter Two of this book that of the four joint parenting types of family the FCMC (both parents warm) family is the most conducive to family harmony whereas the FYMY (both parents controlling) family is the least conducive to it.

The relationship between family harmony and the child's personality, however, has never been investigated before. The present study attempted to find what specific parental attitudes or behaviors are associated with family harmony and what personality traits may develop in children brought up in families varying in the degree of harmony.

The subjects were 2640 Chinese respondents to the questionnaire MTPI as described in Chapter One of this book. They were educated men and women of various ages in four Chinese societies: mainland China, Taiwan, Hong Kong, and the United States. Part I of the questionnaire includes items on the subject's family experiences and parental attitudes or behaviors during their childhood before the age of 12. Part II of the MTPI has 122 items on personality traits. Some subjects were excluded in statistical analyses because their data were missing on some items of the questionnaire.

Subjects completed the MTPI, Part I of which contained questions asking them to recall the child-rearing practices of their father and mother during childhood. First, on 26 4-point scale items (with 13 items to each parent) the parental attitudes or behaviors of fathers and mothers were assessed independently. The scores so obtained were subjected to principal-components factor analysis with oblimin (oblique) rotation as done by my colleagues and me in Lau et al (1990). Three factors were yielded. They were Warmth, Control, and Indulgence.

The first factor Warmth or authoritative parenting (Baumrind, 1971) included items that asked subjects to rate how much or how often their fathers and mothers loved them, talked to them, discussed with them, were pleasant to approach, moralized to them (reverse scored), and didn't like them (reverse scored). The second factor Control or authoritarian parenting included items that asked subjects to rate the extent or frequency that their fathers and mothers were restrictive, strict to them, became angry, kept them in awe, and allowed them independence (reverse scored). The third factor Indulgence or permissive parenting had only two items that asked subjects to assess the degree of their father's and mother's permissiveness (was permissive to or spoiled them) and overprotection (overprotected or overcared for them). Six scales (three each for fathers and mothers) were then constructed by aggregating the items with the greatest factor loadings.

Family harmony was measured in the same part of the questionnaire by one item asking subjects to rate the degree of harmony in their families during childhood on a 4-point scale: 1=very inharmonious, 2=rather inharmonious, 3=fairly harmonious, and 4=very harmonious. The third measure was on the adult child's personality. This measure constituted Part II of the questionnaire which contained 122 trait items yielding nine personality factors as reported in Chapter One of this book.

While family harmony is positively related to parental warmth and negatively related to parental control but unrelated to parental indulgence (Lau et al, 1990), yet what specific parental attitudes or behaviors are associated with family harmony have never been identified. The present study tried to fill this gap in research.

To reduce the probability of obtaining significant effects or relationships by chance due to the large size of the full sample, the alpha level for significance was set at .01 and the four societal samples were broken down by age and sex into 16 subsamples. As shown in Table 1, parental anger and moralization, which are common behaviors of the Chinese parents (especially of fathers), are both negatively related to family harmony while the parent's loving the child, talking to the child, discussing with the child, and being pleasant to approach as perceived by the child are all positively related to family harmony.

The father's attitudes or behaviors may be even more influential than the mother's because the significant correlations with family harmony for fathers in every attitude or behavior were replicated in more subsamples than those for mothers (see Table 1). For example, the significant correlations with family harmony for fathers becoming angry appeared in 10 of the 16 subsamples while those for mothers were replicated in only six subsamples. Although fewer correlations were found in the U. S. Chinese sample, those that did appear in the three U. S. subsamples (r's=.47, .32, and -.59 for young male, older male, and older female respectively) are consistent with those replicated in other subsamples from mainland China, Taiwan, and Hong Kong.

Table 1
**Correlations of Specific Parental Behaviors with Family Harmony
as Perceived by the Adult Child**

Parental behavior during childhood as perceived by the adult child	Mainland Male		Mainland Female		Taiwan Male		Taiwan Female		Hong Kong Male		Hong Kong Female		United States Male		United States Female	
	Y	O	Y	O	Y	O	Y	O	Y	O	Y	O	Y	O	Y	O
	(227)	(407)	(122)	(117)	(96)	(275)	(149)	(88)	(302)	(103)	(250)	(51)	(59)	(101)	(35)	(41)
Becomes angry																
Father		-.23	-.34	-.44	-.36	-.36	-.28		-.33	-.51	-.40					-.59
Mother	-.34	-.30	-.39	-.46			-.33				-.21					
Loves me																
Father	.33	.21	.34		.42	.22	.27		.35	.39	.25					
Mother	.26		.37		.33						.25					
Talks to me																
Father	.25		.25		.36	.27	.28		.26		.26		.47			
Mother			.33				.28				.32					
Discusses with me																
Father	.30		.40	.35		.24	.28		.23	.36	.40					
Mother	.27		.44				.29				.33					
Moralizes to me																
Father	-.25						-.22		-.22							
Mother			-.43													
Is pleasant to approach																
Father	.27		.37	.34			.34		.32	.53	.42			.32		
Mother	.30		.38				.33				.28	.48				

Note. Only the correlations significant at $p<.01$ are listed. Y=young group at age 30 or under, O=older group at age>30. The number in parentheses is the size of each subsample.

Because "the larger the sample the more dependable the correlation" (Cronbach, 1970, p. 133), we pooled all the subjects from the four Chinese societies in calculating the correlations of the adult children's personality with family harmony and parenting. As we note from Table 2, seven of the nine personality factors or source traits are correlated with family harmony and the three parenting factors or dimensions. Extraversion, Self-Discipline, Submission, Other-Orientation, and Independence are positively correlated with family harmony, father's warmth, and mother's warmth; Authoritarianism and Neuroticism are negatively correlated with family harmony, father's warmth, and mother's warmth; Extraversion is negatively correlated with mother's control; Self-Discipline is negatively correlated with mother's control, father's indulgence, and mother's indulgence; Authoritarianism is positively correlated with mother's indulgence; Submission is negatively correlated with father's indulgence; Other-Orientation and Independence are negatively correlated with father's control and mother's control; Independence is negatively correlated with father's indulgence and mother's indulgence; and Neuroticism is positively correlated with father's control, mother's control, father's indulgence, and mother's indulgence. All the correlations are rather low but significant at $p<.01$ or .001.

Table 2
Correlations of Adult Children's Personality Traits with Family Harmony and Parenting during Childhood

Personality Factors (Source Traits)	Family Harmony	Father's Warmth	Mother's Warmth	Father's Control	Mother's Control	Father's Indulgence	Mother's Indulgence
Extraversion	.08**	.09**	.12**	-.05	-.05*	-.01	.01
Self-Discipline	.11**	.10**	.13**	-.04	-.05*	-.07**	-.08**
Authoritarianism	-.10**	-.10**	-.13**	.04	.02	.05	.05*
Submission	.08**	.06*	.08**	.01	.01	.06*	.04
Cautiousness	.02	.01	.01	.03	.04	.03	-.01
Other-Orientation	.12**	.14**	.18**	.07**	.09**	.04	.03
Independence	.13**	.10**	.11**	-.06*	-.13**	-.11**	-.08**
Modernism	-.02	-.01	-.03	.03	.04	.01	-.01
Neuroticism	.18**	-.13**	-.13**	.08**	.11**	.06*	.06*

$*p<.01$. $**p<.001$.

Then we tried to find what specific personality traits or surface traits of the subjects as adult children are associated with family harmony during their childhood. To reduce Type I error, we again divided the four societal samples by age and sex into 16 subsamples. We compared the scores of the 122 trait items of three family harmony groups: Group A=the very and rather inharmonious families (we combined the very and rather inharmonious families into one group because there were not many very inharmonious families during their childhood as recalled by the adult children), Group B=the fairly harmonious families, and Group C=the very harmonious families.

We tested the differences among the three groups in the 122 trait items by ANOVA followed by Scheffe test when necessary. Statistically significant differences were found in 51 of the 122 items. They generally demonstrated that the subjects as adult children raised in harmonious families have developed more positive traits than those raised in less harmonious families. Of the 51 traits in which significant differences were found, only 10 traits are listed in Table 3 because they were the traits in which the significant differences were replicated in two or more subsamples.

To read Table 3, for example, "A,B>C" for the mainland young men in the trait "pessimistic" indicates that the mainland young men raised in very and rather inharmonious families (Group A) and those raised in fairly harmonious families (Group B) are more likely to be pessimistic than those brought up in very harmonious families (Group C). In Table 3 there are four positive traits (calm, good-tempered, self-effacing, and has a stable mood), four negative traits (pessimistic, impatient, unpopular, and suspicious) and two neutral traits (competitive and follows the crowd).

As Table 3 reveals, children brought up in harmonious families have a better chance to develop positive traits and vice versa. For example, Taiwan older men and women in Group C (raised in very harmonious families) are more calm than their counterparts in Group A (raised in very or rather inharmonious families) and Group B (raised in fairly harmonious families). Mainland young men in Group A and B are more impatient than those in Group C, and Taiwan older men in Group A are more impatient than those in Group C and B. Perhaps due to its small size, the United States sample has only one significant difference between groups on the trait "self-effacing" in its older female subsample replicated in another societal sample (in the mainland subsamples of young and older women).

Table 3
Differences in Surface Traits of Adult Children Raised in Three Groups Varying in the Degree of Family Harmony

Item No.	Surface Trait	Mainland				Taiwan				Hong Kong				United States			
		Male		Female		Male		Female		Male		Female		Male		Female	
		Y	O	Y	O	Y	O	Y	O	Y	O	Y	O	Y	O	Y	O
9	Pessimistic	A,B>C								A>C		A>C,B					
15	Calm					C>A,B		C>A,B									
27	Impatient	A,B>C				A>C,B											
44	Unpopular	B>C				A>C											
47	Good-tempered	C>A				C>B		B>A									
67	Suspicious	A,B>C										A>C,B					
72	Follows the crowd			C,B>A				B>A									
73	Competitive			A,B>C		A>C											
79	Self-effacing			C>A	C>A											C,B>A	
102	Has a stable mood			C,B>A		B>A		C,B>A									

Note. Only the statistically significant group differences (p<.05, .01 or .001) replicated in two or more subsamples are shown. A=inharmonious group, B=fairly harmonious group, C=very harmonious group. The subsample sizes are similar to those in Table 1.

Discussion

This study was one of the first to explore the relations between parenting, family harmony, and the child's personality. It extended Chapter Two by providing more information on the relationship of parenting to the child's personality development through family harmony as intervening variable. Like the research reported in Chapter Two but unlike most previous studies that focused on mother's child-rearing practices, this study investigated attitudes or behaviors of both parents as they affect or are related to family harmony and the child's personality. It was interesting to find that fathers seem to play a more important role than mothers so far as family harmony is concerned.

Family harmony is apparently associated with family climate whose four dimensions or variables (supervision, warmth, conflict, and order) are related to children's adjustment (Dishion, Patterson, Stoolmiller, &Skinner, 1991; Kurdek & Fine, 1993; Lamborn, Mounts, Steinberg, & Dornbusch,1991) for family harmony is characterized by parental warmth and lack of conflict between family members. Future research, however, should identify the dimensions or variables of family harmony.

It is evident from Table 1 that father's anger, a common phenomenon in Chinese families, has a disruptive effect on family harmony as its negative relationship with family harmony was demonstrated in 10 of the 16 subsamples. It is also clear from the same table that father's warmth or authoritative parenting style (Baumrind, 1971; Maccoby & Martin, 1983) contributes a great deal to family harmony as all the relevant variables (loves me, talks to me, discusses with me, is pleasant to approach) on the part of the father were found positively correlated with family harmony in eight or nine of the 16 subsamples.

As Table 2 reveals, both family harmony and parenting are related to the child's personality. The correlations imply that family harmony and father's and mother's warmth (authoritative parenting) all contribute to the development of the child's positive source traits (Extraversion, Self-Discipline, Submission, Other-Orientation, and Independence) and that father's and mother's control (authoritarian parenting) lead to the development of the child's negative source traits (Authoritarianism and

Neuroticism). Although parental indulgence or permissive parenting style was not adequately explored in the present study because it was defined by only two items in the questionnaire as factor analyzed, its effect on the child's personality development is generally negative as Table 2 implies.

To further examine the relationship between family harmony and the child's personality, we looked into the differences in surface traits between the three groups of subjects as adult children varying in the degree of family harmony. It was found (see Table 3) that, in general, harmonious families are more likely than inharmonious families to produce children with positive surface traits. This finding is consistent with the results shown in Table 2 which reveals the relationship of the subject's source traits to family harmony during their childhood as they recalled it.

STUDY 2

CHINESE EDUCATION AS EDUCATED CHINESE SEE IT

There are many books (e.g., Chen, 1981; Guo, 1989; Hayhoe, 1985; Lin & Fan, 1990; Stevenson & Stigler, 1992) and articles (e.g., Chen, 1994; Davin, 1990; Fan, 1990; Lo, 1991; Morey & Zhou, 1990; Yin & White, 1994) on various aspects of education in mainland China. Yet none of them looks at Chinese education entirely from the vantage point of the educated Chinese themselves, that is , through the very eyes of Chinese people who have received education in mainland China from primary school through college. The purpose of this study was, therefore, to see Chinese education with the eyes of educated Chinese. The present study asked the subjects to give their impressions of education as they themselves had received and observed it from every possible angle so that a more realistic picture of Chinese education could be presented.

The subjects were 95 students, mostly juniors and seniors of Education Department, out of about 150 students in two classes, each at one of the two universities in two different provinces in China where I taught as visiting professor a course named Developmental Psychology and Education.

As a learning procedure, the students organized themselves into discussion groups of five or six members. Each group discussed as required the following questions in two class periods totaling 100 minutes: (1)How the Chinese teachers teach and discipline their students? (2)What are the problems and their possible solutions in Chinese schools and colleges? (3)How do Chinese schools educate their students in the five domains--intellectual, moral, social, physical, and emotional?

Each group was required to turn in a discussion report on the contents of discussion in two weeks. Out of about 150 students taking the course at the two universities, 95 students in 17 groups met the requirement and the remaining students in other groups failed to submit their group reports. Eight of the discussion group reports were collected from one university and nine from the other. Content analysis (Brislin, 1980) was made of the 17 reports which yielded the findings as follows.

Presented below are the contents that occurred in three or more of the 17 reports, many of them appeared in more than half of the reports, which represent a consensus of the informants or participants in the discussion. It may be interesting to note for the non-Chinese that in Chinese the primary (grade or elementary) school is called "little" school, the secondary (junior and senior high) school "middle" school, and the college or university "big" school. In the following presentations, however, the common English terms will be used instead of the indigenous Chinese ones, which will be used only occasionally.

1. For more than ten years during and after the Cultural Revolution (1966-1976), the school system was operated on a 5-2-2 or 5-3-2 scheme (5-year primary, 2- or 3-year junior high, and 2-year senior high). In recent years the 6-3-3 or 5-3-3 system has been implemented in many cities and some rural areas.

2. Almost without its own aims or functions, nearly every school at the lower level is a preparatory school or stepping stone for the school at the next higher level.

So the kindergarten becomes a preparatory school for the grade school, which in turn is a stepping stone for the junior high school. The junior high is the preparatory school for the senior high, which in turn is the stepping stone for the college or university.

3. The quality of education is generally low, especially in the rural areas, except in a limited number of so called "key" (*dzong dien*) schools or colleges/universities which are found in the cities. The "key" schools and colleges/universities are the favored institutions. Their existence can raise the standard of education but deprive students in the ordinary institutions of their equal educational opportunities.

4. Because there are so many students and so many schools, colleges, and universities (1,080 colleges and universities in 1995), there is a great shortage of qualified teachers at all levels. It is rather common that junior high graduates teach grade school, senior high graduates teach junior and senior high, and college graduates teach freshman courses. The situation has been improving in recent years.

5. Most high schools are academic and college preparatory. During second year in senior high, the curriculum branches off into two tracks, the arts group and the science group. The arts track, regarded as inferior by teachers and parents, prepares students to specialize in liberal arts or social sciences in college while the science track, often chosen by the high achievers, prepares students to major in science and technology. There are some vocational high schools but they are shunned by adolescents because their students are considered inferior to students of academic high schools and their graduates have less chance to go on to college.

6. In educational administration, the school principals and college/university presidents have little autonomy to manage their institutions. Everything from curriculum to personnel is under the control of the government. The final authority rests in the National Commission on Education in Peking.

7. Grade and secondary school teachers are underpaid. This affects their morale

and social status. Their inadequate social status is reflected in the fact that teacher training institutions, including teachers colleges and normal universities, suffer from low prestige and cannot attract students of high caliber.

8. Students are primarily evaluated on their academic achievement. Although a model student is one of "three goodnesses" (*san hau*)--good morally, intellectually, and physically, academic or intellectual goodness carries the greatest weight. Students of three goodnesses are elected or selected from kindergarten through graduate school out of the top 10% in each class.

9. In many primary and secondary schools students are grouped by academic ability into "good and bad" or "fast and slow" classes. The good or fast classes are generally privileged to enjoy the best resources, including the best teachers, available in the school while the slow or bad classes are neglected. This kind of educational arrangement has the same advantages and disadvantages as the "key" schools relative to the ordinary schools in terms of educational standard and equal educational opportunities for all students.

10. When a student fails academically, he or she will lose face and feel inferior in school, in the family, and in the neighborhood. The social and psychological damage thus done is sometimes formidable. Teacher-student, parent-child, and peer relationships are all affected by a student's academic performance. If the student succeeds as a high achiever, he/she will be liked by teachers, loved by parents, respected (often with some jealousy) by peers. If he/she fails, the relations will more or less suffer.

11. Students, particularly in grade and junior high schools, often complain about overcontrolling by their teachers in the name of care and concern. Most teachers are authoritarian, controlling, and moralizing. Favoritism is common; teachers favor good students and students of the opposite sex. They are generally stricter to boys and more lenient to girls. While superior students are favored and inferior students are

disfavored, those in between (the middle or average students) are neglected.

12. As a rule, the class master or mistress (head teacher of a class) is more influential to students than other teachers because he or she is in charge of the whole class and accountable for its performance. His or her influence increases if he or she stays with the same class for two or more years. In most cases, the head teacher is liked by some students and disliked by others.

13. The Cultural Revolution days are gone and traditions return. Chinese schools are still teacher-centered today. Like other authority figures such as parents and bosses, most teachers are characterized by authoritarianism. Teachers in the grade school are, however, more caring, protective, and restrictive while those in the secondary, especially senior high, school and college are less authoritarian and controlling. The change of teacher's attitudes and behaviors toward students from grade school through college is in fact a corresponding response to student's psychological development.

14. The children in the elementary school, especially in the lower grades, tend to obey and respect authority and believe in whatever the teacher says. As they grow, they become less obedient and demand greater autonomy. The adolescents, especially those in senior high school and college, have their own judgment and opinions and demand greater respect and independence as they mature cognitively and physically. Chinese children and adolescents as a whole, nevertheless, respect and obey, at least overtly, their teachers though they prefer some types of teachers to others.

15. While various discipline techniques are used, very much like those by parents at home such as induction, criticism, scolding, punishment, threatening, love withdrawal, and power assertion, moralizing is the most common discipline technique used by teachers. Positive reinforcement like praise, award, or encouragement is sometimes employed, but mostly toward the favored students. Student's negative behaviors are often criticized or punished whereas positive

behaviors are seldom rewarded or reinforced.

16. Lecture is the dominant, and in most cases the only, method of instruction. Students are expected to memorize the textbooks and/or lecture notes for recitation in examinations. Standard answers are the keys to test questions. Even in the university few instructors or professors adopt discussion as a teaching-learning procedure. Students seldom ask questions in class because questioning is discouraged by teachers and derided by peers. Most students pretend to understand all that is taught for fear of displeasing the teacher and displaying inferiority among peers.

17. There are too many tests and examinations (including weekly test, unit test, stage test, monthly test, midterm exam, final exam, graduation exam, regional exam, mock entrance exam, entrance exam) for primary and secondary school students. Most of their time is spent in preparing for those tests and exams,culminating in the most competitive nationwide college entrance examination. The prestige of a school depends on the success rate of its graduates passing the entrance examination and getting admitted to a good high school or a good college/university.

18. Formal education is dominated and directed by entrance examination for a higher level of schooling beginning with junior high school. The most competitive is the annually held nationwide entrance examination for admission to the more than 1,000 colleges and universities in the country. Once admitted to a college or university, a job is almost guaranteed upon graduation. A graduation diploma is the only important thing; little attention is paid to what and how much the diploma holder has learned.

19. Over two million (2.66 million in 1996) senior high school graduates take the nationwide college entrance examination every year. More than 30% (36% in 1996 according to *China Education Daily*, July 5, 1996, p. 1) of the examinees get admitted to a college or university. Many would try again and some would try as often as five times (in five years) if they fail. As residential mobility is restricted and

college graduates are generally assigned jobs in the cities, those from the countryside will have little chance to become urban residents if they fail to get admitted to a college or university (unless they are qualified to join the armed forces, which may also entitle them to become city dwellers). For the young people living in the cities as well as those residing in the countryside, admission to an institution of higher learning is the surest, and for many (especially the peasant's children) the only, road for upward mobility. As a result of economic development in recent years, however, many people including rural dwellers get rich by engaging in commercial activities.

20. Students have been trained since grade school to study passively with little spontaneity under test pressure. They are passive in learning and dependent on teachers for directions as to what to learn (e.g., what to read and what to memorize) and how to prepare for tests and exams (e.g., what areas or questions to prepare for). Ironically, "little" and "middle" (grade and high) school students are kept busy with tests and homework to a much greater degree than "big" school (college or university) students. As a result, most "big" school students become relaxed and lazy as test pressure is relieved. There is little teacher-student interaction outside the college classroom because few students care to call on their teachers for academic or other purposes.

21. Schooling is intellectual education in the narrow sense of the term; it is centered around learning from textbooks and lecture notes. The library is either unavailable, as in many "little" and "middle" schools, or unnecessary, as in many "big" schools. Creativity, originality, divergent thinking, and the ability of independent study are thus stifled. Meanwhile, other domains of education, such as emotional and physical education, are also neglected.

22. Whereas there is a special system to select and train athletes for international competitions, physical education does not receive sufficient attention in the regular curriculum. Moral education is aimed at political socialization focusing on the

cultivation of the Communist world view and Socialist morality. Faith in Communism and Socialism, like a national religion, is officially emphasized although not so well accepted. No other religious faith is allowed officially although religious freedom has been tolerated in recent years. Social and emotional development of the student is hampered by the test-oriented curriculum.

23. Overcompetition for test performance leads to self-centeredness which contradicts the Socialist ideal of collectivism. The competition is so intense and the stress is so keen that social interaction is deformed and emotional outlet is blocked. Consequently, the high scorers in the tests and exams are usually underdeveloped in many ways, particularly in the capabilities of dealing with people and solving life problems. So goes the sarcasm, "High marks but low abilities."

24. Inasmuch as the burden of schoolwork (including tests and homework) is heavy in "little" and "middle" schools, there is not much time and energy left for extracurricular activities. Since the burden is lessened in "big" schools because it is " hard to get in (be admitted) but easy to get out (be graduated)," undergraduates are more relaxed to take part in a variety of activities. Dance on weekends and special holidays is a popular activity on campus for legitimate social interaction between the sexes (presumably because it used to be a favorite recreation for the late Chairman Mao). Dating used to be discouraged or even prohibited but has become frequent recently.

25. Many participants in the 17 discussion groups obviously have a workable knowledge of modern educational theories and are eager to have them applied in China. This is evidenced by their conception of ideal educational practices. The following ideas were found in two or more of the 17 discussion reports:

1) Educational practices should be varied in accordance with the aptitudes and potentials of individual students. [This is also an ancient educational tenet handed down from the times of Confucius but seldom put into practice.]

2) Democracy is the best way of educating the young.

3) All students should be respected.

4) "Bad" or disfavored students should not be discriminated against.

5) The student likes a teacher who is fair, conscientious, calm, warm, and objective.

6) The teacher should praise, support, and encourage the student

7) Teachers may be strict and stern, but should not be harsh and severe.

8) Control and supervision are necessary if rational.

9) Induction (reasoning and persuasion) is the best discipline technique.

10) Teaching should be well-organized but flexible.

11) The ability of independent study must be fostered.

12) Cooperative learning must be encouraged.

13) Textbooks and teaching materials should be updated and linked to the reality of life and society.

14) School principals and college/university presidents should have legitimate autonomy in administration.

15) The nationwide college entrance examination should be reformed.

Discussion

One may wonder how the picture might differ in other two Chinese societies, namely, Hong Kong and Taiwan. I did the same study in both places when I taught the same course in an in-service training program for secondary school teachers there each at a public university. In spite of the fact that the three Chinese societies have been ruled by different governments for more than 40 years, I found far more similarities than differences in their educational scene. This is obviously due to the same cultural traditions and values they have all shared. It is, therefore, unnecessary to report the studies I did in Hong Kong and Taiwan. It is only necessary to point out the differences I found as follows which are considered minor relative to the similarities.

1. While there are few private schools in mainland China, the public schools are generally more prestigious than private schools in Hong Kong and Taiwan.

2. While Taiwan and Hong Kong both have had nine-year compulsory education, education is compulsory in the six-year primary school in many mainland cities and in the five-year primary school in some rural areas of the mainland. Since 1986, however, compulsory education has extended from six to nine years to include the three-year junior high school in some mainland cities.

3. There are some good church-operated schools in Hong Kong where religious faith and church activities are salutary to students moral, social, and emotional development. There are relatively few such schools in Taiwan and the mainland. Due to the extremely competitive nationwide college entrance examination in Taiwan and the mainland, the schools there are even more neglectful of student's well-rounded development than schools in Hong Kong.

4. While the mainland and Taiwan both incorporate political socialization in their curriculum, Hong Kong does not. It may be said that Hong Kong students enjoy a greater degree of academic freedom. As a result of democratization, however, political socialization in Taiwan has gradually faded away in recent years.

5. Under British rule until 1997 when the colony was handed over to the mainland government, Hong Kong was a bilingual society where the medium of instruction was Chinese (mainly Cantonese dialect) in some schools while it was English in others. Mandarin is the medium in all Taiwan schools whereas local dialects are spoken in many mainland schools although *putunghua* (similar to mandarin) is the official national language.

6. Colleges and universities in Hong Kong and Taiwan have larger libraries with more Western books and journals than their mainland counterparts.

7. More college/university faculty members in Hong Kong and Taiwan are

Western trained with Ph.D.s than their counterparts on the mainland.

8. Going abroad to study is easier for students in Hong Kong and Taiwan than for those on the mainland due to financial and political reasons.

9. More professors in Taiwan are interested and play active roles in politics than their counterparts in Hong Kong and mainland China. Many teachers in Hong Kong and Taiwan have commercial interests (e.g., investment in real estate). Recent market-orientation in economy has even commercialized mainland education (Yin & White, 1994).

10. Hong Kong school teachers and university professors are among the best paid in the world. Their Taiwan counterparts are fairly well paid while their mainland counterparts are underpaid.

11. Foreign influences are found on education in the three Chinese societies. While British and American impact is noticeable in Hong Kong and Taiwan respectively, both Russian and American influences are observable on the mainland.

Despite the differences, the common features in education of the three societies are easily seen. Children's academic achievement from kindergarten through high school is the overriding concern of most parents in the three Chinese societies. This concern creates tremendous pressures on and a great deal of anxiety in children. Such phenomenon is probably universal, though different in degree. Even in the United States where education is considered "normal" by many Chinese educators, parental overconcern about their children's academic success is not uncommon. This is vividly described by Lightfoot (1983), a Harvard professor of education, who wrote about good American high schools:

> Parents in Highland Park[near Chicago, also the name of a suburban public high school there] express an early concern for educational excellence. They are anxious that their children get an accelerated head start in learning and that they never lose ground. ... Most parents expect their children will read before formal schooling begins and are critical of kindergarten teachers who stress the social-psychological development of children (p. 129).

Every teacher I spoke with at Highland Park complained of the intense
competition among students and the extreme pressure from parents that their
children achieve in school. ... Yet rarely do students reveal a burning
intellectual curiosity that inspires their interest and commitment. More often
their intensity is linked to winning the academic race, scoring points against
competitors, and gaining a place on top of the pile (p. 131).

Professor Lightfoot also cited (p. 130) a sensible parent, Mr. Cramer, who and
his wife "downplay grades" and encourage their children to think more broadly about
social responsibility and personal happiness. Most important, Mr. and Mrs. Cramer
"try to model these contrary values in their own behaviors, avoiding flagrant
materialism, volunteering for civic functions, and refusing to compete with neighbors
and friends." Mr. Cramer does not believe that the motives of most Highland Park
parents are pure. He says that parents "live vicariously through their children,"
experiencing indirectly all of the successes and benefits of their children's
achievements and status.

What Professor Lightfoot wrote and Mr. Cramer said about American parents
apply as well to the parents in Hong Kong, Taiwan, and mainland China. This
reflects some common values and human nature that we all share. Nevertheless, there
exists much greater difference between American and Chinese education than
between Chinese schools in mainland China, Taiwan, and Hong Kong. According to
Stevenson (Stevenson, 1992; Stevenson & Stigler, 1992; Stevenson, Chen, & Lee,
1993), American parents place a lesser emphasis on academic achievement than
Chinese parents. In the United States, "childhood is a time for many different types
of accomplishments. Doing well in school is only one of them" (Stevenson, 1992, p.
72). Contrary to Stevenson's belief that Americans should learn from Chinese
education, however, I share the views of many Chinese parents in the United States
that American education, especially at the elementary and secondary level, is more
conducive than Chinese education to healthy development of the young. I also agree
with many Chinese men and women who have studied at American institutions of

higher learning that American education at the university level is much better in quality than Chinese higher education.

STUDY 3
A CASE OF EDUCATION REFORM

This was a case study of an educational reform plan in Taiwan which was suspended for nationwide implementation under seemingly overwhelming opposition. The plan was, due to opposition, being carried out on a trial basis in only six localities of the country. The aim of this study was twofold: to describe the background of the reform plan and to detect the personality traits of educated people in Taiwan by observing their behaviors and analyzing their reactions in various situations closely related to the reform plan. To understand the background of the study, a brief account of the reform plan is in order.

The Reform Plan

Taiwan has had nine-year universal education since 1968 which later becomes compulsory for all children six to fifteen years old. On August 4, 1989 Premier Lee Huan instructed the Ministry of Education (MOE) to study the feasibility of a twelve-year universal education plan to be initiated in 1993. On October 9 in the same year, the MOE presented a preliminary report on the plan. In January 1990 a draft of the plan was distributed for public discussion. The preparatory work was to start in the fall semester of 1990, when the school performance of each student entering the junior high school (JHS)from then on will be graded according to a new scheme to ensure equal treatment of all students in all junior high schools . It was planned that beginning in the fall of 1990 students in the first year (7th grade) and later in the following two JHS years (8th and 9th grade) would be assigned to classes by normal distribution instead of ability grouping. Student's performance in the three JHS years would be graded on a 5-point (grade) scale with a quota for each grade according to a normal curve based on class norm without discrimination among classes or schools. The objective was to admit students to the senior high (academic or vocational) school (SHS) on the basis of their complete record of performance during the three JHS years regardless of the class or school from which they were graduated. This would be an improvement over the current scheme by which JHS graduates are selected to enter SHS on the basis of their performance in the highly competitive unified SHS entrance exam. The most serious weakness of the current old scheme exists in the fact that by ability grouping the school's attention is concentrated on the 30% of the student population which constitutes the elite classes while 70% of the student population designated as underachievers are neglected and that the old scheme creates test anxiety in and parental pressure on not only JHS students but also elementary school pupils, which is extremely harmful to their mental and physical health. The new scheme, though more democratic and healthful than the current old one, is not flawless. One of its drawbacks is its overemphasis on academic achievement like the old scheme to the neglect of a well-balanced education for healthy personality development. The academic achievement under the new scheme would be assessed by three "stage" tests each semester. In comparison, however, the new scheme is still better and more balanced than the old one because, instead of relying solely on the annual entrance exam for selection of SHS students like the old system, every course studied, activities attended, and the conduct of the student recorded during the three JHS years under the new plan will be counted, though in differential weight, for assignment to SHS. The assignment is competitive; whether the JHS graduate will be assigned to the SHS of his/her first, second or third choice depends on the student's standing of his/her total performance in class.

The Case Study

The subjects were all those educated adults in Taiwan who had taken actions or expressed opinions about the government's educational reform plan which was a preliminary program for 12-year universal schooling from age six to eighteen, an extension of three more years from the current 9-year compulsory education. They were mostly parents of current or immediate JHS students, school teachers and administrators, college and university professors, legislators, journalists, and government officials.

The data were primarily collected by participant observation and content analysis of newspapers and related literature. I attended committee meetings, conferences, legislative hearings, and debates or discussions with JHS principals, parents, and teachers in addition to professors of various specialties, all concerning the educational reform plan. I analyzed the content of 168 relevant items in ten major Chinese newspapers published during the nine-month period of August 1989-April 1990, which was the interval between the announcement of the reform plan and the suspension of it for nationwide implementation. The 168 items appeared mostly in three largest newspapers; namely, the *Central Daily, China Times*, and the *United Daily*. The items included news reports, features, interviews , and articles. Each item indicated the opinion or attitude of a particular person or group. I also analyzed the contents of relevant conference proceedings, research reports, and magazine articles.

Meanwhile, I observed as participant the behaviors of other participants in the committee meetings, conferences, debates, discussions, and legislative hearings. I also discussed privately with some colleagues and friends the motives of those people who were against the reform plan. The plan was first officially termed the preliminary plan for the extension of free national (universal) education. It was later called the voluntary plan for JHS graduates' promotion to SHS or simply the voluntary promotion plan (VPP). The promotion to the SHS of JHS students on graduation is voluntary rather than compulsory. For convenience, however, it will be often called hereafter the education reform plan (ERP).

It was announced by the Ministry of Education (MOE) on May 3, 1990 that the educational reform plan (ERP) would be suspended until an experiment on a small scale for three years proves it feasible. The announcement coincided with the cabinet reshuffle in which a new premier was nominated by the president of the Republic of China on Taiwan. Premier Lee Huan's stepping down was believed to be a result of personality incompatibility and political incongruity with the president. Although Premier Lee told me that the president approved the educational reform plan at the outset, I suspect that the president suggested its suspension under the pressure of public opinion.

Content analysis of the 168 newspaper items reveals that 23 (14%) of the items supported the ERP, 14 (8%) were against it, 67 (40%) were skeptical of it, and 64 (38%) were neutral in position. The fatal criticism and opposition came from a group of 60 professors (mostly middle-aged, more than 40 of them taught science at several major universities) who signed a statement which appeared in the *United Daily* on February 19, 1990. The theme of the statement was "Please Do Not Use the Junior High School Students as Guinea Pigs." The statement pointed out possible drawbacks of the ERP (e.g., the new selection process for entering SHS is not as fair as the selection by the unified entrance exam). It requested that the ERP be postponed for at least three years pending a thorough feasibility study and solution of all related problems (e.g., shortage of qualified teachers). A month later, the leaders of that science professors group (SPG) claimed to have secured 596 signatures from professors and scholars in support of their aforesaid statement.

The largest gathering for discussion of the ERP was a conference held on March 10 and 11, 1990 in the city of Taichung in central Taiwan. The conference was organized by ten legislators, sponsored by the Taichung Consumers' Rights Promotion Society, and attended by some 200 participants, including secondary school principals and university professors. The conclusion of the conference reads as follows.

All participants in this conference agree that extension of free education for the people is necessary for a progressive nation; we appreciate the benign intent of the government. The proposed plan with the steps to be taken, however, is misconceived, and good intent may not lead to good results. The great majority of the scholars and specialists attending this conference regard the Education Ministry's plan for extending free education as fragmentary which will not make any constructive contribution to the total system of education.

Both the 60 professors' statement and the conference conclusion stressed the hastiness in the decision making process of the ERP planners and the unsolved problems of the current 9-year compulsory schooling. Both urged the suspension of the ERP. Yet both ignored or neglected the fact that the ERP aimed at not only extending free education from 9 to 12 years but also at trying to solve the problems connected with the 9-year compulsory education. One of the problems the ERP intended to solve was the discrimination against the slow learners and underachievers who constitute 70% of the JHS student population and whose chances to enter the prestigious high schools and later the prestigious universities are almost nonexistent.

Now that the ERP would be beneficial to the average and below average students, but why is it that few parents of such potential students speak up to defend it? The reason is two-fold: (1)Such parents are mostly less educated and unable to express their opinions effectively. (2)They are reluctant to speak out for fear of losing face by exposing the weakness of their children.

The ERP's nation-wide implementation in Taiwan was suspended as the opponents demanded it. In the academic year 1990-91 a small-scale three-year (1990-93) experiment was launched in the two largest cities with 21 Taipei JHS classes and 2 Kaohsiung junior high schools participating in the experimental program. Strangely, those who were so enthusiastic about killing the ERP pay little attention to the experiment, the failure of which may defer the 12-year free schooling plan along with the educational reform indefinitely. They disregard the fact that the experimental students are also what they once called "guinea pigs." Since these guinea pigs are volunteers, obviously none or few of the opponents' children are among them. I asked two leaders of the SPG, both being professors of physics, why their colleagues suddenly become so quiet. They were unable to offer any convincing reason. I discussed with one of them, the organizer of the opposition campaign, the motives behind the opposition. He admitted that about a fourth of the SPG members had children who would be affected by the ERP and they were the very people who urged him most strongly to organize the campaign against the ERP.

Because the ERP would treat all students on an equal basis, many professors' children who were to be assigned to the "elite" classes by ability grouping would not enjoy the same privileges under the new plan with grouping by normal distribution. It is understandable that some professors with high-achieving children most likely to enter the JHS elite classes opposed the ERP with a view to protecting their own children. Other professors whose children had passed the JHS age opposed the ERP for other reasons or motives, one of which might be authority defiance.Since most Chinese, particularly the educated, were brought up by authoritarian parents, especially fathers, they were conditioned to defy authority. Because the ERP was believed to be imposed by the premier, the highest authority figure in the government under the president, authority defiance was easily aroused to resist it.

There were other sources of opposition. One was the teachers of the elite classes who, under the new system, would lose some of their extra income gained from coaching their students after school. They also deemed it more difficult to teach a heterogeneously grouped (normally distributed) class than an elite class. Another source of opposition was some of the JHS principals, particularly those of prestigious schools, who were reluctant to cooperate because any change in school operation would bring about inconvenience or extra work for the principals. Still another source of opposition was the parents association of the school, especially of a prestigious one, which was generally monopolized by the parents of the elite students. The parents associations often exert pressures on the principals in the interest of their children. An additional reason or motive of opposition was the bandwagon effect. As the silent majority did not speak out, the opinions of the minority who spoke most loudly against the ERP attracted increasing attention and identification while other opinions were ignored. What made it worse was that the mass media, including TV and newspapers, reported in most cases only the prevailing opinions and sentiments unfavorable to the ERP. The opposition was also caused by the MOE's insufficient effort to explain the merit of the ERP to the public and to improve the plan by objectively considering the criticisms and recommendations. As a result, many opponents failed to see, if not deliberately ignored, the merit of the plan while the sympathizers who made constructive recommendations to improve the ERP felt disappointed.

Because parental decision is usually decisive for the youngster in Chinese society, the Tung Foundation in Taipei conducted a questionnaire survey of 1,000 parents with a return rate of 62%. The survey revealed on April 4, 1990 in the *Central Daily* that 49.7% of the parents would rather choose for their children to take the unified SHS entrance exam and 48.9% preferred the new scheme of the ERP by which their children would be assigned on graduation from the JHS to the SHS according to their three-year JHS record along with their choices (a student's chance for the top choices to be granted depends on the ranking of his or her three-year JHS performance in class, but every student will be admitted to a senior high school, academic or vocational, which may not be his or her best choice). As the survey results show, the pros and cons of the new scheme were about equal in distribution. The reason why nearly half of the parents did not support the new plan was twofold: (1)As mentioned before, some parents had children as potential elite ready to enter the JHS. These children's chances of having the best teachers assigned to them for the most effective preparation to enter the prestigious schools and subsequently the prestigious universities would be lost under the proposed scheme for normalized teaching and learning. (2)Many parents distrusted the teachers who would have greater power in determining the student's chances to enter the SHS of their choice under the new scheme, by which the teacher's evaluation of student's performance determines their ranking in class and, therefore, their probability of being admitted to the right SHS. These parents thought that the current unified SHS entrance exam is a more fair and objective selection mechanism than the individual teacher's testing and evaluation in different JHS classes.

The Tung Foundations survey also revealed two other important findings which were neglected by many people: (1)53.7% of the parents believed that the ERP would normalize the JHS education by making it more balanced than current practice, whereas 32.6% did not think so. (2)51.6% of the parents believed that the ERP would reduce the urban-rural difference in the quality of education, whereas 31.8% did not think so. From these findings it becomes evident that the parents who recognized some advantages of the ERP outnumbered those who did not. Three years later in 1993 when the number of experimental schools had increased to 70 in Taipei and 35 in Kaohsiung with schools in four counties also experimenting, two questionnaire surveys sponsored by the MOE were conducted by two professors of education independently. One survey administered questionnaires to more than 3,000 JHS students, parents, teachers and school administrators in the six experimental localities and four control localities. The results showed a mean of 78% of the total sample supporting the ERP with more people in the experimental group in favor of it than those in the control group. Another survey was conducted among teachers, principals, students and their parents in 127 experimental schools in Taipei, Kaohsiung and Yilang (the largest of the four experimental counties). A mean of 77% of 6604 respondents supported the ERP, a result very similar to that of the first survey. Evidently, a larger number of people considered the ERP feasible after a trial period of three years in the junior high schools of two cities and four counties.

The ERP is, of course, not perfect. It is criticized that the experimental students lag behind the control students in academic achievement as measured by tests. After being assigned to senior high schools, many of the experimental students fail to compete well with the control students who entered the SHS through the joint (unified) entrance examination (SHSJEE).

To oversee and evaluate the implementation of the experimental program, the MOE organized in June 1990 a 12-man committee composed of three presidents of normal universities, two presidents of teachers colleges, four deans or department heads, one director of a science education center, and two professors of education. All the committee members were appointed by the minister of education (ME).The committee was chaired by the president of National Taiwan Normal University and attended by about twelve government (central, provincial, and local) officials of education in addition to the committee members. I was the only committee member not affiliated with any of the normal universities or teachers colleges. I was appointed by the ME simply because I had publicly supported the ERP in principle, though not in every way. The committee met in Taipei about once every two months (sometimes more frequently) for three or four hours to hear reports by local officials and discuss matters requested by the MOE. Most members seldom talked or never said a word throughout the meeting. The chairman did most of the talking. Only one or two members spoke up. Other members and government officials generally talked only when required by the agenda or requested by the chairman.Those who did talk usually defended the government's position. The members also visited the schools with experimental classes and discussed with their principals, teachers, and students.

Out of the 15 meetings the committee had held during the two-year period (June 1990-June 1992), the ME attended twice and one of the three vice-ministers attended almost every meeting. At the 9th meeting when the ME attended, the meeting started at 4:00 PM on August 12, 1991. After hearing the reports by local and provincial officials on the progress of the experimental program, the ME interrupted through his chief secretary the chairman for permission to speak because he had to leave shortly. The ME spoke about 20 minutes, expressing his opinions and making some suggestions which he reminded politely were only his personal views. After the ME left at about 6:00, however, the chairman declared that since the ME had given his "instructions" there should be nothing else we could discuss unless we disagreed with him. At this point, nobody else spoke up although I expressed my views and suggested, but to no avail, that we discuss relevant matters for another hour. The meeting then adjourned at 6:15. This was a good indication of an authority-directed culture because the ME is a higher authority above the committee.

Most members seemed to be lukewarm about the committee and its functions. With administrative duties as presidents, deans, or department heads, they were too busy to fulfill the committee's functions. At the 12th meeting in January 1992, a normal university professor who served as coordinator for the committee raised the question as to the committee's proper functions and the necessity of its continued existence. Two MOE officials and three members spoke in support of the need for the committee. The chairman summarized their opinions. Nobody else talked. Properly speaking, the committee had some authority but no power; it was primarily an advisory body. The decisions made and opinions expressed at the committee were not mandatory.

In he first two years the experimental ERP fared quite well in the two cities, where the academic competition had been extremely intense. In the southern city of Kaohsiung, the principals of the experimental schools and a Bureau of Education official, the division head responsible for the experimentation, were most enthusiastic and conscientious. In the northern city of Taipei, the director of the Education

Bureau was anxious to see the educational reform carried out sooner than scheduled and better than designed by the MOE. Yet after he announced in March 1992 that Taipei would implement the ERP on a city-wide basis starting in the 1992-93 academic year, opposition from various sources surfaced as it had happened two years earlier. The ME and the advisory committee both at first backed up the Taipei decision. But as the opposition gained momentum and became politicized with the support of the opposition party, the ME changed his mind. I was the only one committee member who protested the ME's yielding to political pressure. The director of the Taipei Education Bureau was forced to give up his adventurous attempt.

As a compromise, the city of Taipei decided for the 1992-93 school year to let the first year JHS students (7th graders), with the approval of their parents, have a free choice---to enter either the VPP (ERP) or the JEE (SHSJEE) class. Finally, 24.36% of 48,512 students in 70 JHSs applied for admission to the VPP classes and 19.98% (4,913 boys and 4,781 girls) of them were admitted to 256 VPP classes. Unadmitted were 2,122 or 4.37% of the 48,512 7th graders because they failed to meet the VPP class's normal distribution criterion based on an intelligence test. The aftermath led to a reorganization of the advisory committee. The new committee was made up of 21 members including five college and university presidents, four junior and senior high school principals, and twelve professors. The president of a national comprehensive university was elected chairman. The membership reflects an improvement over the old one in that it has a greater variety in the background of its members. Seven members of the old committee and 14 new members were appointed by the ME, including three female members and two members from the dissenting groups. In addition to professors of education, there are two professors of psychology including one lady from a private university while all other members serve at the public schools, colleges and universities.

The new advisory committee met once a month with about the same group of government officials as the former committee. It had four subcommittees (on planning, research, school visitation, and public opinions) which met whenever necessary. The new committee had met eight times in eight months before its dissolution at the end of June in 1993 with its last meeting attended by the new minister of education. As member of both the old and the new committee, I had attempted for three years to make some modifications of the ERP but found only meager support from other members. One strange thing in the process of the government's endeavor at the educational reform during the three years was that few professors of education at Taiwan's nine teachers colleges, three normal universities, and one university with education department spoke up either to defend or oppose the ERP. Most of those who spoke against it were lay people and specialists in other fields. They constituted the *loudest minority*. The following were their criticisms. The possible rejoinder to each criticism is found in the brackets.

1. Some teachers will be unfair in evaluating the student's performance under the ERP. [In case the teachers are not trusted, an overseeing body can be organized by the parents and/or other independent people.]

2. The 5-point rating scheme with fixed quota for each grade on the basis of normal distribution (e.g., 10% of students in each class will get 5 points, the highest grade) is too rigid. [If so, percentile rank or other relative score such as T score without fixed quota may be used to replace the 5-point grading system.]

3. Low achievers or slow learners should be taken care of separately and not be mixed with high achievers or fast learners in a normally distributed (heterogeneously grouped) class. [The low achievers or slow learners will be discriminated against this way as it has been the case in ability grouping under the current old system. To solve this problem, two sets of teaching materials or textbooks may be used: the basic materials for all students and the advanced materials for those

students interested in learning more at a level beyond the basics.]

4. The pressure on the students would be greater than that exerted by the senior high school joint (unified) entrance exam (SHSJEE) because of the 18 stage tests in 6 semesters and the ratings in five domains of performance or development (intellectual, social, moral, physical, and aesthetical or emotional). [The academic learning in the six semesters of the three JHS years is divided into 18 stages with a test at the conclusion of each stage. This is distributed learning found to be more effective by research than massed learning under the current system dominated by the SHSJEE. The evaluation in five areas of performance would promote a more balanced development of individual students than the old system which relies on book learning in the academic subjects tested by the entrance exam.]

5. The competition among classmates in the five categories of performance or development would be more intense than the competition among all students who take the unified SHS entrance exam. [It is only an assumption. Research has shown results contrary to the assumption.]

6. With a fixed rating scheme for moral and social development, students would become less cheerful and lively. [The rating would promote student's moral and social development which has never been effectively evaluated under the old system. The evaluation could be improved by teacher rating plus peer rating which has never been tried before.]

7. Since vocational schools enjoy less prestige than regular (academic) schools, many JHS students would be unwilling to enter the vocational high school when they are assigned to one on graduation. [The assignment under the ERP is based on the student's choice, although not necessarily the best or first choice. No plan or system can guarantee that every student get admitted to the school of his or her top choice. The educational authorities are urged to establish more academic high schools and/or transform the vocational high schools to comprehensive high schools.]

8. It is unfair for the students in the "good" city schools because under the ERP the same score in the 5-point grading scheme with a class norm is given the same value in the "poor" country school as in the "good" city school. [One purpose of the ERP is to narrow down the gap in education between rural and urban schools. The rural students are already disadvantaged because their schools are generally not as well-equipped and well-staffed as the urban schools; they are entitled to an equal opportunity of education and should be treated on an equal basis as the urban students to ensure social justice.]

9. There are too many uncertainties about the ERP. More assessment is needed. [That is why we must take action immediately by implementing the ERP through action research so that possible uncertainties would be revealed and problems solved as they arise.]

10. No feasibility study or experimental research has been conducted or completed. The educational authorities are just anxious to sell the ERP. [The best way to test the ERP's feasibility is through action research, a research method often used by practitioners in education and management in Western countries. Genuine experimentation is impossible because the largely unchanged school environment contaminates it.]

11. Reform should take gradual steps. More time is needed for the full implementation of the ERP. [We have waited too long and wasted too much time. No real reform in education has been put into practice since Taiwan's restoration from Japanese occupation more than 50 years ago. We must take quick action and implement the ERP without further delay. As a matter of fact, the ERP was tried in only six localities. No date has been set by the new ME for its full implementation in all Taiwan's junior high schools although it was set for 1997 by the former ME.]

12. Some kind of unified written examination should be incorporated in the ERP to counterbalance the difference between classes and between schools in JHS

student's performance. [This can be considered if action research finds it necessary.]

13. The ERP neglects related problems (e.g., large class size with 40 or more students in a JHS class and shortage of qualified teachers, especially in such subjects as arts and music). [The related problems cannot be solved immediately although they are not neglected. If we have to wait until all related problems are solved, we may have to wait indefinitely.]

14. The ERP has no legal basis. The SHS law requires that students be selected by entrance examinations, but the ERP abolishes the SHS entrance examination and admits JHS graduates to senior secondary schools on the basis of their JHS records. [The school law should not interfere with educational reform. If the ERP works well on a limited trial basis, the law should be amended to accommodate it.]

Dozens of studies have been conducted to evaluate the ERP or VPP. The MOE also appointed in 1995 an evaluation committee to assess the ERP at the conclusion of its six-year experimentation. More positive than negative results were found. Worth mentioning were the results of two studies: the MOE evaluation committee's survey study (Ministry of Education, 1997) and a well-designed study done by a female JHS principal in Taipei (Huang, 1993). The MOE study surveyed 153 experimental junior high schools in two cities and three counties by questionnaire and interviewed 84 administrators in schools and local governments engaged in the experimentation. It was found that 83% of the experimental schools preferred the VPP to SHSJEE and about 50% of the schools and administrators endorsed the idea that the VPP be extended to senior high schools. If the VPP is extended to the senior high school, its graduates can go on to college bypassing the CUJEE.

Huang's study mentioned above sampled 1348 students of 36 classes in the three JHS grades with half of them in the experimental (VPP) group and half in the control (SHSJEE) group. Six instruments (five tests and one questionnaire) were used to collect data. The findings indicated that, relative to the SHSJEE group, the VPP students (experimental group) suffered from less academic stress, demonstrated more positive coping behaviors toward stress, had better mental health, and enjoyed more harmonious classroom climate. Yet this study did not receive much attention from the mass media. The reporters and editors of the mass media, especially newspapers, were not as interested in the good news about the ERP as in the bad news about it. Some of them were also parents of prospective elite JHS students. The central concern of most parents remains to be their children's academic achievement measured by tests (especially the SHSJEE), they do not care much about their children's development in personality or other domains of education.

Discussion

Like the civil service examination *ke jiu* that guided Chinese education before the 20th century, the unified college and university entrance examination has dominated education in both Taiwan and mainland China for more than forty years. Taiwan's education, especially at the secondary level, is controlled by two unified entrance examinations, the senior high school joint entrance examination (SHSJEE) and the college and university joint entrance examination (CUJEE). They are held only once a year in the hot and humid summer. They distort secondary education and impede the healthy development of the adolescents. Take the unified SHSJEE for example. It distorts junior high school (JHS) education by making the preparation for SHSJEE its actual aim without regard to emotional, physical, social, and moral development of the students. By the ERP or the voluntary promotion plan (VPP), the JHS graduates may choose to be or not to be promoted to the senior high school (SHS). In other words, the promotion is voluntary rather than compulsory. Yet to which senior high school a JHS graduate may be admitted depends on his/her own free choice *plus* his/her complete record of performance in the three JHS years. When this plan is put into practice, the unified SHSJEE will be abolished. When the complete record of a JHS student's three-year performance is counted for promotion to a SHS of his or her choice, though not necessarily the top choice, the JHS education will be geared to a more balanced development of the student although intellectual development in the form of academic learning still dominates the JHS curriculum.

Certainly, the ERP or VPP is not without imperfections. But why did those, mainly intellectuals, who resist the plan never try to help amend or improve it, or propose a better plan to replace it, if they do have the welfare of future generations in mind? What they have actually done is nothing but to maintain the status quo of secondary education which they know needs improvement. As a matter of fact, no reform plan will ever achieve perfection. It is inconceivable that any reform plan would ever establish an equilibrium that satisfied all students, parents, and teachers. It is not the absence of weakness that marks a good reform plan, but how a reform plan attends to weakness. Weakness, made visible through practice or action research, can be confronted directly and worked with over time.

Since 1968 when universal education was extended from six to nine years, Taiwan has never had any breakthrough in education. The ERP or VPP as the only possible fundamental reform was suspended for nation-wide (in Taiwan) or city-wide (in Taipei) implementation as a result of opposition of a loud minority mistaken as representing the majority. One may wonder why this same group of people or any other group did not oppose with similar impetus the 6-year national development plan (NDP) for economic, social, and cultural reconstruction, which was announced in 1990 and initiated in 1991. It is estimated that the NDP will cost the nation 8,200 billion *yuan* (more than 300 billion US dollars).

Why was there no opposition against the NDP organized on a scale similar to the opposition against the ERP? Even after the new premier admitted that the NDP was only a sketch for national reconstruction, the dissenting voice was still moderate and scattering. Why? My answer is threefold: (1)The NDP did not become an issue affecting individual citizens or their children directly, although it would certainly have a tremendous impact upon the nation as a whole. (2)Although the NDP, like the ERP, was criticized as imposed from above on the people without much deliberation, the NDP was a much larger and more complicated project than the ERP for people to fully comprehend and, therefore, the criticisms were less specific and devastating than those directed against the ERP. (3)The NDP was while the ERP was not endorsed by President Lee Teng-hui. The president as the top leader and highest authority of the country plays a decisive role in national policy. President Lee's primary interest was in political, economic, and diplomatic rather than educational matters although he also considered education reform urgent several years later as he handpicked a new education minister in June 1996 .

The present case study demonstrated the narcissistic and authority-directed personality of the Chinese people, particularly the educated adults in Taiwan. Their love of self is extended to their love of children, who are regarded as parent's "bones and flesh" (*guzou*) in Chinese culture. As love of face stands for love of self, any failure or loss of their children, like their own failure or loss, hurts their ego and leads to loss of face. To prevent their children's failure is, therefore, to save face. Academic achievement is highly valued in Chinese culture because it is a status symbol which can satisfy the need for status, enhance self-esteem, and glorify not only one's face but the face of one's parents as well. That is why the parents (including some science professors) of those prospective privileged JHS elite were so anxious to stop the ERP which would permit no privilege for the elite students and no discrimination against the slow learners and underachievers.

The narcissism of the Chinese people is also characterized by thoughts of omnipotence and tendencies toward criticality and suspiciousness. These narcissistic traits (Raskin & Terry, 1988) were demonstrated in the tough power of the science professors to resist the ERP and their relentless criticism and profound distrust of it. What the critics of ERP have done is simply destructive rather than constructive. None of them takes pains to create a better reform plan or program. It is always easier to criticize others for what they do than do something constructive ourselves.

Self-centeredness is a salient trait of a narcissistic person as measured by the Narcissistic Personality Inventory (Raskin & Terry, 1988). This may explain why some JHS teachers and principals resist the ERP because the teacher's extra income for tutoring would be reduced as tutoring would become less necessary, and the principal's administrative duties would be increased, under the new plan. Self-centeredness may also explain why most professors of education, who constitute part of the silent majority, remain silent about the ERP. They do not speak up because they are not concerned about educational reform but only about their own affairs. Self-centeredness also accounts, at least partially, for the fact that only the loud minority (including parents of the privileged elite students) talk and the silent majority do not. Another reason why the ERP and the suggestions to modify it for improvement are resisted is probably because many Chinese people in Taiwan are inclined to look at the negative side of things instead of examining both the positive and negative side before making a decision. They are either cynical or distrust other's intentions and abilities to make any change in their ways of doing things. They would rather stick to the old habits in which they feel more secure. Any innovation may threaten their feelings of security and, therefore, arouse their doubts and resistance.

The ERP case also attested that Chinese culture and personality are authority-directed. The minority led by the science professors and backed by the mass media against the ERP stood for intellectual authority. They won the battle against the ERP though the silent majority supported the reform plan as shown by opinion survey. In Chinese society, the people without authority or with lesser authority are often dominated by the few with authority or greater authority. The authority may be intellectual, social, or political.

In Taiwan, political, economic, and social issues are usually the focus of attention in mass media. Never before had an educational issue like the ERP attracted so much attention and aroused so much controversy. Since 1987 I have watched this Chinese society as participant-observer in its process of democratization (Simon & Kau, 1992; Tien, 1989). So far I have found in this process four kinds of people, voiced or voiceless, in the light of their attitudes toward public policy at issue. The first kind is the voiceless group who do not express their opinions in public. They may be silent for inability, ignorance, passivity or self-protection, or because they really have nothing to say. This kind of people constitute the silent majority. The second kind is the loudest group who take advantage of every opportunity to speak up and criticize the government. Their voice is so loud or so frequently heard that they are often mistaken to represent the majority. The third kind are those who identify with the government. They support the government's policy and carry out the government's orders. They seldom speak out. They are neither the majority nor the minority. The last and the fewest kind are those who support the government's policy in principle but find room for improvement of it. They make constructive recommendations to improve the public policy or the government's program with a view to promoting the well-being of the people in general.

In any of the first three kinds of people, there are two subgroups: those who really understand the policy at issue and those who do not. The fourth kind of people generally have a good knowledge of the issue. Obviously, the science professors belonged to the second kind; most of them failed to see the merits of the ERP. In a totalitarian society, the first and the third kind of people constitute the great majority. In a society like Taiwan in the present stage of national development, where education for democracy is inadequate but demand for democracy is powerful, all the four kinds of people can be found. In an advanced democratic country where education for democracy in and out of school has equipped its citizens with the qualities needed for normal functioning in a democracy, there will be more people in the third and fourth kind than in the first and second kind.

In sum, the ERP or VPP has failed to be fully implemented not because people in Taiwan want no reform in education. It is just because the VPP was not designed to accommodate the elite student's parents whose primary concern is their children's academic achievement reflected in the performance at the two joint (unified) entrance examinations (JEEs)---first at the SHSJEE and later at the CUJEE. The elite student's parents think that the VPP will reduce their children's chance to get admitted to the prestigious high schools and later to the prestigious universities if the SHSJEE is abolished following full implementation of the VPP. Like most elite students, President Lee's granddaughter did not enroll in the VPP program. After failing to get admitted through the SHSJEE to the prestigious high school of her choice, she left Taiwan in September 1996 under the escort of her mother for Europe to continue her education. Not many adolescents in Taiwan are as lucky as her to have the opportunity of seeking a better education in a Western country.

Most people know that Taiwan's education needs reform. Yet no consensus has been reached so far as to how it should be reformed. Reform is considered urgent by some intellectuals if the personality and talents of the Chinese are to be optimally developed. Under the pressure of some civic organizations (e.g., the Humanistic Education Foundation), the new premier set up in September 1994 the Council on Education Reform (CER) chaired by the president of Academia Sinica (the Chinese academy of research) Dr. Yuan-tseh Li, a chemist and Nobel prize winner. It was hoped by many although doubted by others that with Dr. Li's supreme intellectual authority an effective reform program could be worked out in two years as estimated. In November 1996 when the CER finished its final report, no concrete plan for education reform was produced. The report only reviewed the current problems in

Taiwan's education and made some recommendations for their solutions.

Since the controversy on the ERP (VPP) began, an increasing number of people have shared with me and some other intellectuals the belief that the CUJEE must be abolished in order to carry out a fundamental reform in Taiwan's education. Yet many college and university presidents disagreed with us because, for sloth or effort saving, they would passively accept their students assigned by the CUJEE board according to student's choice and test performance rather than select their students through their own admissions office. Relying primarily on the CUJEE board for student recruitment, the colleges and universities in Taiwan, as a matter of fact, have no admissions offices of their own.

The present case study has mirrored three types of conflict in Chinese culture. One is a political conflict more or less like a power struggle between the president and the former premier. The president has never endorsed the VPP proposed by the former premier as he endorsed other public policies. Another conflict is between two schools of educational philosophy, the developmental school and the psychometric school. The VPP supporters believe in the wholesome development of the students while its opponent's aim of education is to produce students who score high on achievement tests. The third kind of conflict is between two social groups---those who have only their own or their high-achieving children's interests in mind and those who look to the wellbeing of other children and children of future generations. The former outnumbers the latter.

Finally recognizing the urgency of education reform, President Lee Teng-hui handpicked in June 1996 Dr. Wu Jin as the new minister of education. Wu is a 62-year-old scientist who just returned from his career in America two years earlier to become a university president in Taiwan. Unlike most of his predecessors who were politicians, Wu is a scholar and educator uninterested in politics. He has decided to abolish the SHSJEE gradually and the CUJEE eventually. Integrating the opinions and recommendations from various sources, the ministry under his leadership proposed multiple channels for entrance to senior high schools, including the VPP and the American-style application for admission. He also encouraged multiple channels for entrance to colleges and universities.

While many people were expecting Wu to have a breakthrough in reforming Taiwan's education and hoping that he would stay long enough in office to implement his reform plans, he was suddenly replaced by a British-trained veteran educational administrator, Dr. C. C. Lin, in February 1998. Rather unexpectedly, Lin announced in early May that the SHSJEE will be abolished in 2001. I hope the political situation three years later will not affect Lin's plans.

Several other cabinet members also stepped down. This was the fourth major cabinet reshuffle since 1990 under President Lee. The reason for Wu's discharge was not officially announced, but it was hinted by the fourth premier since 1990 that his unique work style was incongruous with teamwork. It was widely known, however, that Wu's quick action and firm determination to reform antagonized a powerful conservative minority consisting of some legislators of the opposition party, Kuomintang dignitaries, public university presidents, cram school owners, and parents and teachers of elite students.

Wu's frequent appearance in the news spotlight and his dynamic and individualistic work style also made his bosses (the president and the premier) and other cabinet members feel jittery, jealous and even inferior. His popularity as shown in various opinion polls hurt him rather than helped him. As an independent intellectual and novice in politics, Wu neglected, or rather, wasted no time to ingratiate his bosses and other influential figures in the government and in the party. Wu's 20-month experience as minister of education clearly indicates that in Chinese politics a civil servant's personal connections with and his conformity to the likes and dislikes of his bosses and influential people count much more than his service to meet the needs of the common people. Both the case of Wu and that of the VPP demonstrate that education reform or any other kind of reform in conflict with the interests of the powerful few is an extremely slow process in Chinese society.

✦ ✦ ✦

CHAPTER FOUR

TYPES AND TRAITS OF PERSONALITY

Chinese intellectuals (in a broad sense) or educated Chinese come in many types. To understand them, we must look at them from every possible angle. Previous researchers have usually treated well-known or high-level Chinese intellectuals (especially writers and educated politicians) rather than ordinary ones, and they have also distinguished establishment figures from those outside. In a conference paper, White (1988) discussed many other dimensions of difference, such as occupations and specializations, generations educated in the 1950s and 1980s, concerns for political ideals or personal livelihood, attitudes toward Westernization, and the classic sociological difference between traditional and technical thinkers. This chapter attempts to supplement prior work by treating the types and traits of personality of the *ordinary* Chinese intellectuals or educated Chinese people. It also explores personality of the Chinese in general, regardless of educational level

This chapter consists of four studies. The first two studies dealt with the personality types and traits of educated Chinese in mainland China and Taiwan respectively. The third study examined the personality of educated Chinese overseas (in Hong Kong and the United States) and of Chinese in general. The last study investigated differences in personality of the Chinese associated with geography, gender, and perception. The first three studies were qualitative while the last one was primarily quantitative.

STUDY 1

MAINLAND CHINESE

The aim of this study was to identify the personality types and traits of educated people in mainland China (ML) as the subjects perceived them. It was a qualitative study. The data were obtained from two sources: free responses to an open-ended question in the questionnaire (MTPI) and to relevant questions in an interview.

There were two groups of ML subjects: respondents to the MTPI and interviewees in a biographical interview. The MTPI respondents were 188 men and 35 women (totaled 223 out of 925 ML respondents to the questionnaire) who answered an open-ended question in the MTPI. The interviewees totaled 120, including 90 men and 30 women.

The open-ended question in the MTPI asked the respondents to list the types and traits of personality they had found among the educated Chinese in general. In the interview, among other questions not intended for this study, I asked the interviewee to mention the salient personality traits of educated Chinese he or she had observed and the differences in personality of the three prevalent generations or age cohorts--the older, the middle-aged, and the young groups --which are the widely used age divisions on the mainland. I also asked the interviewee to compare the educated with the less educated people. In addition, I asked some ML scholars and interviewees subsequently to comment on my preliminary findings and to describe the latest development concerning the personality of ML intellectuals in general.

The types and traits of personality given by the 223 MTPI respondents were categorized and grouped in accordance with their differences and similarities. The information given by the 120 interviewees complemented the questionnaire data wherever relevant. In all, 43 types were found. I regrouped the major types that were similar and omitted the minor ones, which resulted in 13 types. A person belonging to a certain type, however, does not necessarily possess all the traits of that type. A few of his or her traits may overlap with those in one or two other types.

Thirteen Types of Educated Chinese

The analysis of the content of the responses to my questions resulted in the 13 personality types and the traits of each type as presented below.

1. The open type

Extraverted
Cheerful
Sociable
Lively
Eloquent
Assertive
Straightforward
Has broad interests

Dominant
Has leadership abilities
Flexible
Quick in responding
Quick to accept new things
Self-confident
Career-minded
Brave in words and deeds

Dares to change and reform
Interested in politics
Impatient
Imaginative
Has own views and ideas
Insistent on own opinions

2. The silent type

Introverted
Taciturn
Reserved
Prefers to be alone
Cautious
Self-protective
Conscientious
Works hard quietly
Good at deeds but not
   at words

Has own ideas but seldom
   expresses them
Self-effacing
Career-minded
Uninterested in political
   and social matters
Self-confident
Avoids competition with
   others

Uninterested in fame and
   wealth
Has a sense of justice
Has high self-esteem
Highly intellectual
Down-to-earth
Modest, seldom exaggerates
Sincere and kindhearted

3. The pioneer type

Energetic
Ambitious
Bold
Self-confident
Eager to get things
   done
Open-minded
Insightful
Quick to accept new
   things
Quick in thinking and
   responding

Able to grasp the link
   between theory and
   practice
Has a strong desire to learn
Has independent views
   and ideas
Dares to reform, create, and
   open new frontiers
Influential to people
Distrustful and unfearful
   of authority

Considers things thoroughly
Has political brains as well
   as professional capabilities
Skillful at power game
Capable of handling crisis
Is a good leader and
   organizer
Handles life properly

4. The conservative type

Satisfied with reality
Stays with status quo
Unwilling to change
Conservative in thinking
   and action
Moderate in advancing
professionally

Taciturn
Introverted
Stubborn
Self-righteous
Intolerant of different
   opinions
Plays it safe
Careful not to make
   mistakes

Passive
Follows the mainstream of
   society
Avoids competition with
   others
Abhors things new or
   foreign
Upholds personal interests
Seldom discloses own
   feelings and thoughts

5. The reformer type

Advocates social reform
Tries to bring about
   reform in own field
Hopes to have own ideals
   realized
Accepts new things easily

Concerned about politics
Has a desire for power
Despises authority
Has high self-esteem
Has organizing ability
Energetic

Independent
Demanding
Impatient
Impulsive
Radical
Pragmatic

6. The realist type

Faces the reality
Realistic
Contented
Moderate
Tries to improve reality
   gradually
Enjoys a job well done

Traditional in some
   ways and modern in
   other ways
Tolerant
Patient
Cautious
Plays it safe
Adaptable

Self-effacing
Obedient
Cooperative
Honest
Efficient
Maintains a proper interest
   in life and politics

7. The manager type

Has good human relations
Adaptable
Efficient
Active
Cheerful
Has management and
   leadership abilities

Quick in decision-making
Has broad interests
Values self-cultivation
Open-minded
Cooperative
Knowledgeable in
   politics

Democratic
Listens to different voices
Understands the masses as
   well as the intellectuals
Has a desire for power
Careful about words and
   deeds

8. The scholar type

Dedicated to intellectual
   pursuit
Finds the meaning of life
   in academic career

Introverted
Aloof
Has little social life
Arrogant

Awe-inspiring
Wise and moral
Pays no attention to trivia
   of life

Uninterested in politics and non-academic matters
Uninterested in fame and wealth

9. The radical type

Dissatisfied with reality
Idealistic
Extremist
Impulsive
Impatient
Aggressive
Critical
Rebellious

10. The rational type

Guided by reason
Faces reality
Relies on facts
Objective
Flexible
Tolerant
Calm and self-controlled
Self-effacing
Plays it safe

11. The egoistic type

Guided by self-interest
Selfish
Sociable
Ostentatious
Overambitious
Mediocre in abilities
Is a good talker
Self-monitoring

12. The saint type

Has a strong sense of justice
Detached from authority
Uninterested in personal connections
Works hard and whole-

Overestimates own abilities
Autonomous and independent

Imaginative
Creative
Independent
Subjective
Stubborn
Self-confident
Arrogant
Defies authority

Hides own feelings
Keeps a proper distance from people
Cooperative
Democratic
Quick to admit errors
Self-regulated when frustrated
Able to unite others

Crafty and wily
Pursues fame and wealth
Has a strong desire for power
Eager to climb up the bureaucratic ladder
Skillful in exploiting personal connections

Honest and sincere
Erudite and wise
Has own style of life
Has a sense of mission
Insists on the right thing to do

Has no guilt feelings
Takes life easy

Energetic
Controversial
Has both friends and foes
Is a good talker
Aspires to have something accomplished
Brave to challenge evil forces

Has a sense of responsibility
Works ambitiously when trusted by boss
Works as required when not trusted by boss
Works harder when praised
Happy about every success, however small

Is a toady or sycophant
Ingratiates the boss or authority figure
Jealous of those superior in abilities
Arrogant to inferiors
Unkind to peers

Willing to sacrifice for the cherished ideal
Values science
Devalues fame and wealth
Uninterested in politics
Has no fear of failure and

heartedly
Lives a simple and
austere life

Adheres to the chosen
principle

frustration
Never abuses authority or
power

13. The ambitionless type

Has no professional
ambition
Indifferent to career
advancement
Contented with reality
Follows the mainstream
of society
Self-protective
Takes a neutral stand on
controversial issues

Says what people say
Enjoys family life
Lukewarm to people
Interested in material
comfort
Works mainly for a living
Works only as demanded
Calm and patient

Avoids conflict with people
Obedient and submissive
Leads a tranquil life
Mediocre in abilities
Unconcerned about politics
and world affairs

Three Generations of Educated Chinese

Some interviewees and questionnaire respondents described the personality of educated Chinese in terms of age. In most cases, three generations or age cohorts were given--the older (*lao*), the middle-aged (*zhong*), and the young (*qing*). I accept these age divisions because they are widely used on the mainland and interpretable. Roughly as of 1995, the age of the older cohort was above 65, that of the middle-aged ranged from 45 to 65, and that of the young group was below 45 and above 20. Their respective personality characteristics as often mentioned by the interviewees and questionnaire respondents are as follows. These are the general traits of *ordinary* intellectuals or educated people in the three age cohorts. The unique or exceptional cases will not be treated here.

1. The older generation (born before 1930, ràised and educated before 1957)

Circumspect
Has no courage or
willingness to
speak out
Slow in taking action
Plays it safe
Learned, erudite

Conscientious
Conservative
Values fame and reputation
Devalues wealth and
material possessions
Lives a simple life
Satisfied with reality

Tends to impose own
thoughts on others
Stubborn
Introverted
Has little interaction with
peers
Hopes to spend the rest of

Politically sensitive but disinterested
Patriotic
Works hard quietly
Obedient, willing to be led
Sincere and kindhearted

Cherishes old ideas and traditional values
Frowns on things new or foreign
Lacks aggressive energy
Serious of purpose

life peacefully
Contented (for some)
Aspires to have a break-through in career (for others)
Plays a mentoring role

2. The middle-aged generation (born around 1930-50, finished college around 1952-76)

Circumspect
Plays it safe
Works hard
Down-to-earth
Objective
Rational
Concerned for family and livelihood

Career-minded
Dissatisfied with reality but seldom complains openly
Respects authority
Politically sophisticated
Devoted to the new society
Rigid in thinking

Has narrow interests
Taciturn
Less introverted and conservative than the older colleagues but more so than the young ones
Quicker and more willing to take action than the older colleagues

3. The young generation (born, raised, and educated after 1949)

Autonomous
Individualistic
Egoistic
Carefree
Craves independence
Tends to do something new and different
Quick to accept things or foreign
Easily affected by Western culture
Depreciates traditional values

Demands reform
Idealistic
Impatient
Inquisitive
Has a strong desire to learn
Interested in fame
Strives to get ahead
Dissatisfied with reality
Rebellious
Willing to take risks
Bold to speak out

Pragmatic
Politically immature
Lacks self-knowledge
Overestimates own abilities
Unstable in thoughts and emotions
Less introverted, conscientious, and self-disciplined than older and middle-aged colleagues

Types of Educated Chinese by Sex and Leadership Styles

Although the above typology or categorization may be applied to both sexes, it should be more applicable to men than to women since 84% of the questionnaire respondents and 75% of the interviewees were male. As some of them observed, educated women are generally more traditional, submissive, cooperative, and easy to lead. They have little or no desire for power. They may be more interested in material possessions than educated men, but less so than less educated women.

I interviewed a 46-year-old well-informed woman engineer, who was a public relations cadre (officer) of a professional organization and had extensive opportunities to travel and observe people of both sexes. She described three types of female intellectuals with an estimated percentage for each type as follows:

1. The career woman (20%)--extraverted, career-minded like men but does not neglect family duties entirely.

2. The family woman (50%)--introverted, submissive to husband, takes family duties for granted or as obligatory.

3. The ambivalent woman (30%)--submissive to husband reluctantly; feels inferior to men.

The woman cadre also reported seven types of men and five leadership styles with an estimated percentage for each type or style. I must add that this middle-aged lady was one of the most knowledgeable intellectuals I have ever met. The following are the seven types of men, regardless of educational level:

1. The impulsive man (20%)--emotionally unstable, unable to face problems calmly.

2. The crafty man (20%)--taciturn, cunning, and resourceful.

3. The pretentious man (10%)--self-assertive, belittles others, regards self as inevitable in solving problems.

4. The promiscuous man (20%)--interested in sexual novelty, seeks sexual relations with different women.

5. The power-desiring man (5%)--unable to compete with peers intellectually or professionally, jealous of successful peers, desires to secure leadership positions so as to gain power over peers.

6. The office-guarding man (5%)--is already a government or party cadre, very cautious in words and deeds in order to guard his leadership position or hold his office long.

7. The disappointed man (20%)--frustrated by political persecutions, disillusioned, has no more ambition or long-term plans.

The knowledgeable female interviewee also depicted five leadership styles as follows, regardless of sex and educational level:

1. The enterprising leader (10%)--maintains effective communications with superiors, gains strong support from subordinates, creates better working conditions for the unit he or she leads, keeps learning to improve his or her leadership qualities.

2. The mediocre leader (20%)--careful not to offend either superiors or subordinates, agreeable but does not accomplish much.

3. The manipulating leader (30%)--organizes those colleagues who will follow and serve him or her and through them controls other colleagues.

4. The autocratic leader (10%)--irrational and domineering to subordinates but flattering to superiors.

5. The paternalistic leader (30%)--often says to subordinates, "Listen to me because I am always right."

The Three Generations and Their Sociopolitical Environments

The personality traits of the three age cohorts listed above reflect the character of the social and political environments of the time when they were raised and educated. Those traits are, however, more typical of the ordinary Chinese intellectuals than of such well-known but rather exceptional intellectuals as Feng Youlan, Wang Ruoshui, Liu Bingyan, Fang Lizhi, and Chai Ling, who are unique in a certain sense. For example, Feng Youlan, who died recently, was far more productive as a scholar than the average older intellectual, Fang Lizhi is far more outspoken as a reformer than the average middle-aged professor, and Chai Ling is far more rebellious as a student leader than the average educated young woman, while they share some other traits with their respective contemporaries. The older group of the ordinary intellectuals were raised and educated before 1957 and mostly in the "old" society before 1949 under the Nationalist government. Most of the middle-aged intellectuals received higher education during the years of political turmoil (1957-76) including the ten-year Cultural Revolution (1966-76). The majority of the young intellectuals attended colleges and universities in the 1970s and 1980s.

As the cost of higher education was rather high before 1949, most older intellectuals had a well-off family of origin and hence suffered severe persecutions. They were conditioned to fear in a series of political campaigns. They lived, however, for at least twenty years during the Nationalist rule before 1949 witnessing a "weak" nation under foreign (Japanese, Russian, and Western) invasion. They are, therefore, most anxious to see a "strong" nation without foreign oppression. This expectation was partially fulfilled by the Communist regime. The middle-aged and the young generations of educated people, short of similar experiences of the older generations, do not appreciate as much as their older colleagues the Communist accomplishments in building a powerful country. Besides, the general living conditions of the country during the war of resistance against Japan (1937-45) were less satisfactory than today. The older and senior middle-aged intellectuals hence feel more contented than their younger colleagues, who tend to compare their present economic conditions with those of the developed countries like Japan and the United States rather than with those of China before 1949. Some older intellectuals, on the other hand, because of the freedom and privileges enjoyed in the old society, are nostalgic to the good old days. Meanwhile, many older intellectuals are armed with traditional cultural values and thus less vulnerable to Communist and Western influences than their younger colleagues.

The better educated senior middle-aged intellectuals share some traits (e.g., circumspect and taciturn) with the older generation; they are more like the older colleagues than the young ones. Many junior members of the middle-aged cohort received higher education during the Cultural Revolution when most schools, colleges and universities were closed or did not hold classes regularly. These people, as a result, do not have a solid foundation in basic knowledge needed for a professional career. They sometimes complain about the academic loss which hinders their career development. They have a feeling of inferiority and more or less withdraw from social life. To compensate, some of them have a desire for power aspiring to become party or government cadres. Of this group some members had been workers, peasants, or soldiers who were admitted to colleges or universities as a reward for their non-academic achievement, usually political in nature.

The middle-aged are generally affected by economic and livelihood conditions. Most of them are underpaid and have children and parents living together. They have more work to do and bear greater responsibility than both young and older colleagues. They are, therefore, hard pressed by livelihood and family burdens. Many of them feel depressed and unable to concentrate on work, and have been forced to give up original ambition and aspirations. Although they appear to be loyal to the new society and proud of being its "backbone" (*gugan*), they have more complaints than the older generation, wishing to have pay raised, workload reduced, and living conditions improved. The health of many of them deteriorates due to overwork. Some of them die young, in their 40s or 50s. If living and working conditions improve, many would become late bloomers. More members of this group are assigned heavier workload and/or administrative positions than their older and young colleagues because the young are inexperienced and the older are soon to retire or have retired. The administrative work has deprived many middle-aged faculty members and research fellows of much time and energy which would otherwise be devoted to research and writing papers for publication. So they have less income from royalty and less chance for promotion.

The senior subgroup of the young cohort ranges in age from 30 to 45 or so. The junior subgroup is under 30, including those youth participating in the Tiananmen incident of June 4, 1989 (Liu,1990). The senior subgroup shares some traits (e.g., objective and down-to-earth) of the younger middle-aged intellectuals. The junior subgroup is representative of those courageous, idealistic, but doomed Tiananmen youth "calling for democracy in a society that has yet to shed its authoritarian traditions." (Pye, 1990, p. 331).The members of the young generation, especially the junior ones, are more egoistic and individualistic than the older and middle-aged intellectuals. They tend to disguise egoism and individualism with lofty, patriotic demands so as to avoid the criticism of being selfish (Pye, 1990). So they are at once pragmatic and idealistic, egoistic and patriotic. They are more interested in concrete personal matters than the older and middle-aged intellectuals but less so than the non-intellectuals. As regards the less educated or non-intellectual young people, there are roughly three types: (1)the ambitious, hardworking type (30%), (2)the crowd-following, goofing type (60%), and (3)the delinquent type (10%).

The well-educated young people feel rather arrogant while the less educated feel inferior. They are, however, both affected by the relaxation of traditional values during the Cultural Revolution. They are thus less polite and less respectful to elders and parents than the older and middle-aged people. They have weaker family ties and are less willing to look after younger siblings and aging parents than the older and middle-aged.

The young people in the cities, regardless of sex and educational level, are more dependent on their parents for economic reasons (housing and financial support) than those in the countryside because most parents in the urban areas have paid jobs, public housing, and pensions after retirement, which are the privileges unavailable to the peasant's parents. If married, the city young people usually live with the husband's parents because of housing shortage.

After the June Fourth Incident of 1989, some mainland scholars tell me that the psyche of the older and middle-aged intellectuals has become even more realistic and stabilized while the young colleagues have turned out to be generally depressed with less motivation for professional achievement and less hope for lofty aims. An increasing number of young people are anxious to go abroad to escape from the distressing reality. It is no wonder that in 1992 the mainland Chinese studying at American institutions of higher learning outnumbered foreign students from any other country to reach a total of 42,949. Many of those young people who are unable or unwilling to leave the country engage in profit-making or commercial activities to improve their living conditions and raise their socioeconomic status.

Distribution of Educated Chinese in the Thirteen Personality Types and Some Common Traits

In some of the thirteen types of personality, one or two age groups may dominate. For example, we may find more older intellectuals in the conservative type and the scholar type; more older and middle-aged people in the silent, the rational, and the saint types; more young and middle-aged persons in the open, the pioneer, and the reformer types; more middle-aged ones in the realist and the manager types; and more young intellectuals in the radical type. There are many ambitionless people, we find them in all age cohorts. Purely egoistic people are rare; there may be more of them, if any, in the young and the middle-aged generations than in the older generation. There are not many people in the saint and the pioneer categories, either. The new generation of leadership, the so called "technocrats," all middle-aged, may fall in the rational or the realist group while the older elite are mostly in the conservative group.

There are presumably more people in some types than in other types. The demarcation line between the types is, however, not clearcut. There may be people in between or in an intermediate position between any two types. For example, there are more silent people than open people, but there may be many people in between who lean a little to one of the two types or sway between the two types. In general, there are more educated Chinese in the silent, conservative, rational, ambitionless, realist, and scholar categories than in the open, radical, egoistic, pioneer, reformer, manager, and saint categories. Some mainland scholars told me that since the June Fourth Incident in 1989 the number of educated people has increased in the conservative, silent, ambitionless, manager,and egoistic types, but has decreased in the reformer, pioneer, and the radical categories. According to the same informants, the number of intellectuals in the PRC remains stable in the rational, the scholar and the saint groups.

As a whole, the majority of ordinary educated Chinese have the following personality traits in common: egocentric, authoritarian, narcissistic, self-protective, self-defensive; modest, unassuming, and submissive outwardly but proud, self-inflated, and rebellious inwardly; introverted, distrust extroverts, jealous, other-directed, lack a sense of humor, uncooperative, inhibited in heterosexual relations, deemphasize individuality, hesitant to display individuality or differences from peers, criticize others behind their back, reject as well as flatter authority figures and advanced Westerners (Americans and Europeans), and lack adventurous and exploratory spirit. In comparison with less educated people such as peasants and workers, the intellectuals are less interested in material enjoyment, less obedient and cooperative, less altruistic, more objective, more circumspect and sophisticated, more inclined to blame others and shun responsibility, and less devoted to the new society.

Almost all Chinese have feelings of inferiority or insecurity due to harsh and unstable economic, social and political conditions centuries old. The intellectuals believe that their destiny and the destiny of the nation are inseparable. So they earnestly hope that China will become wealthy, powerful, and democratic.

The average Chinese, especially the average educated person, is egocentric and authoritarian as a result of egocentric and authoritarian parenting, schooling, and governing. He or she is dignity-conscious and sensitive to matters of "face"--deeply concerned about his or her status, reputation, and self-esteem. A strong need for achievement is another universal trait for educated Chinese under normal circumstances. Many will, however, lose the need for achievement and become ambitionless in exceptionally hopeless or helpless situations.

Other Observations on Educated Chinese

The responses to the questionnaire and my personal correspondence with mainland intellectuals also revealed the following observations which may add to our understanding of educated Chinese.

1. There are more educated people who are expert but not red (loyal to socialism and the Communist party) than those who are red but not expert.

2. Few intellectuals with political ambition are academically successful. Those who are really interested in scholarly career seldom have political aspirations.

3. Quite a few intellectuals join the Communist party not to serve the country and people, but for self-interest and self-protection.

4. Some intellectuals become politicians. They no longer have the time for or interest in intellectual pursuit. They seek power instead of knowledge.

5. The positive factors for an educated person's prestige are diploma, achievement, expertise, authority or power, other's respect, and public attention. The negative factors are lack of opportunity for professional development, change to an unwanted job, and work without autonomy.

6. There are some intellectuals who, for some reasons, are neither properly trained nor assigned the right position. It is even worse if their career is entirely determined by others. Consequently, many of them turn out to be ambitionless and just work for living.

7. The older generation of intellectuals are generally better trained than the middle-aged and the young generations. Some of them have received graduate education in Europe, Japan, or the United States. Many of them have reached the retirement age but are still active in the institutions of higher learning, usually teaching graduate students and/or mentoring junior colleagues.

8. Since Deng Xiaoping's proposal for an open-door policy in 1978, some young and middle-aged people have gone abroad for further education under official auspices or private supports. Since the June Fourth Incident, most of those who have not yet returned have chosen to remain abroad. Meanwhile, a growing number of young people are seeking unofficial financing (including sponsorship from friends and relatives outside the mainland) to leave the country.

9. Few intellectuals make good administrators or managers. Most of them lack leadership and organizing abilities, for which no formal training is provided.

10. Regarding authority relations, a good leader is one who appreciates talents, unites colleagues for a common cause, and is considerate to subordinates. Unfortunately, many of those in authority abhor being excelled by others and consciously or unconsciously suppress their colleagues.

11. The potentials of most educated Chinese have not been properly developed. That hinders China's progress in democratization and modernization.

12. Many educated people would like to change their present conditions but find it impossible under the existing system. They often expect more than they can bring it about, which leads to disappointment and frustration.

13. Regardless of age, the interpersonal relations of the educated people are characterized by outward friendliness but inward apathy.

Discussion

This was a first study by an outside researcher of the personality of commonplace but typical Chinese intellectuals or educated people in the Peoples

Republic of China (PRC). This study differs from previous researches which have treated distinguished or high-level Chinese intellectuals rather than ordinary ones. Previous researchers, for example, have studied those intellectuals in terms of their relationship with the state (Goldman et al, 1987). Some scholars dealt with the educated Chinese elite in a historical perspective (e.g., Grieder, 1981), others illustrated essential Chinese traits and predispositions by the actions of students and political leaders in key events (Chow, 1960; Pye, 1990). This study tried to supplement prior work by looking at the educated Chinese (including intellectuals in both the Chinese and the Western sense) from a new angle. What I accepted in this study were primarily the first-hand data collected by myself on the mainland of China. The research methods I used were interviewing and questionnaire survey rather than documentary research.

This study reveals the differences in personality of the ordinary educated Chinese and, to a lesser degree, distinguishes them from the less educated compatriots. It also depicts the personality of the Chinese people as a whole, educated and less educated alike. The differences in personality reflect the variations in nature (heredity) and nurture (experience) of the individuals, and also the different periods and environments in which the Chinese people have lived. The similarities are reflections of the time-honored culture of traditional China which all Chinese share.

While both nature and nurture exert significant influences on personality development or formation, theories of interaction indicate that differences in personality can be explained in terms of the interaction between the person and the environment, or between personality traits and situations in which the person functions (Feshbach & Weiner,1982; Mischel, 1976). That is why people living in different periods of time and/or under different conditions develop or manifest different personality traits or types. Which, the person or the situation, is more influential in the interaction process depends upon which is more powerful in his (her) or its impact.

The changing or changed political environment as a powerful situation may lead to the change of a person by activating some of his or her personality traits and making other traits dormant. For example, Mao Zedong was radical and rebellious as a revolutionist during his revolutionary years, but became a conservative and egoistic ruler after he seized power (Chou, 1980). Deng Xiaoping was more open as a reformer in 1978 when he delivered a speech to the National Science Conference announcing the favorable change in approach to intellectuals (Schwarcz, 1986). But he turned out to be a conservative and coldblooded leader during and after the June Fourth Incident in 1989.

In line with the theory of person-situation interaction (Mischel, 1976), the personality of the people in general and the educated in particular fluctuates with the political situations created by Mao Zedong and Deng Xiaoping, the two most powerful figures in the PRC. The Chinese had high hopes for the new regime before the Hundred Flowers campaigning of 1957 and the anti-rightist campaign that followed. They were conditioned to fear in 1957 and afterwards, especially during the Cultural Revolution. They were again hopeful after Mao died in 1976, but felt disillusioned after the 1986-87 student unrest and especially after the June Fourth incident. The older and the middle-aged generations are, however, more stable in thoughts, feelings, and actions than the young generation, who are more sensitive and responsive to the unpredictable political situation and, therefore, more subject to change.

Although the personality of an individual normally becomes stabilized in early adulthood, its manifestation is largely determined by situations. A situation may be neutral or irrelevant; it may elicit or inhibit a certain or some traits. That explains why educated Chinese were distrustful of their friends and relatives during the

Cultural Revolution, why they returned to a more active life after Deng Xiaoping rehabilitated the political and social status of "mental laborers" in 1978, and why they became silent again after the Tiananmen drama in 1989. Yet the various types and traits of personality reported above are already there, they will manifest themselves at the right time and in the right situation in days to come.

If we use the "two large, loose groups" termed liberal and conservative by Nathan and Shi (1996, p. 522) to characterize my 13 types of mainland Chinese, 4 types (the open, pioneer, reformer, and radical) would belong to the liberal group and the remaining 9 types to the conservative group. Among the three generations of educated Chinese, the young generation are generally more liberal and less conservative than the middle-aged and older generations. As a whole, there are more conservative intellectuals than liberal ones. The less educated Chinese are generally conservative. As Nathan and Shi (1993) pointed out, "the reservoir of confidence" in the Communist government among the less educated Chinese "may have helped the authoritarian regime to survive (p. 111).

According to many of the 120 educated people I interviewed, the people China needs most for modernization are of the pioneer type. Yet this type of people are rare and hard to find even among the well-educated elite. Standing in the way are the authoritarian child-rearing practices (though relaxed somewhat in the one-child family), the rigid educational methods, and the totalitarian political system. Democracy as a way of life is called for in family, school, and society at large if we wish to facilitate the modernization process in China. Mao Zedong and Deng Xiaoping had turned the mainland of China into a Communist country. The new society with absolute power in the hands of its top leaders had in turn changed Mao and Deng from two radical revolutionists into two relentless dictators. Perhaps someday the educated and the less educated Chinese in a united effort under the leadership of some men or women of the pioneer type will successfully transform their beloved motherland into a modernized country of genuine democracy. I hope that Jiang Zemin and Zhu Rongji can help make this dream come true.

STUDY 2

TAIWAN CHINESE

The purpose of this study was to describe and discuss the personality traits and types of Chinese in Taiwan as the questionnaire respondents and I observed them. The data were collected from two sources: my own participant observation and my subject's responses to the open-ended question in the MTPI.

I have lived in Taiwan since 1949 when I left the mainland except the 19 years I spent overseas (6 years in the United States and 13 years in Hong Kong). During the 27 years in Taiwan, I observed as a participant the people around me, especially the educated. I recorded what I had observed from which I gained insight into their personality.

The subjects who responded to the same open-ended question in the questionnaire (MTPI) as used in Study 1 were 93 educated people (55 men and 38 women). They were a subsample of the 651-subject Taiwan (TW) sample who completed the MTPI.

The questionnaire data were analyzed in the same way as in Study 1. However, no interview data were used because relevant information was not sought in the interview of TW subjects. Data obtained from participant observation were useful in supplementing and interpreting the questionnaire data.

Nine Types of Educated Chinese in Taiwan

The analysis of the data collected by questionnaire and participant observation resulted in 27 types of personality which were then reduced to nine types in the same way as in Study 1. The nine types and the traits of each type are presented below.

1. The conservative type

Conservative	Values intellectual life	Moral
Contented with reality	Devalues material life	Self-controlled

Respects authority
Follows the mainstream
   of society
Other-directed
Values traditional culture
2. Self-protective type
Self-protective
Self-monitoring
Circumspect
Self-effacing
3. The rational type
Rational
Calm
Patient
Emotionally stable
Tolerant
4. The scholar type
Devoted to scholarship
Engrossed in intellectual
   work
Introverted
Has little social life
5. The reformer type
Eager to reform
Desires to influence people
Strives to realize own
   ideals
Takes initiative
Has a sense of mission
6. The radical type
Radical
Disappointed about reality
Dissatisfied with own
   identity
Upset by unfulfilled
   ambition
Angry at the world
7. The power-desiring Type
Has a strong desire for
   power
Interested in politics
Eager to be a leader
Extraverted
Is a good talker

Introverted
Reserved
Has a sense of mission
Has a sense of justice

Modest
Obedient
Passive
Self-controlled

Advocates gradual reform
Consistent in word and deed
Planful
Principled
Objective

Ignores social norm
Independent
Autonomous
Detached from politics

Idealistic
Active
Upright
Self-confident
Defies authority

Criticizes government
Demands drastic reform
Rebels without a program
Overestimates self
Egocentric

Ingratiates the boss
Is a sycophant
Submissive to superiors
Domineering to inferiors
Self-centered

Tolerant
Sober
Hardworking
Thrifty

Unassertive
Even-tempered
Tolerant

Realistic
Moderate
Conscientious
Has a sense of humor
Enjoys life

Honest
Sincere
Has own ideas but seldom
   speaks out

Has moral courage
Strives for perfection
Interested in political and social
   matters
Values Westernization
Devalues traditions

Too idealistic
Emotional
Impatient
Authoritarian
Poor in social adjustment

Self-monitoring
Seeks fame and wealth
Skillful in exploiting personal
   connections
Crafty and wily
Shrewd and snobbish

8. The self-righteous type

Self-righteous	Egocentric	Enjoys being flattered
Self-important	Defies authority	Tends to blame others
Arrogant	Respects no one	Promises much and delivers
Boastful	Isolated	little
Stubborn	Has few friends	

9. The egoistic type

Self-serving	Never self-examining	Values material life
Guided by self-interest	Self-assertive	Prefers things foreign
Lacks social responsibility	Domineering	Snobbish
Devalues morality	Dissatisfied with reality	Manipulates inferiors and
Opportunistic	Over-estimates self	subordinates
Easy to be tempted	Inconsistent in word and deed	Exploits personal connections

Like the mainland (ML) educated people, a person belonging to a certain type does not necessarily possess all the traits of that type but is characterized by most of them. A few of his or her traits may overlap with some traits in one or two other types. The nine Taiwan (TW) types, like the thirteen ML types, are more applicable to men than women because there are more educated men than educated women. It is estimated that there are proportionately more young men (aged 20 to 45) in the self-righteous, radical, and egoistic groups; more middle-aged (45-65) men in the self-protective, power-desiring, and reformer groups; and more older men (above 65) in the conservative, rational, and scholar groups.

Four Types of Educated Women in Taiwan

As to educated women, content analysis of my questionnaire and participant-observation data revealed four types as follows.

1. The traditional type

Traditional
Conservative
Contented with reality
Values family
Tries to be a good wife and mother

2. The confused type

Confused about own identity
Emotional, sentimental
Feels inferior
Sometimes docile, sometimes willful
　or stubborn
Has no firm, independent outlook

3. The idealist type
Idealistic
Seeks own identity
Devalues traditional roles
Desires to change reality
Values career more than family

4. The independent type
Independent
Ambitious
Competes with men
Dominant
Career-minded

It is estimated that there are proportionately more young (aged 20-35) women in the idealist and confused groups, more middle-aged (35-55) women in the independent group, and more older (above 55) women in the traditional group. Like men, there are some women characterized by traits of more than one types, for example, by traits of both the idealist and independent types.

Discussion

ML and TW Educated People Compared

In general, six types of personality overlap out of the thirteen ML types in Study 1 and the nine TW types in the present study. They are the conservative, rational, scholar, reformer, radical, and egoistic types. Although some descriptors vary, the essential traits of each of the six types are identical or similar for both ML and TW Chinese. Many ML Chinese of the silent type and of the conservative type are similar to the TW Chinese of the self-protective and the self-righteous type respectively. As regards the educated women, the three ML types in Study 1 find their counterparts in the four TW types in the present study. The family, ambivalent, and career types of ML women correspond to the traditional, confused, and independent types of TW women respectively. Again, the descriptive terms vary, but the essential characteristics are similar for the three corresponding types.

For the men, we find neither the power-desiring type among the ML intellectuals nor the ambitionless type among the TW intellectuals. An increasing number of educated people in Taiwan are similar to the manager type of their mainland counterparts. For the women, the idealist type is lacking on the mainland. A reason for the absence of some types on either side of the Taiwan Strait may be that the missing types are not conspicuous or important enough to attract the attention of my informants (questionnaire respondents and/or interviewees). It may be fair to say that all the types found on one side also exist on the other side but their salience and magnitude vary.

We have no quantitative data on the size of each type of people. We can only estimate the relative size on the basis of my participant observation and discussion with colleagues on both sides of the Taiwan Strait. Table 1 shows the rank ordering of the estimated size of each type. For example, there are more ML men in the silent group than in any of the other twelve groups and more TW women in the traditional group than in any of the other three groups.

Table 1
Rank Order (RO) of Relative Size of ML and TW groups of Intellectuals by Personality Type

Mainland				Taiwan			
Male	RO	Female	RO	Male	RO	Female	RO
Silent	1	Ambivalent	1	Self-protective	1	Traditional	1
Conservative	2	Family	2	Conservative	2	Confused	2
Realist	3	Career	3	Self-righteous	3	Independent	3
Scholar	4			Reformer	4	Idealist	4
Rational	5			Power-desiring	5		
Ambitionless	6			Egoistic	6		
Open	7			Scholar	7		
Manager	8			Rational	8		
Reformer	9			Radical	9		
Egoistic	10						
Radical	11						
Pioneer	12						
Saint	13						

Besides genetic factors, personality is influenced by culture. Culture exerts its influence on personality development through family, school, and society at large.

Taiwan as a fast-developing Chinese society is characterized by urbanism, economic prosperity, feminism, equalization of educational opportunity, and political democratization. Lasswell's eight basic values of social life and four modes of their enjoyment (Lasswell & Kaplan, 1965; Lasswell, Lerner, & Montgomery, 1976) may be used to examine the behavior and personality of the educated adults in Taiwan. The eight basic values are power, enlightenment, skill, wealth, well-being, respect, rectitude, and affection. The four modes of value enjoyment are security, liberty, equality, and growth. The importance attached by TW intellectuals to the eight values and four modes of their enjoyment can be rank-ordered as in Table 2 according to my participant observation.

Table 2
Rank Order (RO) of Importance Attached to Lasswell's Eight Basic Values and Four Modes of Their Enjoyment by Educated Chinese in Taiwan

Basic value	RO	Mode of value enjoyment	RO
Respect	1	Security	1
Wealth	2	Growth	2
Enlightenment	3	Liberty	3
Skill	4	Equality	4
Power	5		
Affection	6		
Well-being	7		
Rectitude	8		

As a "face-treasuring" people, the Chinese, regardless of age, sex, and educational level, place the greatest value on respect, which is ranked 1 in Table 2. They consider dignity, status, fame, honor, glory, prestige, recognition, or reputation more important than anything else. Wealth, enlightenment, skill, and power are all but means to the end of gaining face (Ho, 1980) or respect. Affection (love, friendship, and loyalty) and well-being often come along with respect. It is ironical, however, that rectitude (conduct according to moral principles), though emphasized in Confucian teachings, is not actually valued in Taiwan, a Chinese society claiming to uphold cultural heritage.

To enjoy the basic values, the greatest importance is attached to security without which no value can be long enjoyed. Growth in the basic values, especially in respect, wealth, and power, comes only second to security in significance. Then come liberty and equality. While both sexes seek respect and wealth, men are more enthusiastic about power, growth, and liberty whereas women are more interested in affection, security, and equality.

Comparing the two Chinese societies, we find both differences and commonalities. The commonalities have resulted from the shared traditional culture on the one hand and Western impact on the other hand. The differences are mainly the outcomes of the distinct economic and political systems, which have developed separately in the two societies since 1949 when China was divided. Traces of cultural traditions are, however, discernible in both societies. Even after the 1996 popular presidential election, Pye's (1985) view still holds that the cultural potential for authoritarian rule remains in Taiwan although the society and polity have become more democratic and pluralistic.

For what is common, people of all types of personality are found on both sides of the Taiwan Strait. A type, such as the pioneer type or the power-desiring type, not reported by my informants on one side does not imply its non-existence. The fact that it was not reported might be due to less attention drawn to it. The pioneer type, for example, is too much needed on the mainland for modernization to elude attention of my subjects. As a matter of fact, the pioneer type is needed on both sides for optimal national development.

With regard to the dissimilarities, we find more people of the silent, realist, scholar, and ambitionless types on the mainland and more people of the self-righteous, reformer, power-desiring, and egoistic types on Taiwan. As for the pursuit of values and their modes of enjoyment, respect, enlightenment, security, and liberty are equally treasured on both sides. The mainland, however, attaches greater importance to affection, skill, well-being, and equality while Taiwan takes keener interest in wealth, power, and growth. Meanwhile, wealth has been much sought after in recent years on the mainland by the educated and the less educated people alike as a result of changed government policy on economic development. Rectitude is somewhat neglected by people of both societies although both governments occasionally remind the populace of its necessity. For self-interest, people on both sides, particularly on the mainland, rely on connections with people of influence to achieve personal goals.

Quite a number of Chinese, especially men, are narcissistic. Most of the clinical criteria of the narcissistic personality as defined by the American Psychiatric Association (1980; Raskin & Terry, 1988) can be applied to the description of many educated men in Taiwan. They are egocentric, self-important, unrealistic, exhibitionistic, exploitative, defensive, and unable to tolerate criticism. As one's face symbolizes one's self, love of face (*ai mien dzi*) in Chinese culture is in essence love of self, which is characterized by self-absorption, self-admiration, and self-aggrandizement. This observation is given further support in Study 3 of this chapter and elsewhere in this book.

STUDY 3

OVERSEAS CHINESE AND CHINESE IN GENERAL

This study was carried out before 1997 when Hong Kong was still a British colony. The term "overseas Chinese" in the present study refers to Chinese in both Hong Kong and the United States. The term "Chinese in general" here means the Chinese people as a whole, including Chinese in the four regions (mainland China, Taiwan, Hong Kong, and the United States) under study.

This study had two aims: first, to reveal the personality types and traits of the educated overseas Chinese in Hong Kong and the United States with data derived from questionnaire survey and biographical interviewing; second, to detect the commonly found personality traits of Chinese in general based on data collected through participant observation.

The subjects who provided the questionnaire data were 57 men and 35 women in Hong Kong and 16 men and 14 women in the United States. They were among the respondents to the MTPI as described in Chapter One of this book. The subjects of biographical interviewing were 16 educated Chinese immigrants in the United States, including 6 married couples. The subjects of participant observation included all the Chinese people, regardless of educational level and socioeconomic status, whom I have observed as participant in mainland China, Taiwan, Hong Kong, and the United States.

The questionnaire respondents answered the same open-ended question as those in Study 1 of the present chapter. The plan of analysis of data derived from the responses to the open-ended question was also the same as that used in study 1. The 16 cases of Chinese Americans will be presented in brief to illustrate the mentality and personality of educated Chinese in the United States. For participant observation, I have both systematically and casually observed the Chinese people, particularly the educated adults, as participant in their daily life and activities for various lengths of time in mainland China (4 months systematically and 4 years casually), Taiwan (6 years and 21 years), Hong Kong (4 years and 9 years), and the United States (2 years and 4 years). The systematic observation was recorded and content analyzed while the casual observation had left only impressions to be tested by systematic observation.

Personality Types and Traits of Overseas Chinese

Content analysis of the responses to the open-ended question in MTPI revealed 13 types of personality for the Chinese in Hong Kong (HK) and the United

States (US), including 9 types shared by both HK and US Chinese and 4 types with two (the reformer and the self-righteous) applied to HK Chinese and the other two (the silent and the confused) applied to US Chinese only. The nine shared types are the self-protective, conservative, scholar, radical, egoistic, realist, manager, ambitionless, and adaptable. The first five are also shared by mainland China (ML) and Taiwan (TW) Chinese and may be considered the most common types characterizing the educated Chinese in the four populations under study (many ML Chinese of the silent type can also be categorized as self-protective).

The realist, manager, and ambitionless types also exist in mainland China. There is an increasing number of educated people in the manager type in Taiwan not identified by my MTPI respondents. The silent type of US Chinese have their counterparts in mainland China and the self-righteous type of HK Chinese is also shared by ML and TW Chinese (Many people in the ML conservative group can be categorized as self-righteous). HK and US Chinese, however, have two types not identified among the ML and TW compatriots, namely, the adaptable and the confused. The adaptable are found among both HK and US Chinese while the confused among US Chinese only. In all, there are 18 types of personality identified in the four Chinese populations as shown in Table 1.

Table 1
Personality Types of Educated People in Four Chinese Populations

Personality type	Mainland China	Taiwan	Hong Kong	United States
Silent	x			x
Self-protective	x	x	x	x
Conservative	x	x	x	x
Scholar	x	x	x	x
Radical	x	x	x	x
Egoistic	x	x	x	x
Reformer	x	x	x	
Realist	x		x	x

Table 1 (Continued)
Personality Types of Educated People in Four Chinese Populations

Personality type	Mainland China	Taiwan	Hong Kong	United States
Manager	x	x	x	x
Pioneer	x			
Saint	x			
Ambitionless	x		x	x
Open	x			
Rational	x	x		
Self-righteous	x	x	x	
Power-desiring		x		
Adaptable			x	x
Confused				x

Note. x indicates existence of the type.

The personality types of HK and/or US Chinese which are also found among ML and/or TW Chinese have already had their component traits listed in Study 1 and/or 2. They will not be repeated here for the component traits for each shared type are either identical or similar for the relevant populations. Presented below are the traits of the two types applied to HK and/or US Chinese only.

1. The adaptable type (for both HK and US Chinese)

Adaptable	Has a good career
Realistic	Has a good identity
Flexible	Gets along well with Occidentals
Independent	Has both Chinese and Western friends
Rational	Speaks fluent English
Extraverted	Westernized to an appropriate extent
Cooperative	
Emotionally stable	

2. The confused type (for US Chinese only)

Introverted	Has poor human relations
Passive	Has poor career development
Self-pitying	Complains about many things
Emotionally unstable	Feels marginal in American culture
Lacks self-knowledge	Unhappy in America but unwilling to

Has identity confusion   return to homeland
Lives an aimless life
Mediocre in ability

Educated Chinese in the United States

The Chinese population in the United States is currently dominated by middle-class educated people rather than uneducated laborers as it was during late 19th and early 20th century. Large numbers of Chinese have left mainland China for Taiwan, Hong Kong, Southeast Asia, and the United States since 1949 when the Communists seized power (Wang, 1991). Meanwhile, those who went to the United States were later joined by Chinese from Taiwan, Hong Kong, and Southeast Asia. After President Nixon reversed the American policy of containment of Communist China and visited Peking in 1972, the exodus of Chinese emigrants from Asia to the United States accelerated and continues to the present day. These large waves of Chinese included graduate students, professionals, and merchants. The Tiananmen tragedy on June 4, 1989 hastened another wave of Chinese, primarily intellectuals, to flee the mainland for refuge in America.

There is a significant difference between the Chinese who arrived in the United States before and those who came after 1949. Most of the former chose to return to their homeland whereas most of the latter choose to settle in America permanently. In recent years, however, quite a few from Taiwan have returned to the island after completing graduate education because of the shrunk American job market. Meantime, a handful from Taiwan and the mainland return home for patriotic motives.

The Chinese in the United States, as in other countries, are fragmented. Most of them associate only with members of in-groups---a few close friends and relatives. There is little communication and cooperation among people outside the in-groups except for occupational or professional necessity. For more than a century, there has always been racial discrimination against them, although much less today than before due to American's changed perception of the Chinese people. Most Chinese Americans perceive themselves as marginal men and women no matter how successfully they have adapted to the American culture. They do not mind losing their Chinese citizenship, but they cannot tolerate losing their face or dignity. To help the reader to have a better understanding of them, 16 cases of educated Chinese in America are presented below in concise form. Their names are represented by alphabetical letters.

Born and raised in mainland China, A and B are a happily married couple aged over 60. A is a realistic and emotionally stable man with a Ph.D. earned at Stanford. He is a brilliant scholar in mass communication and the author of six books. His wife B is an outgoing and dynamic woman. She is a real-estate broker and amateur opera singer. A was satisfied with his job as journalist in Taiwan 30 years ago. It was B who persuaded him to seek a better career in the United States. He also had two very supportive mentors at Stanford who helped him a great deal in graduate study and career development. A and B both say that America gives them a better opportunity for self-actualization. A adds, however, that no matter how successful a Chinese is in America, he or she still feels marginal. A speaks flawless English, yet his relations with Americans are only professional. A and B have two daughters and one son who are also faring well.

C is 50 years old and his wife D is three years younger. C is aggressive, ambitious, and energetic while D is charming, docile, and patient. Both were born, raised, and educated in Taiwan and received their Ph.D. in psychology at American universities. C has taught at the University of California for more than 20 years and was promoted to full professorship at age 37. He has published about 50 articles and presented about 60 conference papers. His wife D has worked as a researcher and coauthored many papers with him. Three years ago C decided to return to Taiwan but was hesitating because his only child did not like Taiwan's schools. Like the children of most Chinese Americans, C's son feels happier in American than in Chinese schools. After careful consideration and discussion with D, however, C finally quit his American job and accepted an offer from a national university in central Taiwan. C and D are now teaching at the same university in Taipei. Their son is attending a local American school. C says that it is morally, socially, and emotionally more rewarding to serve his own people.

E is an active, patient, and religious woman. She is an educational administrator. She gets along well with both Americans and Chinese. Her husband F is a nuclear engineer. They both work in the federal government. E is 54 and F is 59 years old. Both were born on the mainland and educated in Taiwan and America. F is sincere, prudent, and introverted. He is not as adaptable to American culture as his wife. He is, however, cooperative and supports whatever E does, such as community service and activities of Asian American organizations. An important thing they have in common is that they both have their humanitarian and nationalistic sentiments developed since junior high school days. During the early years of their settlement, they organized a demonstration in New York protesting the killing of a Chinese youth by American police. Recently, they have been raising library funds for rural mainland schools. They are anti-Communist but sympathetic with the mainland people. They have two daughters.

G and H are a married couple in their early 60s. Both are doctors of Chinese medicine trained in China and emigrated to America in 1982. Yet their two sons fled the mainland to the United States as refugees ten years earlier. They live with their unmarried elder son in California. Their married younger son lives nearby and visits with them once a week. Both sons have received B.S. at Purdue University. G and H have only a few patients a day and live on meager income, but they do not expect their sons to support them. They say that most Chinese come to America for economic and political reasons. They miss China because of greater job satisfaction and better human relations there. Their life in the States is quiet and calm but rather dull with few outside activities. They relax and watch TV when there is no patient. G is more cheerful and easygoing than her husband H.

J is a professor in social science. He claims to be fully Americanized but is extremely thrifty. He has bought four houses with his savings, one for residence and three for rent. He is aggressive, energetic, and sociable. He left for Taiwan in 1949 after graduation from a university in Shanghai. Several years later he went to the States for graduate study and earned his Ph.D. Then he started his teaching career at the university. He married a girl from Taiwan at age 45 and divorced her eight years later because his wife was barren and sensually cold. He sometimes had sex with American women. At 58 he married in Hong Kong a girl aged 28 from the mainland. Two sons were born in less than two years. Since late 1970s he has visited the mainland often, usually as leader of a study tour with American colleagues and students. He also takes timeout to have reunion with his mother and siblings on the mainland.

K is a 58-year-old Harvard man. He teaches international law at a university near Washington, D.C. He left the mainland at age 13 with his parents and siblings for Taiwan where he received high school and college education. Then he went to the States for graduate study. He is loyal to the Republic of China (ROC) on Taiwan and has never applied for American citizenship. Like many Chinese intellectuals at home and abroad, he advocates peaceful unification of Taiwan with the mainland under a democratic government. Tall, handsome, active and circumspect, he is a leader in the circle of pro-ROC social scientists in America. He is chairman of a research committee in the university law school. He has authored and edited about a dozen books. K has always wanted to do something for Taiwan and has worked on the island twice. He was once invited to join the cabinet but resigned due to disagreement with some colleagues on the mainland policy. His biochemist wife also got a doctorate from Harvard. They have a son.

L and his wife M are the president and vice president respectively of a small telecommunication company. They are both 37 years old. Both were born and raised in Taiwan with parents from the mainland. They have known each other since childhood when attending the same kindergarten in Taipei. They went to the States for graduate study together at age 24. Immediately after receiving an M.S. in electrical engineering, L was hired as design engineer by an American company. Like many Chinese who want to be their own boss, he started his own business at age 32. He has both Americans and Chinese on his board of directors with investors from both America and Taiwan. To promote his business, L travels frequently outside the United States. M assists him in management after completing her graduate study in comparative literature. She is a good wife and tender mother of two children (a son and a daughter). She is a Christian and prays often. She has a charming personality except that she sometimes gets irritated with her husband and children when things get out of control. Unlike the average Chinese man, L is extremely patient and rational. Both L and M like to live and work in the States, they are also filial to their parents in Taiwan.

N and her husband O are both 35 years old from Taiwan. N's parents are mainland Chinese while O's father is a Taiwanese and mother is a Japanese. O is thrifty like his father and has a very good temper like his mother. He got a Ph.D. in biochemistry and works as senior scientist for a biotechnological company. N has an agreeable personality and works as attorney for a law firm after completing professional training in Taiwan and the States and passing the Bar examination in California. She would rather, however, work in Taiwan because she would not have to use a foreign language there. Yet language barrier is not a problem for a Chinese scientist in America. So her husband prefers to work in the United States at least until he is ready to set up his own technological firm in Taiwan. Being the youngest of her parent's five children and the only child abroad, N thinks she could take care of her aging parents when working near them. She says that she will wait for her husband to go home together with their daughter in the foreseeable future.

P is a 45-year-old senior officer in the United Nations. He was born on the mainland and raised in Taiwan. He came to the United States after receiving college education in Taipei. He is a political scientist with a Ph.D. He taught in college before working for the U.N. in New York. He is well paid and highly satisfied with his present job, although it takes three hours a day to drive to work. Unlike most Chinese men who are introverted, P is cheerful and hospitable; he talks and laughs a lot. His wife is also sociable but not as good-tempered as he. P's father died when he was 13. His mother once in a while comes from Taiwan to stay with him but does not get along well with his wife. He would like very much to have his mother to live with him. Yet like most Chinese folks who do not speak English, P's mother finds it uncomfortable to live in a foreign culture. His wife works part-time. They have two sons.

Q is a 44-year-old democratic movement leader from mainland China. He is as patriotic as most Chinese intellectuals; he is also as resolute and fearless as those massacred at Tiananmen Square on June 4, 1989. He quit his job as physician in Peking eleven years ago and has since organized anti-Communist activities in America to promote his cause of democratizing China. He first thought of democracy as a 9th grader and aspired to be a social reformer sometime later. He says that many college students on the mainland talk about democratic movement, but only privately; few would dare to do so in public. He hopes what he does abroad will contribute to China's democratization. He will return to the mainland at the right time. Most Chinese, especially the educated, cherish the hope that China will become prosperous and democratic; yet not many really do something about it as Q does.

There are still, however, some Chinese who are pro-Communist at home and abroad.

Personality Traits of Chinese in General

As I observed the Chinese adults in general, regardless of educational level and socioeconomic status, a number of traits of a modal (most frequently found) personality had been repeatedly observed. Although we cannot say that every Chinese displays these traits or characteristics, we can probably say that a majority of Chinese or at least about 50% of the educated I have observed show most of the traits presented below.

A. **Major Traits**. There are four major traits or personality dimensions as follows.

1. Narcissism. The Chinese love of face implies narcissism (love of self). The Chinese are generally face (self)-loving and egocentric. They display such narcissistic traits (Raskin & Shaw, 1988; Raskin & Terry, 1988) as self-centeredness, a sense of self-importance, a tendency toward interpersonal exploitation, an exhibitionistic need for attention and admiration, an inability to tolerate criticism, and a dependency on external sources of gratification. They tend to use more first person singular pronouns (they often say " I " or "I personally") and fewer first person plural pronouns in speech and writing, which is a reflection of narcissism (Raskin & Shaw, 1988). They are often jealous and critical but seldom appreciative of other people.

2. Achievement motivation. The Chinese people have a strong need for achievement (Atkinson, 1977; McClelland, 1961) or achievement motivation. Striving to excel, to get ahead, to win in competition with others is a mainspring of the upward social mobility that has characterized Chinese society since Confucian times. Although Confucius taught people to excel in *jen* or humanity (Chan, 1963), the average Chinese works hard and strives for wealth, power, prestige, higher learning, social position, public acclaim,

and/or approval of family and friends. The achievement motivation of the Chinese generally aims at self-interest and interest of the family; it seldom contributes to social wellbeing and often implies lack of public spirit.

3. Authoritarianism. Many Chinese display to some extent the major components of the authoritarian syndrome (Cherry & Byrne, 1977) --- conventionalism (adhering to conventional values though somewhat accepting Western, especially American, values), submission (obeying though sometimes resenting authority figures), aggression (verbally or physically aggressive, advocating punishment for violators of conventional values), cynicism (having a negative view of people, distrusting others), superstition (believing in ghosts and gods), and projectivity (overly concerned with sexual morals, projecting own sexual motivations onto others). Authority figures (e.g., parents, teachers, government officials) often abuse authority. The resentment or defiance of authority is often repressed or suppressed.

4. Introversion. Most Chinese are introverted. To use Eysenck's (1967) adjectives as trait descriptors, they are quiet, passive, unsociable, reserved, careful, and rigid. Some of them are emotionally unstable (anxious, impulsive, aggressive), and others are emotionally stable (controlled, calm, carefree). They are socially incompetent. They lack language skills. They do not have many friends. They seldom talk to strangers.They prefer doing things alone to working with others. They make neither good leaders nor good followers.

B. **Minor Traits**. There are fifteen minor or secondary traits which are more or less related to one or more of the major or primary traits presented above. They may be briefly described as follows.

1. Conservatism --- conservative; cautiously moderate; inclined to oppose

change in methods and institutions.

2. Perseverance --- persistent in pursuing a goal, for self-interest, survival, or a lofty cause, in spite of difficulties.

3. Dependence --- dependent on parents, children, relatives, mentors, friends, superiors, group, government, and any external source of influence (including connections with people of influence).

4. Dominance --- tending to control or lead others but resenting being controlled or led.

5. Aggressiveness --- Authoritarian parenting and schooling plus authoritarian governing produce an authoritarian personality, usually in men, tending to be aggressive, advocating punitive measures to control another's behavior.

6. Emotionality --- emotional; overreacting; irrational; subjective; verbally or physically aggressive when frustrated.

7. Double-facedness --- hypocritical; insincere; self-monitoring; acting differently in different situations or toward different people (e.g., superiors and inferiors, members of in-group and out-group); inconsistent in words and deeds.

8. Double standard --- judging or treating others by a stricter standard than self and in-group; critical; demanding; self-protective; seldom admitting own error; overestimating own abilities; rarely praising others (especially peers and inferiors).

9. Snobbery --- attaching great importance to authority, power, wealth, and social position; admiring and courteous to superiors or people in authority and condescending to inferiors.

10. Feelings of both superiority and inferiority --- looking down on others with a feeling of superiority, but feeling inferior and insecure with and

jealous of peers who achieve greater success in some respect (e.g., in career, wealth, social position).

11. Extrapunitiveness --- extrapunitive; when frustrated or having committed an error, tending to blame others or showing aggression toward the source of frustration.

12. Superficiality --- superficial; concerned with only the easily apparent and obvious; not thorough; not profound; not precise and painstaking; not exacting; not efficient; name is more important than essence or quality.

13. Sense of mission --- This is a potential trait for many educated Chinese, but only a minority of them display it. They love their motherland or the world as a whole and aspire to do something for the good of their country or mankind, but not many of them take any concrete action.

14. Sense of justice --- This is a potential trait for Chinese people in general but not many manifest it in action. They hate injustice, but few of them have enough motivation to do something about it.

15. Altruism --- This is a potential trait for many. It may be observable when the circumstances call for it. Normally, it is manifested in some Chinese people, usually with some religious intention. Many mothers of the traditional type, are self-sacrificing for their children with or without hope of being repaid.

C. **A Core Trait**. If a single term for the core trait is to be used to characterize Chinese culture and personality, I prefer *authority-directed* to situation-centered (Hsu, 1981), social-oriented (Yang, 1981), collectivist or individualist (Triandis, McCusker, & Hui, 1990), tradition-, inner-, or other-directed (Riesman, 1961). I found this core trait by inferring from the common traits (e.g., obedient, respects authority figures) of salient personality types (the conservative and the self-protective) shared by the four populations and from the prevailing traits (authoritarianism, conservatism, dependence, and snobbery) of the Chinese regardless of educational level. It was also a result of my observation as a participant in the daily life of my compatriots in Taiwan, Hong Kong , mainland China, and the United States. The finding is consistent with Confucianism which "explicitly directed that children should be taught to have proper respect for all forms of authority" (Pye, 1985, p. 61). It is further borne out by the results of studies on parenting and schooling reported in this book that parents and teachers as authority figures direct the behavior of their children and students. Chinese history abounds in relevant evidences. The Cultural Revolution was a dramatic example of authority-directed mass behavior motivated and directed by the highest authority Chairman Mao.

According to Friedman (1990),

> a person may be said to "have authority" in two distinct senses. For one, he may be said to be "in authority," meaning that he occupies some office, position, or status which entitles him to make decisions about how other people should behave. But, secondly, a person may be said to be "an authority" on something, meaning that his views or utterances are entitled to be believed. (p. 57)

In Chinese society, the two senses mentioned above are not clearly distinguished; the person in authority is often treated as an authority. So the parent, teacher, specialist, government official, or religious/ideological leader has authority; he or she is an authority as well as a person in authority. The higher the office, position, or status a person occupies, the greater authority he or she has. In discussing the need for authority, Finnis (1990) has this to say and I would like to substitute the word "consensus" for his "unanimity" in order to suit my argument:

> There are, in the final analysis, only two ways of making a choice between alternative ways of coordinating action to the common purpose or common good of any group. There must be either unanimity, or authority. There are

no other possibilities. (p. 175)

The Chinese are often egocentric, narcissistic, and authoritarian. Each individual is inclined to think that his or her opinion is better than others, which makes consensus difficult to achieve. In Chinese society, intelligence and dedication to the common purpose or common good of a group are often mixed with selfishness and folly. In such a society, people are authority-directed because authority is usually the only way of coordinating action. Authority is, however, often abused. It sometimes leads to misbelief, defiance, or rebellion. Solomon's (1971) view substantiated by his interview data still holds today that the Chinese have an ambivalent attitude toward authority---a combination of the desire for a strong leader and the resentment against the demands of the powerful authority on the individual.

Discussion

It is no wonder that almost all personality types of HK and US Chinese, like their counterparts in Taiwan, find equivalents among the 13 or 15 (when the self-protective and self-righteous are added) types of ML Chinese. This is because all the Chinese, particularly the educated, share a common traditional culture. The most common are the six types (self-protective, conservative, scholar, radical, egoistic, and manager) shared by all the four populations under study. Many of the ML silent and ambitionless type can be categorized as self-protective and many of the ML conservative type are also self-righteous people. So the number of ML types in Study 1 can be extended to 15.

A new trend exists in the increasing number of educated Chinese of the manager type found in Taiwan as well as in mainland China, Hong Kong, and the United States. So the number of TW types in Study 2 can be extended to 10 (with the manager type added). The demarcation between types is, however, not clearcut because some common traits are found in two or more types. As a matter of fact, all types can be identified in the four Chinese populations but some types are more conspicuous to the observers (respondents to the MTPI open-ended question in this case) than other types.

Of the 18 types listed in Table 1, the last three were not discerned by most ML observers, namely, the power-desiring for TW Chinese, the adaptable for HK and US Chinese, and the confused for US Chinese. This is due to societal differences. The power-desiring type is conspicuous in Taiwan for the island is in a process of political transformation from authoritarian rule to democratic government and the people there have more opportunities of political participation to gain power. The adaptable type is noticeable in Hong Kong and the United States because the Chinese there have a Western culture to adapt to. The confused type is observable in the United States for the Chinese there are a minority group and American society where they find themselves is strikingly different from the three Chinese societies---mainland China, Taiwan, and Hong Kong. Most US Chinese, no matter how long they have settled in their adopted land, have a feeling of marginality. They feel more or less confused in identity. Racial discrimination still exists in the United States.

As for the Chinese in general that I have observed, particularly the educated men with whom I have come into contact most frequently for many years, four primary (major) traits or personality dimensions and fifteen secondary (minor) traits or characteristics plus a core trait have been commonly found. The core trait and most of the primary and secondary traits have a negative connotation. This finding is not only consistent with the findings in Study 1 and 2 of this chapter but also consistent to some extent with the observations of two renowned Chinese writers Po-yang (1986) and Sun Lung-kee (1985). Po-yang's (1986) controversial book *The Ugly Chinese* has been a best seller on both sides of the Taiwan Strait.

It is hypothesized that, along with other factors, the major and minor personality traits plus the core trait found in the present study may account for both success and failure of China and her people. The success: one of the world's oldest civilizations and a fast-growing economy. The failure: a country divided and less modernized than Japan and the West. This rather bold hypothesis, however, needs further research.

STUDY 4
PERSONALITY DIFFERENCES BY GEOGRAPHY, GENDER, AND PERCEPTION

In contrast to Study 1 2, and 3, which were based on qualitative data, this study mainly employed quantitative data derived from the responses to the MTPI. Some qualitative data derived from interview and participant observation were used in the present study only to describe personality differences associated with geographical factors.

Sex difference in personality has been widely studied (Brabeck, 1983; Brody, 1985; Coates, 1974; Schiedel & Marcia. 1985; Stewart & Lykes, 1985; Veroff, Reuman, & Feld, 1984), yet personality differences related to geographical and perceptual factors have not received as much attention. We will here report first the differences in personality of the people living in various areas, parts, or regions of mainland China and Taiwan. Then the sex differences and perceptual differences in personality will be reported.

Personality Varies with Geography

Culture varies with geography, so does personality. Differences in personality are found between the people living in the city and those residing in the countryside, regardless of the region or province where they dwell. According to my interviewees, the city dwellers in mainland China are more knowledgeable, sophisticated, modernized, liberal, egoistic, aloof, shrewd, and circumspect than the country residents, who are more naive, kind, sincere, simplehearted, straightforward, loyal, obedient, friendly, hospitable, traditional, conservative, altruistic, enthusiastic, and hardworking than the city dwellers. For instance, the neighbors in the city seldom visit each other, they are just nodding acquaintances while those in the countryside often visit, chat with, and help each other. Far more country men than city boys join the army. They are more loyal, obedient, courageous, and willing to sacrifice for the nation. Parent-child and husband-wife relations are more egalitarian in the city than in the country.

The urban-rural differences in personality were further supported by the results of a questionnaire survey. I divided my male and female subjects in mainland China and Taiwan into two age cohorts (those aged 30 or under and those above 30) and three geographical groups--the country village, the small town, and the city where they were reared before the age of 12. For the 122 items in my MTPI, one-way ANOVA was performed to examine the differences among the geographical groups. The analysis was repeated for the subjects in the different sex, age, and area groups separately. Out of 122 items in the MTPI, statistically significant differences, mostly at .01 level, were found on 26 items between at least two geographical groups in at least one generation of at least one sex in the mainland and/or Taiwan, mostly between the country people and the urbanites.

In the statistical analysis of the questionnaire items, the significance level (p) revealed by the F (ANOVA) plus Scheffe tests ranges from .0006 to .0451 with a mean of . 0178 for the difference between groups on the 26 items or trait descriptors. For example, relative to their rural or village counterparts, the Taiwan city young men are more imaginative and more inclined to try new things , but less realistic. And compared to their urban or city counterparts, the mainland rural or village women of the older generation are less democratic but more submissive; they are also more likely to believe in god or gods. The details are shown in Table 1.

Personality also varies with the province or the region within a province where a person lives. As examples of provincial or regional differences in personality, the following observations were reported by my interviewees from various parts of the mainland:

1. The Shanghaiers are generally independent, knowledgeable, even-tempered, self-controlled, tolerant, emotionally stable, and quick in learning and responding. They are also crafty, face-loving, and look down on compatriots outside Shanghai. Shanghai women are particularly self-willed and their husbands are hence henpecked.

2. In general, the inlanders, like the country people, are more naive and simplehearted than the coastlanders. For example, people from Gansu, a province of NW China, are not as sophisticated, crafty, and shrewd as people from Chekiang, Fukien, and Kwantung. People in the western mountain areas of Shantung or in the northern mountain areas of Fukien are more conservative and unsophisticated than people along the eastern coast of Shantung or along the southern coast of Fukien.

3. As a whole, northerners in China are less egoistic, sophisticated, crafty, and shrewd than southerners. For example, Peking and Shanghai are the two biggest metropolises in China, one in the north and the other in the south. Both are more modernized than the average Chinese city and the people of both are more extraverted than the average Chinese. Yet Pekingese are more sincere, friendly, and generous to outsiders than are Shanghaiers.

Table 1
**Personality Traits of Mainland and Taiwan Chinese of Both Sexes and Two
Generations Reared in the City and Country Village**

Personality trait	Mainland				Taiwan			
	Male		Female		Male		Female	
	Young	Old	Young	Old	Young	Old	Young	Old
Flexible						V< C		
Bold	V< C							V< C
Democratic			V< C					
Passive								V< C
Prefers things foreign	V< C					V< C		
Is a person of deed	V> C							
Interested in money	V< C							
Realistic			V> C		V> C			
Eloquent			V< C			V< C		
Self-protective	V< C							
Feels superior			V< C					
Feels inferior						V> C		
Works quietly	V> C					V> C		
Boastful			V< C					
Imaginative					V< C			
Believes in god or gods				V> C				
Self-effacing	V> C							
Has leadership abilities			V< C					
Sociable							V< C	
Anxious	V> C					V> C		
Submissive		V> C			V> C			
Inclined to try new things					V< C			
Often self-examining						V> C		
Accepts new things easily	V< C				V< C			
Over-estimates self			V< C					
Advocates restrictive child training		V> C				V> C		

Note: Young=young generation aged 30 or under, Old=older generation above 30,
V=reared in rural village, C=reared in city, the sign > means more than, < means less
than.

Sex Differences in Personality

Now we come to sex differences in personality. We compared our male and female respondents to the MTPI on the nine personality factors yielded by factor analysis of the 122 items in the questionnaire. Each of the four geographical or societal samples were further divided into two age groups, young (30 or under) and older (above 30). The sample size varies as reported in Chapter One.The results of statistical analysis with *t* test are shown in Table 2. As the scores on the 6-point scale indicate, all educated Chinese perceive themselves to be moderately extraverted, quite self-disciplined, rather democratic or unauthoritarian, moderately submissive, moderately cautious, quite other-oriented, rather independent, fairly modern, and fairly healthy or unneurotic.

Statistically significant sex differences in personality were primarily observed on two factors, namely, Independence and Other-orientation. In terms of self-perception scores, the educated men are more independent than the educated women whereas the latter are more other-oriented than the former, regardless of age and the place where they live. This is consistent with prior work by Western scholars and will be discussed later. Other sex differences were found significant in some samples but not in others. For example, the Hong Kong men are more modern or less traditional than Hong Kong women, regardless of age. The Hong Kong and mainland women are less healthy or unneurotic than their male counterparts, regardless of age. Worth noting is the finding that in mainland older group the men are more cautious than women while the reverse is true for the young group, which is consistent with the findings in Study 1 and is apparently due to the differing social and political circumstances the two age groups of men have experienced. The sex differences on other personality factors in other groups or samples are not conspicuous.

Table 2
Sex Differences in Personality of Young and Older Intellectuals in Four Chinese Populations

Personality Factor	Age	Mainland			Taiwan			Hong Kong			U.S.A.		
		M	F	t	M	F	t	M	F	t	M	F	t
Extraversion	Young	3.97	3.81	2.15*	3.86	3.86	.02	3.88	3.76	2.27*	3.86	3.99	-.90
	Older	3.78	3.93	-2.17*	3.79	3.80	-.12	3.83	3.81	.16	3.99	3.85	1.16
Self-Discipline	Young	4.39	4.38	.04	4.19	4.29	-1.39	4.22	4.30	-1.94	4.33	4.32	.04
	Older	4.51	4.55	-.73	4.58	4.51	1.07	4.35	4.34	.12	4.45	4.50	-.52
Authoritarianism	Young	2.99	3.05	-1.17	2.97	3.00	-.64	3.11	3.08	.84	2.99	2.91	.97
	Older	2.91	3.06	-2.59*	2.80	2.92	-2.07*	3.09	3.14	-.71	2.99	2.99	-.06
Submission	Young	3.36	3.37	-.01	3.43	3.45	-.31	3.48	3.53	-1.24	3.45	3.64	-1.71
	Older	3.72	3.79	-1.29	3.69	3.74	-.77	3.54	3.69	-1.87	3.56	3.65	-.81
Cautiousness	Young	3.34	3.51	-2.51*	3.66	3.58	1.18	3.66	3.61	1.11	3.52	3.53	-.05
	Older	3.45	3.26	2.65**	3.67	3.64	.45	3.64	3.50	1.34	3.43	3.60	-1.35
Other-orientation	Young	4.26	4.41	-2.75**	3.93	4.09	-2.66**	3.88	4.04	-4.21***	3.91	4.01	-.94
	Older	4.35	4.51	-2.39*	4.22	4.29	-1.10	3.89	4.11	-2.39*	4.00	4.23	-2.42*
Independence	Young	3.92	3.63	5.11***	3.68	3.54	2.06*	3.72	3.33	8.82***	3.77	3.33	3.63***
	Older	3.97	3.75	3.75***	3.92	3.69	3.32**	3.77	3.37	4.22***	3.91	3.49	4.13***
Modernism	Young	4.06	3.90	2.73**	3.80	3.77	.41	3.71	3.54	3.84***	3.79	3.81	-.19
	Older	3.83	3.76	1.20	3.67	3.54	1.84	3.71	3.45	3.06**	3.87	3.63	2.53*
Neuroticism	Young	2.83	2.95	-1.89*	3.06	3.09	-.37	2.99	3.29	-6.35***	2.89	3.07	-1.80
	Older	3.01	3.15	-2.36*	2.94	3.09	-1.99*	3.02	3.26	-2.43*	2.94	3.05	-.97

Note: *$p<.05$, **$p<.01$, ***$p<.001$

Difference in Personality between Self-Perception and Perception of Others

In the MTPI there are two responses to each of the 122 trait items: the first response is self-perception which yields a self score and the second response is the perception of other educated people in general which yields an other score. On the nine personality factors derived from the 122 trait items, the four Chinese samples generally perceive themselves more favorably than they perceive others in terms of the 6-point scale, regardless of sex, notably on seven factors. As the *t* test shows in Table 3 where the level of significance is set at $p<.01$, almost all men and women perceive themselves to be significantly more extraverted or less introverted, more self-disciplined, less authoritarian, more submissive or less dominant, less cautious or more adventurous, more other-oriented, and less neurotic. On the other two factors (Independence and Modernism) the difference between self-perception and perception of others is not conspicuous or consistent.

Table 3

Differences in Personality between Self-perception and Perception of Others
by Chinese Men and Women in Four Societies

Personality Factor	Sex	Mainland			Taiwan			Hong Kong			U.S.A.		
		Self	Other	t	Self	Other	t	Self	Other	t	Self	Other	t
Extraversion	M	3.85	3.54	8.8*	3.80	3.63	4.2*	3.87	3.67	5.0*	3.94	3.40	7.6*
	F	3.87	3.59	5.2*	3.82	3.75	1.0	3.74	3.73	.4	3.96	3.48	5.5*
Self-Discipline	M	4.45	4.23	8.6*	4.48	3.76	17.6*	4.25	3.91	10.5*	4.41	3.72	12.5*
	F	4.46	4.38	1.7	4.36	3.87	9.7*	4.30	3.98	8.1*	4.41	3.84	7.4*
Authoritarianism	M	2.94	3.35	-15.7*	2.86	3.57	-19.7*	3.10	3.61	-16.2*	3.00	3.67	-12.6*
	F	3.06	3.28	-4.7*	2.98	3.55	-13.4*	3.09	3.65	-18.1*	2.97	3.64	-8.7*
Submission	M	3.57	3.49	2.8*	3.63	3.43	5.8*	3.49	3.40	2.5*	3.52	3.57	-.7
	F	3.51	3.43	1.7	3.55	3.35	3.9*	3.55	3.35	5.5*	3.66	3.66	-.1
Cautiousness	M	3.42	3.90	-13.8*	3.65	3.84	-4.7*	3.66	3.77	-3.1*	3.47	3.90	-5.9*
	F	3.37	3.92	10.0	3.58	3.73	-2.7*	3.59	3.82	-4.9*	3.62	3.99	-4.4*
Other-Orientation	M	4.31	3.86	16.2*	4.14	3.36	20.1*	3.89	3.41	13.8*	3.96	3.17	12.6*
	F	4.46	4.01	10.1*	4.16	3.42	16.7*	4.04	3.45	15.8*	4.12	3.33	9.6*
Independence	M	3.95	3.99	-1.4	3.82	3.68	3.9*	3.73	3.73	-.2	3.83	3.47	6.0*
	F	3.69	3.95	-6.0*	3.59	3.64	-1.2	3.33	3.71	-9.4*	3.44	3.47	-.6
Modernism	M	3.92	3.75	5.7*	3.71	3.74	-1.0	3.71	3.71	-.2	3.83	3.59	4.0*
	F	3.82	3.77	1.0	3.68	3.85	-3.4*	3.52	3.73	-5.1*	3.70	3.53	2.2
Neuroticism	M	2.95	3.20	-8.6*	2.98	3.26	-7.4*	3.00	3.25	-7.9*	2.94	3.44	-9.1*
	F	3.03	3.22	-4.5*	3.08	3.27	-4.8*	3.28	3.27	.4	3.01	3.38	-5.3*

Note: *p<.01

Discussion

This study (Study 4) provided some quantitative data to supplement Study 1, 2 and 3 which were qualitative. Individual differences among people living or brought up in different geographical regions have been heard about but seldom investigated. The findings in the present study lend empirical support to the common sense and add to the understanding of Chinese people from various parts of China and those living overseas.

Consistent with prior research (Stewart & Lykes, 1985), sex difference in personality of the Chinese people, like that of their Western counterparts, is not as great as traditional notions would suggest. On nine personality dimensions or source traits, educated Chinese men and women in the four societies differ on only two of them as detected by the t test: men are more independent and women are more other-oriented. This is in agreement with research results in Western literature that women value relationship to a greater extent than men (Gilligan, 1979,1982) and that men are more field independent than women (Witkin & Goodenough, 1977). Women's care for and sensitivity to the needs of others are the traits that have traditionally defined the "goodness" of women (Brabeck, 1983; Gilligan, 1977). These traits of other-orientation characterize the Chinese as well as Western women. Dependence in their interpersonal relationship on others also makes women less independent than men.

According to Borkenau (1990), "the main purpose of trait terms is not so much to describe but rather to evaluate people" (p. 394). Person perception in terms of personality traits is, therefore, person evaluation. Self-perception is in fact self-evaluation and perception of others is evaluation of other persons. Messick, Bloom, Boldizar, and Samuelson (1985) studied people's perception of their own and other's fairness. They demonstrated that people listed more of their own fair behaviors than other's fair behaviors. Allison, Messick, and Goethals (1987) have found the same pattern for behaviors that are explicitly good. This self enhancing tendency was also observed in my study of the difference between self-perception and perception of others in terms of the nine personality factors or source traits as reported in Study 4. On seven out of nine source traits, the educated Chinese of both sexes in four societies perceive themselves more favorably than they perceive other educated Chinese. This finding supports the assumption (Beggan, Messick, & Allison,1988; Myers & Ridl, 1979) that people tend or prefer to think of themselves as being somewhat above average on evaluative dimensions. This preference or tendency may also be interpreted as a sign of narcissism, which is a basic trait of Chinese people as found in Study 3 of the present chapter.

Additional data on age, sex, and geographical differences in personality of the Chinese people are available in Study 2 and 3 of Chapter Six on personality traits and values.

General Discussion

Typological approaches in personology aim to discover the types or categories of personality. Only a few researchers (e.g., Pulkkinen, 1996; York & John, 1992) have studied adult personality with a typological approach since Block (1971). If we intend to classify the personality of educated Chinese, particularly of educated men, we may find as many as 18 types as shown in Table 1 of Study 3 in this chapter. But the most common types are only six in number, namely, the self-protective, conservative, scholar, radical, egoistic, and manager. However, the person of a pure type is not easy to find; most people demonstrate traits of more than one type with some traits of one type more dominant than those of other types. For example, one scholar may be at once conservative and self-protective, and another scholar radical and egoistic. It may appear complicated to understand the personality of a Chinese, yet if we grasp the major and minor traits described in Study 3, we will have no difficulty understanding the average Chinese adults, regardless of age, sex, education, geography, and socioeconomic status. A Chinese may not display all the major and minor traits, he or she often possesses most of them with some traits more dominant than others. In general, the less educated country (rural) people, particularly women, are more naive, simple, and unselfish.

It must be noted that due to social desirability and self-enhancing tendency the Chinese, like Westerners, perceive themselves more favorably than they perceive others (see Study 4). So the Chinese are not as extraverted, self-disciplined, democratic, submissive, adventurous, other-oriented, and unneurotic as they self-reported in the questionnaire. This assumption is supported by the results of my participant observation (see Study 3). My assumption is also partially supported by the results of a study of Chinese personality traits by a research team in mainland China using the Minnesota Multiphasic Personality Inventory (MMPI). The mainland study (Song, 1985) found that Chinese are reserved, introverted, considerate, and cautious.

One may wonder why I accepted the typology proposed by the woman cadre in Study 1. The reasons are: First, her opinions were based on her many years' informal participant observation of many people in various parts of China. Second, her typology of mainland women find equivalents in mine of the Taiwan counterparts---her career, family, and ambivalent women correspond to my independent, traditional, and confused women respectively. Third, six of her seven types of men coincide with similar ones in my typology---her impulsive man is similar to my radical type, her crafty man to my realist type, her pretentious man to my self-righteous type, her power-desiring man to my power-desiring type, her office-guarding man to my self-protective type, and her disappointed man to my ambitionless type. As for her promiscuous man, I found such men (though not too many because Chinese men, especially the educated, are self-controlled and/or controlled by their wives) in almost every (except the saint) type of mine. Lastly, I could not have a better typology of the leaders in Taiwan than the woman cadre's five types of mainland leaders except that I found more mediocre leaders than other types in Taiwan. I also found combinations of types; some leaders, for example, are autocratic and manipulating simultaneously.

As we note from the 16 cases of US Chinese in Study 3, most Chinese in the United States have a feeling of marginality. They suffer more or less from identity confusion. Fortunately, the majority of them are adaptable and able to conquer their identity crisis to a tolerable extent. According to my interviewees, they choose to remain in their adopted country primarily for the following reasons: political uncertainty in their homeland, good living and working conditions in their host country, and a much better education for their children in American schools and institutions of higher learning. As I have observed, there is another important reason. It is the untold fact that their relatives and friends at home (in Taiwan, Hong Kong, and mainland China) deem it a status symbol to live in America, the promised land of many Chinese, regardless of age, sex, and educational level.

CHAPTER FIVE

LIFE SPAN PERSONALITY DEVELOPMENT

There has been a vigorous call for a life span developmental approach to the study of personality (Baltes & Schaie, 1973; Lamb, 1978; Veroff, Reuman, & Feld, 1984). Erik Erikson (1963, 1968) is probably the most influential theorist who has demonstrated the significance of the life span approach. A life span or life-stage approach to the study of personality assumes that " certain universal life tasks demand certain kinds of personal reorganization and hence certain structures in personality emerge at one stage of life more powerfully than at another." (Veroff et al, 1984, p.1143) Such a developmentally normative perspective is explicit in the Erikson's eight stages of man (Erikson, 1963, 1968). Previous studies, qualitative or quantitative, of personality development with a life span approach have generally been done by Western scholars using Western subjects (e.g., Haviland, 1984; Helson, Mitchell, & Hart, 1985; Levinson et al, 1978; Ochse & Plug, 1986; Veroff et al, 1984). No such study employing a Chinese sample has ever been conducted.

This chapter will report two studies to test the validity of Erikson's theory. Study 1 concerns the personality development in the first six stages of 28 brief Hong Kong (14 male and 14 female) cases. Study 2 deals with six mainland Chinese cases in greater detail, three men and three women. Two of the six cases cover the first six stages of psychosocial development. The other four cases extend over the whole life

155

span. For convenience of reference, a brief overview of Erikson's theory is in order (Bee & Mitchell, 1980; Erikson 1963, 1968; Ochse & Plug, 1986; Owen, Blount, & Moscow,1981; Woolfolk & Nicolich, 1980) .

Erikson's Theory of Personality Development

Erikson belongs in the psychoanalytic tradition, but he focused his attention on the ego, on the conscious self. He described the way in which a person's sense of *identity* develops through a series of *psychosocial* stages over the life span. Erikson sees personality development as resulting from the interaction of the child or adult with his cultural or social environment. Over the life span, each individual goes through eight distinct developmental periods or stages with a specific developmental task, crisis or ego quality as a bipolar personality dimension at each stage, such as trust vs. mistrust at the first stage.

At each stage conflict arises between newly emerging personal needs and social demands, and culminates in a crisis. A crisis is a normal event. It connotes a turning point in development. In order to go through future stages successfully, a person must resolve the crisis of the present stage. The way in which a person resolves a crisis will have a lasting effect on the person's self-image and view of society. Thus a successful resolution has a positive effect and an unsuccessful resolution a negative effect on later development or on the resolution of crises in subsequent stages. On the other hand, healthy development at later stages may correct or readjust to some extent the unhealthy development (estrangement or developmental failure encountered) at earlier stages.

Now let's look at the eight stages Erikson proposed, which are summarized in Table 1. The table also gives approximate ages and the significant people involved at each stage. The age covering each stage is approximate. It may begin or end somewhat earlier or later, depending on the individual and the society in which the individual lives.

1. Trust vs. mistrust (age 0--1)

The first developmental task or crisis occurs during the first year of life. A favorable ratio of trust over mistrust constitutes a psychosocial strength which is a foundation for all future strengths. The issue is whether or not the child will develop a sense of basic trust in the predictability of the world and in his ability to affect the happenings around him or her. The behavior of the mother or her surrogate is critical to the baby's successful or unsuccessful resolution of the crisis during this stage. Children who emerge from the first year with a firm sense of trust are those with parents and/or other caregivers who are loving and who respond predictably and reliably to the child. The infants whose early care has been erratic or harsh may develop mistrust toward others and self.

2. Autonomy vs. shame and doubt (age 2--3)

The second stage occurs during the second and third years of life. The child's greater mobility is the major change at this stage. The child can now move around in the world with autonomous will and enjoy doing things without help. This forms the basis for the sense of autonomy or independence. If the child's attempts to exercise his or her autonomous will are restricted without proper guidance, the failure to take advantage of the new opportunities for mobility and exploration may result in a sense of shame and doubt. Meanwhile, proper toilet training is important at this stage. Too rigid or too early toilet training may deprive the child of the opportunity to freely and gradually control his or her bowels and bladder, and thus hinder the development of autonomous will. Excessive shaming as well as improper toilet training may lead to the child's feeling of shame and doubt.

3. Initiative vs. guilt (age 4--5)

This period may be called the play age. Language and locomotion permit the children to expand their imagination. They are energetic, curious and aggressive. They enjoy playing and fighting with other children. They are developing a conscience and will feel guilt about aggression, failures, and erotic fantasies. Initiative is the quality of playing and doing something for the sake of being active. Parents should allow children to initiate action and to ask questions without encountering ridicule or shaming. They should also help children learn self-control. If initiative is over-restricted or derided, the children may develop a sense of guilt. Such children, when grown up, may have a conscience so cruel and oppressive that they will judge themselves and/or others too harshly.

4. Industry vs. inferiority (age 6--12)

This is the school age corresponding to the six years in grade school. The child is now more ready than before to learn skills (cognitive and social), to share obligation, to make things, and to win recognition for being industrious, competent, and productive. The danger at this stage is an estrangement from him or herself and from his or her tasks--the sense of inferiority. This may be caused by an insufficient solution of the preceding conflict: the child may still want his or her mother more than knowledge and skills; he or she may still prefer to be the baby at home rather than the big child in school; the boy may compare himself with his father and the girl with her mother, and this comparison arouses a sense of guilt due to the Oedipus complex as well as a sense of inferiority.

5. Identity vs. identity confusion (age 13--19)

This stage marks the end of childhood. Not until adolescence does the individual begin maturing in physiological, cognitive, and social development to experience the crisis of identity. The adolescent needs a moratorium to integrate the identity elements ascribed earlier. Failure to integrate various roles or identity elements results in role diffusion or identity confusion. Each of the earlier accomplishments serves as a foundation in the search for identity or for a sense of self. Having established a sense of basic trust, the adolescent is now searching for people and ideas to have faith in. The sense of autonomy developed in childhood leads to the autonomous will to decide about future careers and life styles. With the sense of initiative the young person probably has had a chance to play at various roles in preparation for performing one or more of them at some future date. The sense of industry achieved during the school age leaves the adolescent with a sense of competence in his or her ability to make meaningful contributions to the world.

6. Intimacy vs. isolation (age 20--40)

Some forms of identity crisis may return in the later stages of the life cycle after adolescence. The first of these is the crisis of intimacy. True intimacy is possible only when identity formation is well on its way. Intimacy refers to a person's willingness to relate to another person in a deep sense, to have a relationship based on more than mutual need and reciprocity. Sexual relations are only a part of intimacy. A true psychosocial intimacy exists in friendship, in erotic encounters, or in joint inspiration. A person who does not accomplish such intimate relationships with others during this period may have a sense of isolation. Isolation is "the incapacity to take chances with one's identity by sharing true intimacy, such inhibition is often reinforced by a fear of the outcome of intimacy: offspring--and care." (Erikson, 1968, p. 137)

7. Generativity vs. stagnation (age 41--60)

Generativity " is primarily the concern for establishing and guiding the next generation. There are, of course, people who ...do not apply this drive to offspring of their own, but to other forms of altruistic concern and creativity" (Erikson, 1968, p. 138). The task of mid-life is to "generate in the most inclusive sense ...children, products, ideas, and works of art" (Erikson 1974, p. 122). Any activity or production that contributes to the well-being of others strengthens one's sense of generativity. Those who do not achieve a sense of generativity, either because they do not generate in Erikson's sense or because they are not satisfied with what they have done or produced, may experience a sense of stagnation.

8. Integrity vs. despair (age 61--plus)

Integrity refers to the fact that the fruit of the preceding seven stages gradually ripens "in the aging person who has taken care of things and people and has adapted himself to the triumphs and disappointments of being, by necessity, the originator of others and the generator of things and ideas" (Erikson, 1968, p. 139). It means the acceptance of one's life as one has lived it and of the people who have been significant in one's life. It is the acceptance of the fact that how one's life has been lived is one's own responsibility, and that it is futile to wish that the things and people had been different. Without that sense of integrity, there will be despair and fear of death. Despair refers to "the feeling that time is short, too short for the attempt to start another life and to try out alternate roads to integrity" (Erikson, 1968, p. 140).

Table 1
Erikson's Eight Stages of Personality Development

Stage	Approximate Age	Important people and institutions involved
Trust vs. mistrust	0--1	Maternal figure (mother or mother surrogate)
Autonomy vs. shame and doubt	2--3	Parental figures (parents or their surrogates)
Initiative vs. guilt	4--5	Parents, playmates
Industry vs. inferiority	6--12	Parents, teachers, playmates
Identity vs. identity confusion	13--19	Family, school, and peers
Intimacy vs. isolation	20--40	Spouse, friends, and acquaintances
Generativity vs. stagnation	41--60	Family, friends, and work world
Integrity vs. despair	61--plus	Family, friends, and humanity

STUDY 1

TWENTY-EIGHT BRIEF HONG KONG CASES

Most of the research based on Erikson's theory has been confined to studies of adolescence and youth, and some tested its validity concerning the development of personality from adolescence to the onset of old age (Ochse & Plug, 1986). This study examined the validity of Erikson's first six stages of personality development with 28 Hong Kong Chinese cases.

The subjects were 14 men (age range 22-35, mean age 26) and 14 women (age range 21-30, mean age 25). All of them had received at least two years of higher education. Most of them were graduate students in a developmental psychology class taught by me at the Chinese University of Hong Kong. All the subjects had reached the 6th stage of Erikson's eight stages of psychosocial development.

As a course requirement, I asked my graduate class in developmental psychology to write a retrospective case report of personality development to test the validity of Erikson's theory. Most of my students wrote about themselves and a few reported the development of their friends or relatives. They were advised to ask the subjects' parents and other family members for additional information concerning the subjects' development, especially during the first three stages which were beyond recall by the subjects themselves. Twenty-eight well-written case reports on 14 men and 14 women were selected. With the assistance of a former graduate student Mr. Tsoi Fa-shu, the contents of the 28 reports were analyzed in terms of Erikson's stages.

The analysis of the content of the 28 case reports was conducted by scoring the subjects' perceptions and the observations of their family members (primarily their parents). If there are significantly more points on the positive side, the development is counted positive, viz., the ratio of the positive side over the negative side is favorable like "a favorable ratio of trust over mistrust" (Erikson, 1968, p. 105) at the first stage. If there are significantly more points on the negative side, viz., the ratio of the positive side over the negative side is unfavorable, the development is counted negative. If the scores on both sides are tied or not significantly different, the development is considered mixed.

The outcomes of the subjects' development at each stage are shown in Figure 1. The positive and negative experiences encountered and relevant behaviors manifested at each of the six stages are presented below. After that, four cases, two most favorable and two least favorable, will be reviewed to illustrate what contributed to positive and negative outcomes at each stage of development.

Development at Each Stage with Relevant Experiences and Behavioral Manifestations

Stage 1 (age 0–1)

Positive development. As shown in Figure 1, the development of the 12 men and 11 women was positive at this stage, viz., their development demonstrated a favorable ratio of trust over mistrust. They were in general cared for warmly and fed properly and regularly by mother or her surrogate. They also slept well and excreted well.

Negative development. Two men and two women had a negative development during this period either because the mother was too busy and/or poverty-stricken to take good care of them, or because the baby experienced difficulties in sleeping, taking food, and/or excretion due to illness.

Mixed development. One woman had a mixed development because of premature birth and being taken care of by a maid although she was loved by both parents who were too busy to attend to her most of the time.

Behavioral manifestations. The behavioral manifestations included trust and confidence in self and others (positive behaviors); and mistrust in and suspiciousness of others, and lack of self-confidence (negative behaviors).

Figure 1

The Personality Development at Erikson's First Six Stages (from Infancy to Early Adulthood)
of 14 Males and 14 Females in Hong Kong

Stage	M1	M2	M3	M4	M5	M6	M7	M8	M9	M10	M11	M12	M13	M14	Total P	N	X
								14 Males									
1	P	P	N	P	P	P	P	P	P	P	P	X	N	P	12	2	0
2	P	P	N	N	P	P	P	P	P	P	N	X	N	P	8	5	1
3	X	X	X	X	P	X	P	P	N	P	X	X	P	X	6	1	7
4	X	N	P	P	N	N	P	X	X	P	P	N	N	P	5	5	4
5	X	X	X	P	N	N	P	N	P	P	P	N	N	P	6	5	3
6	N	N	N	N	P	N	N	P	X	P	P	N	X	P	5	7	2

	F1	F2	F3	F4	F5	F6	F7	F8	F9	F10	F11	F12	F13	F14	Total P	N	X
								14 Females									
1	P	P	N	P	P	P	P	P	P	P	X	P	P	N	11	2	1
2	P	X	N	X	P	P	N	X	N	P	N	X	P	N	5	5	4
3	X	P	N	N	X	P	X	P	P	P	N	P	P	X	7	3	4
4	P	P	X	X	X	P	X	X	N	P	N	P	P	X	6	2	6
5	P	N	N	N	X	P	X	N	X	X	X	X	X	X	2	4	8
6	P	N	X	X	P	P	N	N	N	N	X	P	X	N	4	6	4

Note: P=Positive development, N=Negative development, X=Mixed development.

Stage 2 (age 2--3)

As the infant is delicate during the first year of life. He or she is usually given good care to prevent any possible danger or harm. When the child enters the second year of life and becomes a little more resistant to disease, parents tend to be less careful in handling him or her. The unintentional neglect hurts the growth of the child to some extent. Starting from Erikson's second stage, therefore, the child's development is generally not so smooth as during the first stage.

Positive development. At this second stage, 8 men and 5 women had positive development, i.e., with a favorable ratio of autonomy over shame and doubt.

Negative development. The development of 5 men and 5 women was negative, i.e., the ratio of autonomy over shame and doubt was unfavorable.

Mixed development. The remaining 1 man and 4 women experienced mixed development.

Positive experiences. At this stage, the positive experiences included permissive and gradual toilet training, parental warmth, and praise, which are conducive to positive development.

Positive behavioral manifestations. Independence, self-control, and cheerfulness were among the positive behavioral manifestations as a result of development at this stage.

Negative experiences. Parental shaming, punishment, overcontrol, too early toilet training, and strict discipline in kindergarten were all negative experiences conducive to negative development.

Negative behavioral manifestations. Dependence, anxiety, stinginess, withdrawnness, excessive cautiousness, and overconcern about "face" are negative behavioral manifestations resulted from negative development during this stage.

Stage 3 (age 4--5)

Positive development. At this stage 6 males and 7 females experienced positive development.

Negative development. One male and 3 females experienced negative development.

Mixed development. Mixed development was experienced by 7 males and 4 females.

Positive experiences. The positive experiences of the subjects in the development at this stage included freedom and opportunity to play with agemates, entering kindergarten, praise and/or encouragement by parents or other adults, and permissive child rearing practices.

Negative experiences. The subjects' negative experiences at this stage of development included lack of freedom and opportunity to play, punishment, accident resulted from play, being discriminated against, parental overcontrol or restriction of activity.

Positive behavioral manifestations. The subjects' behavioral manifestations indicating positive development at this stage included industriousness, activeness, extraversion, adventurousness, courage, optimism, curiosity, perseverance, and a sense of accomplishment.

Negative behavioral manifestations. The subjects' behavioral manifestations indicating negative development at this stage included guilt feelings, pessimism, self-centeredness, fearfulness, timidity, and lethargy.

Stage 4 (age 6--12)

Positive development: 5 males, 6 females.

Negative development: 5 males, 2 females.

Mixed development: 4 males, 6 females.

Positive experiences: academic achievement, praise, prize, new friends, loving parents, good teachers, being elected or selected student leader, church activities, having good models.

Negative experiences: poor test results, frightful teachers, being neglected by parent or teacher, poor relations with peers, sibling rivalry, death of a parent or a beloved family member, punishment at home or in school, home moved to a strange environment without friends, worsen family conditions, unsatisfactory body image, family conflict, divorce of parents, illness.

Positive behavioral manifestations: working hard, getting along well with schoolmates, enjoying reading and/or schoolwork, becoming a Christian, helping with house work, looking after younger sibling, serving as class monitor, having a sense of self-respect, identifying with hardworking parent, showing curiosity, having a need for achievement, having a sense of responsibility, obedient, cooperative, enjoying exercises.

Negative behavioral manifestations: underachieving, feeling inferior, having school phobia, running away from home, thinking of suicide, being jealous of peers or siblings, fooling around, being emotionally unstable, feeling frustrated or depressed, being rebellious, being nervous, avoiding activities or social interaction, being oversensitive, being self-conscious.

Stage 5 (age 13--19)

Positive development: 6 males, 2 females.

Negative development: 5 males, 4 females.

Mixed development: 3 males, 8 females.

Positive experiences: academic achievement, being admitted to a prestigious school or university, good teacher, praise, prize, proper guidance, religious faith, friendship, good human relations, work experience, student activities, becoming student leader, parental encouragement, enlarged social circle, Christian fellowship, improved family conditions.

Negative experiences: frightful teacher, overstrict parent, unfavorable relations with parent, poor test results, poor school record, failure in college entrance exam, failure in love affairs, sibling rivalry, poor peer relations, family conflict, father's career failure, death of a parent, impoverishment, male preference (favoritism for sons, negative experience for daughters), pimples on face, obesity or skinniness.

Positive behavioral manifestations: having high need for achievement, working hard, identifying with parent, becoming interested in a profession, entering college, enjoying school work, participating in student and/or church activities, becoming a Christian, having an improved self-image, identifying life goals, feeling satisfied with own roles, being conscientious and responsible, working for self-support.

Negative behavioral manifestations: being jealous of siblings or classmates, conflicting with parent or peers, disliking activities, feeling extremely dissatisfied with status quo, feeling confused about own roles or self-image.

Stage 6 (age 20--40)

Positive development: 5 males, 4 females.

Negative development: 7 males, 6 females.

Mixed development: 2 males, 4 females.

Positive experiences: college and/or graduate education, teaching and/or working, occupational identity, Christian faith, intimate friend, being consulted by parent on family matters, being liked by students when teaching, extracurricular activities, church activities, emotional outlet, good relations with parent and/or peers, many friends, having identified life goals, community service, winning prize in school contest, success in love affairs, boarding in college, baptism, traveling abroad, having a good job, getting married.

Negative experiences: dull or lonely college life, death of a parent or sibling, failure in romance, loneliness, poverty, poor or mediocre academic performance, difficulty in finding a job, conflict with parent or parent-in-law, loss of confidence, inability to find an intimate friend, lacking a sense of belonging, interpersonal complications, poor relations with family and/or colleagues, failure to achieve intimacy, unfavorable change of jobs, a fussy spouse, one-sided love, disappointment in work or people.

Positive behavioral manifestations: saving money for further study abroad, improving relations with family or peers, believing in God, making progress in relations with friend of opposite sex, taking part in student or social activities, playing active role in church work, winning social support, finding life goals, joining in community service, having an intimate friend, traveling abroad, enjoying marriage life, becoming a provider in the extended family, acting as a filial child to parents, accepting reality.

Negative behavioral manifestations: avoiding opposite sex or social activities, longing for but fearing intimacy, indulging in fantasies about opposite sex, suppressing interest in opposite sex, being passive in work and play, becoming shiftless, having difficulties in social adjustment, quarreling with parent, losing self-confidence, feeling inferior, separating with intimate friend, acting rebelliously, feeling impatient, anxious, timid, lonely, or lost.

Four Illustrative Cases

Of all 28 cases as shown in Figure 1, there were one man and one woman whose development was the most favorable, i.e., positive at all six stages. There were also one man and one woman whose development was the least favorable, i.e., negative at four of the six stages. It may be instructive to review briefly how these four subjects, two men and two women, developed through the six stages.

Case 1: M10, age 30. M10 (male #10) was born in an impoverished family with an unemployed father but received warm care from a loving and patient mother throughout the first three stages of development. At stage 4, both parents worked but father indulged in gambling. Fortunately, he had enough time to play and study while receiving proper guidance from mother. He was both a filial son at home and a diligent pupil in school. At stage 5, he had a heuristic teacher who helped him develop broad interests and the aspiration to go on to college. He also associated with several high-achieving schoolmates as models. He lived in school dormitory and worked after graduation from high school, which made him more independent. At stage 6, he entered college and did part-time teaching. He tried to establish intimate relations with girl friends but failed. Under the encouragement and guidance of his mother, he finally got married and enjoyed family life as well as work.

Case 2: F6, age 23. F6 (female #6) was the only child of her parents. She grew healthily and achieved the sense of basic trust and autonomy under parental love and care of the best kind during the first two stages of development. Meanwhile, she had a lovely dog as her companion. With full autonomy, however, she was somewhat stubborn and willful. She entered kindergarten at the third stage when she had more little friends to play with and teachers to adore her. She was active and self-confident, although still stubborn and willful. She was industrious and often praised by teachers at the 4th stage. She learned to take care of herself when father's business encountered difficulties and both parents were too busy to pay much attention to her. She was a cheerful, lively, and optimistic girl although still somewhat willful at the 5th stage when she entered a girls high school. She enjoyed school and took part in various student activities. Father became ill-tempered because of frustrations in business, which drove her nearer to mother. She found fellow students friendly in college and joined in many extracurricular activities at the 6th stage when she enjoyed intimacy with friends. She was extraverted, natural, enthusiastic, and responsible at the age of 23.

The above two cases illustrated positive development at all six stages from infancy to early adulthood. The following two cases are negative in development at four of the six stages; the first two stages were both negative, thus having laid a poor foundation for subsequent development.

Case 3 (M13, age 25). M13 (male #13) was inadequately fed and often woke up during sleep due to hunger at the first stage when parents were busily struggling against poverty with six mouths to feed. At the second stage, another mouth was added to the family when a younger sister was born. With five children to attend to, mother was impatient, often scolding and hitting him, and toilet training was strict. This made him feel shame and doubt and become stubborn and stingy. He had sufficient freedom to play and run around, however, during the third stage with a budding conscience. At the 4th stage he was an academic underachiever scorned by teachers, which made him feel inferior. Meanwhile, another brother was born. The family moved to a strange place where he had few friends. At the 5th stage father died and mother was still strict. He was withdrawn and secretly loved a female teacher, aspiring to be a teacher himself. Soon he began to have some contact with the church and entered college at the end of Stage 5. He was then a self-aware, obedient, and polite young man. He did not, however, achieve a complete identity until the next stage when he had a sense of accomplishment in his work after graduation from college. He had a girl friend and some roommates in college who gave him constant encouragement and inspiration. But he alienated his girl friend when taking the graduation exam. He again felt isolated and lonely at age 25.

Case 4 (F3, age 23). The case of F3 (female #3) was similar to that of M13. With four children and a house of six mouths, F3's mother was too busy to give her the care and attention she needed as an infant. Like M13, she did not sleep well either. So she developed a sense of mistrust and turned out to be pessimistic about the world. At the second stage when toilet training is important, her mother used shaming as a method to control her bowels and bladder. She was even forbidden to cry by both parents as she cried a lot to seek parental attention. A deep sense of shame and doubt was thus developed. At the third stage when play promotes healthy growth, she was restrained to go out of the house. Her father disdained girls to use makeup or dress up, hence a sense of initiative could not properly develop in her. At the 4th stage when she started school, mother had to go out working and only attended to her occasionally. She helped with housekeeping and made progress in school. Her academic achievement, however, failed to draw parental attention. Father even scolded and hit her as usual. The family had to move to a different area and she was forced to leave her friends in the neighborhood. She also suffered from parental favoritism toward younger brother. She realized that she must study hard but still could not get rid of a sense of inferiority. So her development was mixed at this stage. At the next stage during adolescence, her life circle enlarged with more friends and more teachers to interact with. Her academic performance was good through industry, but still failed to win any praise from parents and siblings. Her parents favored boys and neglected girls. Her relations with two elder brothers and one younger brother deteriorated. She had a boy friend but the friendship did not last long. She then avoided contact with boys, feeling inferior and confused. She now became very sensitive and taciturn. At the 6th stage she learned positive and negative lessons from her mentor and father respectively. She had difficulties in search of occupational identity. She taught for a while before working as a nurse. Then she returned to the teaching profession because of inability to adapt to the hospital environment. Probably aware of the harm done to herself by parental neglect and control, she was permissive to her students and liked by them. Finally she had a boy friend and expected to achieve identity and intimacy at the same time, although still feeling somewhat lonely and confused at age 23.

Discussion

Although the sample was small and its representativeness could not be claimed, we are still able to discern a trend of development with or without sex differences. For both sexes as demonstrated by the four illustrative cases, the number of cases of the most and that of the least favorable development are the same. For both sexes and most cases, the first stage witnessed a general smooth development dominated by positive outcomes with almost identical distribution of cases in the three categories of development (12 male and 11 female cases positive, 2 male and 2 female cases negative, no male and one female case mixed). The subsequent five stages were, however, not so smooth in development. Probably because of more rigid toilet training and greater use of shaming for females than for males at the second stage, the development of autonomy at this stage was not so easy for girls as for boys with 8 male cases but only 5 female cases positive.

Another sex difference appeared at the 4th stage. There were three more negative male cases than female cases (5 males and 2 females) at this stage. It is probably because boys encountered greater pressure from parents for academic achievement than girls did that lead the boys to a deeper sense of inferiority at this school age, the period when formal education begins. Three of the five negative male cases evolved from a mixed or partial resolution of the crisis at the preceding stage while the remaining two cases experienced positive development at Stage 3.

The third major difference between sexes was found at Stage 5 when four more males than females (6 males and 2 females) had successfully resolved the crisis of identity. For this disparity two interpretations may be offered. First, it may be that women as a group suffer from more obstacles than men in their identity resolution. Their development becomes more complicated when we consider society's expectations for the particular roles they are to fulfill (Franz & White, 1985). Many females may have to keep their identity incomplete until they know (or find) their man (Evans, 1967). In other words, many women, like most females in my sample, have to deal with intimacy issues successfully prior to identity issues, whereas men tend to follow a more stepwise developmental pattern proposed by Erikson; viz., identity comes before intimacy (Schiedel & Marcia, 1985).

Second, it is possible that females have a "diphasic identity development pattern" (Schiedel & Marcia, 1985, p. 158): some of them pursue a more occupationally and/or ideologically oriented track, and achieve an initial identity before age 20; others follow a more home-oriented track (O'Connell, 1976) and do not form a self-constructed identity after fulfilling the socially prescribed roles of wife and mother (Marcia, 1980). The former are career women and the latter are family women (Helson et al, 1985). Besides these two groups of women, there are those who attempt to play both roles (career woman and family woman) equally well, but usually to no avail. While the number of career women is increasing in Chinese society, most women, like most female subjects in my sample, are more home-oriented or family centered, or they are at best "modern traditional" (Helson et al, 1985).

My findings differ from those of Ochse & Plug (1986). Their findings suggest that the white woman in their South African sample resolved their crisis of identity at a younger age than did the white men. They offered two explanations. One is the women's premature foreclosure (the tendency to foreclose their identity by accepting the traditional roles of wives and mothers). The other explanation is that "the critical stage in the formation of identity occurs when intimacy and generativity have already developed to some extent, and that the white women have a start on the men as far as this is concerned" (Ochse & Plug, 1986, p. 1249). Their findings confirm the commonly held view that" white women develop intimacy before their male counterparts and are already relatively well imbued with a sense of intimacy in adolescence" (Ochse & Plug, 1986, p. 1249). Their findings differ from mine probably because most Chinese women in my Hong Kong sample neither foreclosed their identity nor developed intimacy before their male counterparts. The female subjects in my sample were still in school during adolescence, most of them had neither made a vocational choice nor had an intimate friend, especially a boy friend, because they were discouraged by both parents and teachers to develop an intimate relationship with boys at such a young age. Most Chinese, particularly educated Chinese, need a moratorium in adolescence to integrate the identity elements ascribed to the childhood stages. For both Chinese men and women, notably for men as Ochse and Plug (1986) have suggested, the critical period in the development of identity occurs well after adolescence. That may explain why most men and women in my Hong Kong sample failed to resolve identity crisis during adolescence.

Achievement of identity in adolescence or after it does not guarantee intimacy, however. Two men (M4 and M7), for example, achieved identity at Stage 5 but failed to gain intimacy at Stage 6. Failure to resolve identity crisis at Stage 5 as a moratorium may lead to achievement of identity and intimacy simultaneously at a later stage, like cases M5 and M8. Less educated Chinese without a high school or college education might resolve the crisis of identity and intimacy more successfully than well educated Chinese through foreclosure (without passing through much searching and questioning) and through early marriage respectively.

The distribution of both sexes in the three categories of development (positive, negative, and mixed) is similar at Stage 6; most men and women did not achieve satisfactory intimacy at this stage. Only one woman (age 27) and four men (mean age=28) were married, but marriage does not guarantee intimacy. The married woman (F4) and one (M9) of the four married men resolved the crisis of intimacy with only partial success; their development was mixed at this stage. On the other hand, intimacy may be achieved without marriage. All the four women and two (M8 and M14) of the five men who had achieved intimacy were unmarried.

Overall, the overview of the 28 cases and the separate review of the four illustrative cases evidenced support for Erikson's theory of epigenetic development of personality. Since Erikson also suggests that all the personality components develop to some extent throughout the life span, the components are interdependent and they develop to some extent in parallel (Ochse & Plug, 1986). This has also been demonstrated in the case studies presented above, such as F3 (female #3) who expected to resolve at once the crises of identity and intimacy very soon. Identity formation is not confined to adolescence, it is the consequence of a lifetime of experience (Erikson, 1968). Several researchers (Conger, 1973; LaVoie, 1976; Adams & Jones, 1983) have demonstrated that different parental socialization styles may either enhance or hinder the ego-identity process. This has been supported by the case of F6 (female #6)whose relationship with both parents was generally warm and positive. The case of F6 demonstrated moreover that the only child is not necessarily doomed to develop negatively in personality as in many mainland Chinese children who are overindulged as a result of one-child policy (Jiao, Ji, & Jing, 1986).

STUDY 2

SIX DETAILED MAINLAND CHINESE CASES

This study consisted of six mainland Chinese cases, three male and three female. The first two cases cover the first six stages of psychosocial development like those in Study 1. The other four cases extend over the whole life span. The six cases will be presented individually and the psychosocial development in each case will be discussed to see if Erikson's theory can apply validly.

The first two cases were one young man and one young woman who were approaching the midway of the 6th stage of psychosocial development. The other four cases were two men and two women who had entered the last stage of Erikson's eight stages of personality development. Three of the four subjects were in their 60's and one man was 91 years old. All the six subjects were well-educated Chinese adults.

The two young subjects were students in a class I taught as visiting professor of developmental psychology at a university in eastern China. They wrote a case report as a major course requirement. The four older subjects were interviewed by me when I was teaching at another university in southern China. Three of them were faculty members auditing my class in developmental psychology. The other man was a chemical engineer whom I had known for more than 40 years. All the six subjects have kept corresponding with me up to the present day. The case reports of the two young subjects and the interview protocols of the four older subjects plus their letters constituted the primary sources of data for the present study.

The six cases are presented below. In each case, more details are given in some stages than others due to uneven distribution of data provided by the subjects.

Case 1 (Female, age 27): A Compromised Identity before Intimacy

L is a 27-year-old female psychologist. Her father is a medical doctor and mother a nurse. She is their youngest child and only daughter with two elder brothers. After she was born, her mother hired a maid to take care of her. She was also suckled by a neighbor's mother because mother's milk was insufficient. She was later entrusted to the maternal grandmother's care after age 3 in the countryside. Grandparents were better-off than the average country people. They lived in a large house with a big yard. Grandma was kind to other kids around as well as to L. So L had quite a few playmates. They often played in the big yard. L was willful and quarrelsome. Grandparents loved her; they were neither restrictive nor too permissive to her. L lived with them for about three years.

At age 6, L joined her mother who was sent down during the Cultural Revolution to work in a country hospital. Willful as before, L stuck to mother wherever she went. Father was sent to another place while the second brother stayed with paternal grandparents and the first brother with maternal grandparents. The two bothers joined mother one and two years later respectively. L started school at age 7. She was active and lively, but still willful. She developed a need to excel and win. She played with both young adults and peers.

L was class head (monitor) for the first five years in the grade school. She took part in extracurricular activities such as ping pong, arts, and basketball teams. She had a feeling of superiority as she excelled in many ways and became the center of attention among teachers and peers. In the neighborhood outside school, however, she was a follower rather than a leader of the group as she had to play with boys and girls one or two years older. Playing with boys, including her two brothers, led her to take on some boyishness.

Though boisterous with peers, L remained sticking to mother and often listening silently to her talking with other adults. So she was also a quiet and docile girl in the eyes of adults at the time. Starting from the third grade, she enjoyed reading novels which were borrowed by brothers from school and by mother from the hospital. By reading novels, she learned a lot about the world and its people.

In the year when L completed the 6-year elementary education, there was a great change in the political environment as the radical Gang of Four was overthrown. When she entered the junior high school, academic achievement was again emphasized as before the Cultural Revolution. Ability grouping put her in the "super-fast" group in the second year (8th grade) that was to complete the second and third year courses in one year. Being one of the top students in her class, she was nevertheless the target of criticism by her over-demanding class master. The criticism added to her pride instead of shame because it attracted more attention which was exactly what she needed.

To create the impression that she is smart, L pretended to be careless about the frequent tests while her test results remained superb. At age 14, she was conferred the membership of the Communist Youth Corps, which is a symbol of honor for outstanding young people in Communist China. One year later, her performance in regional joint entrance exam qualified her for admission to the best senior high school in the area.

After entering senior high, everybody seemed to be "buried in books," studying hard for the highly competitive nation-wide joint college entrance exam. The class climate was thus rather dull. L, along with several younger classmates, was, however, not so immersed in study. She even watched TV in the evening while other students were studying. The two-year high school course (as found then in most mainland Chinese senior high) soon came to an end before L was ready for the college entrance exam. So she failed in the exam and felt disgraced. Then she worked hard in a review class for another year and finally won admission at age 17 to one of the best universities in eastern China.

In choosing the major field of study, her father recommended medicine, but she refused to follow her father's career as physician. She chose the science track in senior high mainly because science students enjoy higher prestige than arts students. Another reason for her choosing science was to contradict the general belief that women are unfit for science. She, however, finally made a compromise by choosing psychology as major, which, she thought, was a a field of study having the qualities of both arts and science.

Before entering college, L had never gone anywhere without being accompanied by adults. Her first trip to the university campus was also escorted by mother. Since coming to the big city where the university is located, she has known more about the injustice and selfishness of people, which led her to feel rather disappointed about the world in which she lives. She also found that the college is different from the elementary and secondary schools where she was always the center of attention. Her current peers are a select group of high school graduates from the same and other provinces of the country. She is, therefore, no longer paid much attention by people around, which made her feel rather inferior and cautious in doing things and dealing with people.

Though changed outwardly, L's personality remains basically the same. She appears to be indifferent to the happenings on campus, but strong ambition and high self-esteem still dominate her inner world. As a junior, she was one of the few students in a class who turned in the major assignment to a visiting professor who taught the class. Several years later in 1991, she was the only former student in the class who wrote to that professor reporting her life experiences in the recent past.

L entered the graduate school of the same university in 1986 at age 21 and got a Master's degree three years later. Then she began a teaching career in a college of education in the same city. Meanwhile, she was planning to take TOEFL and go to the United States for further education. Then at age 24 she fell in love for the first time with a colleague. The man was a fine arts instructor from Peking, an activist supporting the June 4th movement in 1989 for political reform. Though she warned herself when she discovered that the man was irresponsible in heterosexual relations, she could not resist his dating until he developed a romance with an American girl a year later during summer vacation in Peking, his home town. The unhappy ending, of course, hurt her ego. She had hoped that she would become more mature after this incident. In the following year, to the surprise of her friends and relatives, she married a doctoral student of physics from her native province studying at an American university in California. She met this man two years earlier and he returned home for the wedding. She decided that this man is more suitable for her than the fine arts instructor. She joined her husband abroad in early 1992. A year later when she wrote me last, L was applying for admission to a graduate program in cognitive psychology at the University of California.

Case 2 (Male, age 29): Simultaneous Achievement of Intimacy and Identity

H is a 29-year-old male graduate student in educational philosophy. His family consisted of three generations: grandparents, parents, two elder brothers and two younger brothers. Grandfather was a gambler and lost all his property in gambling. Father ran a hospital which was later nationalized. Mother worked in the same hospital. Having eight mouths to feed, living was rather hard for the family. Life was peaceful, however, the whole family lived in harmony.

Grandfather was authoritarian and irrational but permissive to grandchildren. All adults in the house were fearful of him. Grandmother was a religious vegetarian. She seldom minded others' business and never lost her temper. Brought up under a strict and ill-tempered father, H's father was introverted and somewhat rebellious. He worked as an apprentice during adolescence, then joined the Red army for ten years, and returned to his native place afterwards. In contrast to grandfather, father was a responsible family man. He encouraged children to be honest, humble, and down-to-earth. He valued their academic achievement.

Mother came from a well-off family in the "old" society before 1949. She learned to be a hardworking housewife and worker in the "new" society. She loved children but was too busy to take good care of them. H was not properly fed during infancy. While permissive to children, mother was ill-tempered. H would rather stay closer to father. Good relations with parents, especially father, led H to be extraverted, self-confident, independent, bold, have a sense of humor, and feel secure. He is the only member in the family to receive a university education.

Cared for by a wet nurse while mother was too busy, H's development during infancy was more negative than positive as he was not well-fed, did not sleep well, and cried a lot during the day. Then he got seriously ill at age 3. In sickbed and to the surprise of adults, he comforted sorrowful parents with songs and said before singing, "Don't worry, I'll be all right. Let me sing for you in case you don't believe." Since then, parents had taken better care of him. Meanwhile, he had been taught since age 2 to speak, sing, and count. His development has thus turned to be generally positive except that he has been underweight since then. He is now tall and thin.

In the 3rd stage, he was full of curiosity and imagination. His language ability was better than his peers who often came to play with him in the house. As both parents were working, they asked his maternal grandmother to help with housekeeping and childrearing. Grandma was, however, too busy with housework to give him sufficient attention. So he had enough time and space to develop his initiative.

At the beginning of the 4th stage before starting school at age 7, H had a strong desire to learn. He asked adults a lot of questions and listened outside the classroom in a nearby school to teachers inside. He told peers the stories heard from adults (mostly father). His quality of industry was fully developed with a good start. Since entering school, he has been an outstanding student. He was made class monitor every year, praised by teachers, and adored by parents. Being class monitor wakened his sense of responsibility. He reasoned that he must set himself as an example for peers and stay ahead of the class in every way.

In the 4th grade, he began to read novels and tell what he read to peers. His abilities in reading, speaking, and writing were thus greatly improved. He was soon made a student leader of the school and chosen to participate in all national (e.g., labor day, national day) festivities of the school. He now became more self-confident and proud of himself. Outside school, he was also a leader of peers in the neighborhood. He made some good friends both in and outside the school.

The junior high school provided him with a new environment for development to which he had been looking forward since the later years in grade school. He again was appointed class monitor by his class master. In the 8th grade, he was assigned to the "fast" class. Now he became haughty and was the target of peer's jealousy and teachers' favoritism. He made several good friends, however. The friendship has continued till the present day. Entrance to senior high is a difficult hurdle he must overcome. To help him pass the hurdle, his parents hired a tutor for him to review the subjects to be tested in the entrance exam.

In senior high school, H found that the academic competition was keener than before and parental pressure was also stronger. The reason was simple: everybody aspires to go on to college while the places are limited. This was the first time that H left home to attend a school in another town. He therefore had to learn to live independently and take care of himself. In the 11th grade (the second and last year in most senior high schools in mainland China then), H fell in love for the first time with a girl classmate. This was unusual at the time because heterosexual friendship was discouraged in high school. While enjoying intimacy, his academic performance dropped sharply. He and his pretty girl friend then both failed in the nationwide college entrance exam.

Fortunately, his parents, teachers, and friends, especially his girl friend, continued to give him support and encouragement. His girl friend quit school to work while H was preparing for a second trial in the following year. But test anxiety made him miss the target by a narrow margin. He wanted to give up but his parents would not allow him. For a change of environment, parents made arrangements for him to stay with his aunt and join the review class in another school. The failure in two trials had a profound impact on H's personality, at least for the time being. He turned introverted, lost confidence and pride in himself. His interest in his girl friend also waned.

After a year's hard work with a loss of about ten pounds in weight, H eventually passed successfully the nationwide college entrance exam and got admitted to a prestigious university in a big city of his native province. Yet a success in the third trial was not something to be excited about for him. He even shunned social interaction on campus at the beginning. His personality soon became stabilized, however. He acted freely within the limits of social conventions. Academically, he did well and felt that he is worthy to be called a college student. He believed that it is his responsibility to contribute what he has learned to mankind, however poor his capability may be. Socially, he did not feel as happy as in high school because he could hardly find a real friend in college as he did in high school and outside school. He also lost his girl friend who did not go to college. His parents more or less objected their continued association, implying that the girl was not worthy of him. Though H still loved the girl, he sensed that the work world must have changed her as she was no longer the same girl he used to know so well.

During the senior year in college, three events contributed to H's psychosocial development: falling in love with a female classmate, being elected a member of the student council, and the practicum in his major field of study. He did extremely well in all three--as a happy lover, as an efficient organizer of student activities, and as a successful practice teacher. These positive experiences recovered his self-esteem; he once more felt confident in and proud of himself. After graduation, the girl went on to study for a Master's degree at the same university while he was assigned to work at a university in another city. Nearly all the abilities and qualities developed so far were found useful in his job as personnel officer of the university. For three years he had succeeded in dealing with colleagues of various kinds while adhering to his moral principles whenever possible. His boss liked him and wanted to promote him, but he decided to quit the job and take the examination for admission to the graduate program at his alma mater. He did so for three reasons: to marry and live with the girl he loves in the same university city, to match his training with that of his prospective wife, and to search for the identity as a scholar or college instructor.

Thus after three years working in another city, H came back for graduate studies and joined his girl friend in the city where she was already working as a college instructor. They got married on the Mid-autumn Day in the same year. His wife is an intelligent gentle woman. Their matrimony has been the outcome of four years' mutual understanding and mature romance. It is certainly a much more sophisticated romantic relationship than the one with his former high school girl friend. During the four years, he has learned to tolerate, yield, and sacrifice for the well-being of the woman he loves. The intimacy he enjoys is most conducive to a favorable development of his personality from now on.

H wrote in 1991 that he expected to receive the Master's degree in July 1992. He hoped to be assigned a job in the same city where his wife is working. If not assigned to work in the same city with his wife on graduation, he planned to apply for admission to the doctoral program at the same institution. He would rather be a scholar or college instructor than an administrator. Though he handled well the complicated human relations when he worked in the personnel office of another institution, he abhorred to deal with so many of those hostile and selfish people.

Case 3 (Male, age 91): Extended Generativity

W is a 91-year-old retired professor. His father was an illiterate peasant and mother an illiterate housewife. W is the second child with one elder brother, one younger brother, and two younger sisters. He started schooling at age 12, worked and studied in grade school. At 17, he entered a 5-year normal school which was free. Then he taught in junior high school for four and half years. He married at 22, and lived with parents until 26 when he left for Japan to receive higher education financed by the Nationalist government. He returned to China six years later, taught at a high school and became its principal in the following year for 18 years until 1949 when the Communist seized power. Then on completion of one-year ideological study at the "revolutionary university," he was assigned to teach at a teachers college till retirement at age 86 in 1987.

Taken good care of by mother during infancy and early childhood, W began tending cow and working in the rice paddy at age 5. Mother was strict, especially to daughters. Father had better temper than mother. They occasionally scolded him but never hit him. Since attending school at age 12, he had learned to hate the rich and sympathized with the poor because during childhood his family was maltreated by wealthy people. Father sent him to school in order to raise his own social standing.

Father had higher expectations for him than mother did. He studied with a view to saving his country and family, and decided to become an educator when entering the normal school at age 17.

He served as educator for 62 years and as associate professor of education since 1950 till retirement in 1987. He never applied for promotion, thinking that a full professor or a Ph.D is nothing better than an associate professor without a doctoral degree. His interest in fame and profit has been relatively trivial. That may be one reason why he is still sound in body and mind at age 91. Other things that keep him mentally and physically fit include early morning jogging since age 31, cold water bath since 47, singing revolutionary songs since 71. He goes to bed at 9: 00 p.m., gets up at 3 : 00 a.m., and takes an afternoon nap for half an hour. He lives with his younger son and daughter-in-law, never drinks or smokes, and never quarrels with wife.

His wife was four years younger and died at age 78. She was an uneducated peasant and married by parental arrangement through an intermediary. He taught wife up to the level of primary school. They have two sons, who both have received higher education and teach in college. His wife was good-tempered, never scolded or hit children. He scolded sons when they were little and naughty but never hit them. Family relationships have been good but sons are not so nice to parents after marriage. "You lost a son when you got a daughter-in-law," he said.

W is very pleased with the fact that some former students of the schools where he taught or served as principal have now become university presidents who call on him when they come to the city where he lives. He wrote to me at 88, nearly two years after official retirement, that he was living " a second life" happily. He was trying to do some meaningful things that he did not have a chance to do before. For example, he donated his savings (about 9000 yuan equivalent to US$1800) to some schools and educational organizations, and wrote an observation report on rural education in his native province with recommendations for improvement. Since age 78 he has edited or translated three books, and wrote many papers on education. He cited for emulation some long-lived Chinese and Western intellectuals (e.g., George Bernard Shaw and Bertrand Russell) as examples of people who still made significant contributions to society in their 80s or 90s. He says he is still active at 91.

Case 4 (Male, age 66): A Rebellious Identity and Overdue Intimacy

C is a 66-year-old retired chemical engineer. His father had only two years of informal education by a tutor and later became a private banker. C's mother was illiterate. He is the youngest of their four sons with two elder sisters and one younger sister. He lived with parents until they died (father at 76 and mother at 70). His brothers and sisters lived with parents until marriage. Father believed in fortune-telling (the eight-character telling) and favored the first and the third sons because they had "better" fortune. C was, however, disfavored since birth by father because of "bad" fortune as told by a fortune-teller. He was frequently hit by father during childhood.

Mother loved all children and sympathized with C but could not stop father's maltreatment of him. C was the most filial child to mother but feared and hated father. The entire family believed in fate and C accepted his "fortune" with little doubt. Father acted like a tyrant in the house but was less strict to daughters than sons. The three daughters were later more filial to father than their brothers. Of all the seven children, the first son was the only one to receive a four-year higher education and thus became father's favorite.

Father was as tyrannical to wife as to children but mother was extremely tolerant as many traditional Chinese wives. Grandmother was stingy and fussy, and unkind to mother and C. She died when C was 24 years old. Due to unstable social factors, C received six-year elementary education in two forms and in four schools. Two years were spent with two tutors separately at home and one year each was spent in four different schools. In one school he did well in drawing, singing, and performing on stage, which won him teachers' praise. Then Japanese invasion interrupted his schooling for two years. During that time at about age 14, he came across pornography owned by his second elder brother. From then on C suffered nocturnal emission for more than 30 years, which tormented him physically and emotionally.

C entered junior high school at age 15. He did well in extracurricular activities and was popular among peers. As a 9th grader near graduation, C rebelled against the school authorities for a cause he deemed just. He made several good friends of the same sex in and out of school then. The friendship of two of them lasts till the present day. One of them left the mainland for Taiwan in 1949. The other friend is a versatile talent with whom C shares ideas and inspirations, joy and sorrow.

Apparently C found it difficult to concentrate on studies. In recollection, C thinks he had a talent in music and performing arts but was not given an opportunity to develop it. Academic achievement was then as is today the primary, if not the only, goal in climbing the educational ladder. Lacking a good academic preparation, C failed in the entrance examination of the senior high school and stayed home for one year.Then the Japanese surrendered and the civil war between the Nationalists and the Communists broke out. With no self-confidence in further pursuing a regular education, C attended an accounting school aspiring to work in bank through his father's connections. He was, however, unable to get a bank job after finishing the one-year accounting course. He felt shame and stayed home for two more years until 1949 when the Communist army occupied his home town. He was then 24 years old.

To risk a way out, C joined the Red army under parental objection. He taught the soldiers to sing and engaged in recreational activities in the army.Three years later, he was recommended by the army to take the entrance exam of an institute of technology. He was admitted to a two-year program in chemical engineering. He found the program difficult, but with the help of peers he managed to complete it. After graduation, he worked as a technician in Peking for four years before being sent to a remote region in northwestern China. After seven difficult years, he got a job in a mountain area in southeastern China through the help of a former boss in Peking. Having served in a factory there as a chemical engineer for 25 years, he was ordered to retire at age 65.

C is a nice person, but sometimes so nice as to become gullible. He often helps friends and relatives financially or otherwise. He is generous to others but thrifty to himself. He trusts others but lacks self-confidence. He is self-conscious, especially of his baldness. Probably as a result of psychological tension caused by paternal maltreatment and physical disorder caused by nocturnal emission, C began to get bald in his twenties and became completely bald around 30. He has since then had the habit of wearing a cap wherever he goes for fear of being laughed at. Although the cap is a painful burden, psychologically and physically, on him, especially in hot weather, he has no courage to take it off in public.

Worth noting is C's overdue romance. Before age 22, C had been thirsty for love. Yet until then he had only secretly loved several girls with no courage to let them know. He was, however, not shy otherwise. While in the accounting school at age 22, he was fairly active. There he loved singing, played volley ball, and read English aloud every morning, which attracted peer attention. One evening, a female schoolmate showed interest in him when taking a walk together. From then on, they fell in love. Being loved by a girl for the first time, he was so ecstatic that his heart and mind were completely occupied by his girl friend. The girl wanted to marry him but he was hesitant to give her a definite answer because he did not have the means to support a family and psychologically he was not ready to do so. The girl felt disappointed and broke up with him.

C subsequently dated two girls, but lost them shortly. He waited and waited, for the right girl to come along. His friends and relatives were more worried than he himself about his chances to find one. When he was 44 years old, one day in 1969 on his way home with his nephew to spend the Lunar New Year (LNY) holidays, he met two young women walking on the same country road behind them. The younger woman was a rather shy teenager and the older one in her early twenties was more talkative. C chatted, joked, and sang to them on the road for about half an hour before parting. He promised to send them some songs he knew and had their address. Soon C fulfilled his promise by sending them the songs with a note. The older girl replied calling him "uncle" according to the Chinese custom of greeting a man similar to father's age. The correspondence went on about three or four times in half a year. Then its frequency increased. With a landlord family background much disgraced in Communist China then, the girl was a high school graduate sent down to the countryside for labor reform during the Cultural Revolution. She was given much encouragement and comfort by C during those bitterest years of her life.

Two years later in 1971 during the LNY holidays, C invited his girl friend to meet his folks in town. This was the second time they saw each other. But C refrained from any romantic thoughts because of the age difference (he was then 46 and she was 24). They kept corresponding afterwards, however. Having corresponded for three consecutive years, they came to know each other's inner world quite well. His sincerity, empathic concern, and heart-warming letters had won her sympathy, gratitude, and love. In 1972 during the LNY holidays again, they met for the third time. This time C was invited by the girl to meet her folks. To avoid unusual attention from curious people, C asked his nephew to escort him. He spent three days with her family. Her parents were obviously satisfied with their daughter's boy friend, ignoring the age difference. Finally, with unusual courage, C kissed his girl friend. This was the first time she had ever been kissed by a man.

C then got the girl a chance to join a commune in the province where he was working. Her performance in the commune often won her praise and commendations. So she was given the job as a country school teacher. Eventually on New Year's Day of 1974 at the age of 48, C married his 28-year-old girl friend to the surprise of his friends and relatives. Three years later in 1977, a year after the Gang of Four was crushed, the college entrance examination was resumed. C's wife took the exam and successfully passed it. Then on completion of a two-year course in a teachers college with an outstanding record, the college wanted her to join the faculty and teachers urged her to go on for further training. She politely refused their kindness, however, because she thought that her husband needed her. So she would rather teach in the staff children's school of the factory where C was working. Since then she has been taking very good care of her husband while teaching full-time at the factory school.

Without a complete formal education from grade school through four-year college and with a job in a factory far away from urban areas, C was dissatisfied with his career development. Yet on the contrary, he considered himself most lucky to have a happy, though belated, marriage. "God was kind in bestowing a considerate and loving wife on me, though unfair to me otherwise." he said. Probably due to nocturnal emission suffered for more than 30 years, C lost his fertility. Having waited for seven years under curious or suspicious eyes of people around, C and his wife, as advised by a friend, adopted a three-month-old boy.

Brought up under a tyrannical and prejudiced father, C has a deep feeling of inferiority. He is impulsive, impatient, and very sensitive to others' reactions. He is, on the other hand, altruistic and self-sacrificing to friends and relatives. For over 20 years before marriage, he had given one-third or half of his income to his second elder brother who had less income but more children than other siblings.

When officially retired at age 64, C still went to office every day trying to offer his service whenever possible until totally retired a year later. Staying home all day makes him feel lonely while wife and son are both in school. Sometimes he regrets the adversities of life and the failures in self-actualization. If there were a next life, he says he would live it differently except that his wife would be the same one again and he would love her with all his heart as he does in this life. To spend his retired life meaningfully, he keeps himself busy by reading, growing vegetables, and helping his wife with housekeeping and child-rearing. He had three reunions on the mainland in the last 14 years with his old friend who left for Taiwan in 1949. Since their last gathering C has repeatedly asked for another reunion. He communicated with his friend often. His last letter reached Taiwan in April 1997.

Case 5 (Female, age 64): Identity Achievement without Intimacy

Y is a 64-year-old female professor of psychology. Her grandfather was a well-off businessman. Father had a mental breakdown as graduate student studying chemistry in Germany. Mother was a grade school teacher. Y is the only child of her parents. Mother had to look after both husband and daughter. She was strict and impulsive but rational most of the time. She had T.B. when Y was in junior high school. Y had to take care of both ill parents then. Father's mental illness had made her interested in psychology since high school days. Though somewhat less introverted now, Y's personality (introverted, sensitive, conscientious, patriotic) has remained basically the same since late teens.

Y has received complete formal education from kindergarten through college, all operated by American or English churches in China. One year before graduation from college and on the eve of Communist takeover, Y left the mainland for Hong Kong with her uncles. She returned home alone two and half years later, however, because of patriotism and filial piety. She has resolved to save her country and people since high school days when her native place was occupied by Japanese army. Her ideological identity was also shaped by the translated Russian novels she read in those days at the persuasion of a schoolmate. Her patriotism coupled with belief in Communism prompted her return to China from Hong Kong. In addition, filial piety hastened her return home to take care of parents who, because of ill health, had not fled the Communists along with her uncles.

Y finished higher education at a teachers college in a southern city and went on for a two-and-half year graduate study at a normal university in Peking. Then at age 27 she was assigned to teach at a college in another southern city until 24 years later when she was transferred to serve the same teachers college from which she was graduated 26 and half years ago. Married at age 31, husband was her former classmate at the college where they met eight years earlier. She never had another boy friend. She got married only because she was constantly urged by mother. The traditional Chinese notion is that a woman should get married before she is too old. She had attended single-sex schools and college until the senior year in college when she transferred to a co-educational college where she met her husband. Lacking sex education and having little heterosexual interaction, she did not even know how a child is delivered at age 20. She said that she did not have any sexual interest until she was in graduate school.

After marriage, her sexual interest has been negligible and husband has been dissatisfied with sexual life, Y said. Most of the time, they work and live in two different places far apart. Unable to have their own child, Y adopted a son as suggested by mother without the consent of husband. Y and husband had been together only for seven years when both taught at their alma mater before she applied at age 57 for transfer to a prestigious university in another city where her mother and adopted son live. So she left her husband alone again. The adopted son, now a school teacher, has been living with Y's mother since adoption and has seldom seen Y's husband.

Y has been a successful college instructor admired by her students. At age 58, she was offered, through the help of a friend in the United States, a chance for advanced study as a visiting scholar at a prestigious American university. She returned to China a year later. She translated a book by her internationally known American mentor and had the translated version published in China in the following year when she was 61 years old. Since then her prestige as a psychology professor has been mounting. Although a woman is supposed to retire at age 55 and a man at 60 in China, Y still enjoyed teaching and research at 64 in 1992 while almost totally ignoring married life. In 1993 she edited a book in psychology for nationwide sale and immediately told me about the publication.

Case 6 (Female, age 66): An Identity Achieved the Hard Way

F is a 66-year-old retired college professor in psychology. Her father was a farmer and country tutor. Mother was illiterate. F has two elder brothers, two elder sisters, and one younger brother. She was born in a rural community of male chauvinism where women have to work harder than men outdoors as well as indoors and are often deprived of educational opportunity. As the third daughter born at a time when father was expecting to have another son, she became the unwanted child in the house. Both elder brothers have received college education while the younger brother, against parental will, joined the army after graduation from high school. Both elder sisters had little schooling. F wanted to go to school but father objected it. She insisted, however, and was secretly supported by mother. So she went to school while working during Sundays and vacations. As demanded by father, she cut firewood in the mountains and sold it in town until graduation from high school. To save face, she avoided teachers and schoolmates in the street when carrying firewood for sale.

Father was extremely strict and hit F often. All children and mother were fearful of father. Since childhood F has hated unequal treatment of women. She angered at father's maltreatment but did not openly rebel against him. She learned some basics as auditor in father's tutoring class. Though objected by father, she nevertheless managed to start formal education at age 12 in the 4th grade and finished high school at 21. She saw schooling as a way, and for her the only way, to raise the social standing of her family in general and her own socioeconomic status in particular. She took the college entrance exam three times. She failed twice but succeeded at the third trial in getting admitted to a teachers college at age 25. In college, she acquired at the call of the Communist party a new mission--to serve her country.

After graduation from college, she served as assistant at the same college for three months before being selected for graduate study in psychology at a normal university in Peking under Russian professors. Two and half years later, she returned to teach at the same college which sent her to Peking. Promoted from teaching assistantship to lecturership at age 34, F had remained in that position for 26 years until becoming associate professor at age 60. She retired in the following year from the institution, now a normal university, where she had served for 30 years. After teaching part-time at a private college in the same city for one and half years, she was no longer needed there and had to retire completely. She regretted at first that she had to stay home almost all day. To reduce the feeling of loss and loneliness, she decided to take part in some outdoor activities (e.g., shadow boxing and outing) organized by the university club of retired colleagues in addition to housekeeping and reading. Three years later when she wrote in 1992, she said she is well adjusted to retirement life now and occupies herself with voluntary counseling service for adolescents and recreational activities for the elderly. She seldom feels lonely and lost at age 66.

F had known her husband for seven years before marriage. He was the first man she had ever loved. She got married at age 30 after completion of graduate study in Peking. Husband is a biological researcher. They have two sons, both of them have received college education. She was lenient to children while husband was strict to them. She had been determined not to repeat her father's way of treating children. Husband is impulsive and she is stubborn. Despite occasional bickering, they get along happily and enjoy satisfactory sexual life. They have always lived together except in early 1970 when she was sent down to the countryside for rustication during the Cultural Revolution until husband joined her several months later.

Grown up in a rural family with a male-chauvinist father who treated her harshly and having to mingle with schoolmates from well-off families, F was, even as a college instructor, very sensitive to others people's reactions for fear of being looked down upon. On the other hand, she also felt proud of herself because few of her peers during childhood and adolescence who were rich or poor, with loving or controlling parents, were able to go on to college like her.

Discussion

The six cases will be discussed one by one.

Case 1 (L, female, age 27): A compromised identity before intimacy

L has developed quite well during the first three stages of life cycle. Her willfulness reflects her autonomy and her quarrelsomeness reflects her initiative. Her sense of basic trust is later demonstrated by willingness to turn in a case report on her own psychosocial development as required by a visiting professor whom she has only seen in the classroom while most of her classmates did not do the same.

L's industry during the 4th stage is indicated in her being active and lively in school, her budding need to excel and win, reading novels, and serving as class head for five consecutive years in the grade school. Her industry extends to the next stage of life cycle when L is ability-grouped into the "super-fast" class in the junior high school. The teacher's criticism adds to her pride instead of shame while she has no feeling of inferiority and needs the attention from others. The conferment on her the membership of the Communist Youth Corps and her winning the admission to the best senior high school in the region further testify L's industry as a salient personality trait.

L is not so industrious, however, in senior high. So she fails once in the nationwide college entrance exam and only succeeds in passing it the following year at age 17. In identity searching, she makes a compromise by choosing a field of study (psychology) between medicine as recommended by father and science/technology as preferred by most elite students and their parents.

L experiences some identity confusion in college and in the city where the university is located. On the one hand, she is no longer paid much attention by people on campus as she was in grade and high schools. On the other hand, the injustice and selfishness of people in the big city disappoint her. She therefore loses some of her faith in people on campus and those in the community. She also feels somewhat inferior when she finds herself among peers in college who are a select group of elite. She nevertheless wants to be different from peers. She trusts a visiting professor from outside the mainland and hands in the major assignment of the course he teaches while most of her classmates fail to do the same. In addition, she corresponds with that professor several years later and answers his questions about her recent development.

L enters the graduate school at age 21. She tastes generativity in the teaching career at 24 and tastes intimacy at 25 with the first man she has ever loved. That romance does not last long because the man betrays her. A year later she marries another man she met two years earlier but seldom had time to see each other. This man is a doctoral student at an American university, who she believes to be the right choice for intimacy. The fact that she marries a man she only knows superficially reflects her easy trust in people and her willingness to take a risk for a significant life goal. Her industry continues to manifest itself in her preparation to study at a prestigious American university. By doing so, she aspires to strengthen her identity as a psychologist.

Case 2 (H, male, age 29): Simultaneous achievement of intimacy and identity

H apparently does not develop very well during the first two stages of life cycle. His development in these two stages is not too negative, however, as he is able to sing in sickbed at age 3 to comfort his parents. Since then his development has been generally positive in ratio, which must have compensated whatever was negative in the preceding stages. For example, his trust in people, like his female classmate in Case 1, is later manifested in meeting the course requirement of a visiting professor from outside the mainland of China; and his autonomy is subsequently reflected in quitting the administrative job to attend the graduate school for a change of career.

H's industry in the 4th stage is developed in grade school as shown by reading novels, telling stories, and being a student leader. In the 5th stage, industry continues to be a central feature until the last year at age 18 in a 5-year junior (three years)-senior (two years) high school when he falls in love with a pretty classmate. While temporarily tasting intimacy, he experiences identity confusion after repeated failure in two trials at the nationwide college entrance exam. He wants to quit another trial but parents do not allow him. He does not feel happy even after succeeding in the third trial. He soon, however, recovers his composure. At the beginning of the next stage when he is 21 years old, he gains his identity as an educated person aware of the responsibility to serve the mankind. Although he does not feel so happy socially and, moreover, has lost his first girl friend, the situation as a whole improves gradually. So in the senior year when he is 22 years old, he does well again socially and academically. Now he has a new girl friend, is elected to the student council, and performs well in the practicum. All these favorable experiences have added to his identity achievement, though a little late in terms of Erikson's schedule.

The three years spent in the personnel office of a university serves as a period of moratorium for H to integrate the identity elements (trust, autonomy, initiative, and industry) developed earlier and to carefully consider all relevant factors in search of an occupational identity. He finally decides to quit the personnel job even with a prospect of immediate promotion. He prefers the career as a scholar or college instructor probably because he detests to deal with people of various kinds, many of them are so hostile and selfish. Soon after he becomes a graduate student with a view to having himself trained to be a scholar, he marries the girl he has loved for four years. It may be said that H achieves identity and intimacy simultaneously at age 25 in the 6th stage of psychosocial development.

Case 3 (W, male, age 91): Extended generativity

W seems to have developed psychosocially well in every stage of his life cycle. His basic trust and autonomy are later shown in his willingness to be interviewed by a visiting researcher and to correspond with the researcher after he leaves mainland China. When tending cow and working in the rice paddy during the 3rd stage, he must have the opportunity to develop initiative by playing and working with peers and adults. Although he does not start school until the end of the 4th stage, he must have developed the quality of industry (in learning skills, sharing obligation, and winning recognition) by helping father (e.g., tending cow and working in the rice paddy) during the 4th stage of psychosocial development.

During the 5th stage, W learns to hate the rich and sympathize with the poor. He regards schooling as a means to the end of saving his family and country. He also makes the decision to become an educator at age 17 when entering the normal school. He is married at age 22 by parental arrangement as practiced in traditional Chinese society. His wife is illiterate but good-tempered. He tutors wife up to the level of primary school. They have two sons. Family relationships have been harmonious. W no doubt enjoys true intimacy during Stage 6 of his life cycle.

W experiences generativity at Stage 7 as his two sons have grown up, received college education, and got married. He has not only established and guided his own children who have become college instructors, but also his numerous students, some of them have become college or university presidents of whom he feels proud. His sense of generativity even extends to the last stage of life cycle. He does not retire at the normal retirement age as his service is still needed by the university until age 86. He continues to teach, write, edit, and translate far beyond age 60. He even starts "a second life" as he claims following retirement at age 86 and does something he did not have a chance to do before. He still aspires to make some contributions to society, emulating those long-lived distinguished intellectuals in Chinese and Western history. W's case is one that demonstrates the fact that even in the 8th stage of life, as in the preceding stage, any activity or production which contributes to the well-being of others strengthens one's sense of generativity.

Case 4 (C, male, age 66): A rebellious identity and overdue intimacy

Abused since birth by a superstitious and tyrannical father, C does not develop well during the first six stages of life. With a loving and tolerant mother, the unfavorable development is counterbalanced to some extent. His total development of the six stages may thus be termed mixed with both positive and negative elements. While trusting people, he does not have enough confidence in himself. His lack of self-confidence is vividly reflected in his self-consciousness of baldness. While he has enough autonomy to join the Red army against father's will, he also demonstrates shame and doubt about his ability in scholastic pursuit and career development.

C's initiative is over-restricted by father, which is indicated in his secretly loving some girls without the courage to let them know. On the other hand, his initiative is reflected in his loving to sing and his bold rebellion against school authorities. During the school age, his development is also mixed because of frequent change of schools and tutors. At the 5th stage, he experiences identity confusion, especially in late teens when he is unable to receive formal education in senior high school. He has potential talent in music and performing arts which, however, finds no channel for development. Realizing that he has no propensity for academic pursuit, he studies accounting but fails to get a job.

Identity confusion continues until the beginning of the next stage when he risks a way out at age 24 by joining the victorious Red army near the end of the civil war. He does so as a rebellion against his bad "fortune." Three years later he is recommended for admission to a two-year chemical engineering program at an institute of technology. He finds the program hard but manages to complete it. While he has seemingly achieved occupational identity as a chemical engineer, he cannot get rid of confusion as he does not feel quite fit for the job.

C does not yet accomplish lasting intimate relationship with a woman in the 6th stage, but some intimate relationship does exist between him and one or two friends of the same sex. True intimacy with a woman does not come about until the

7th stage which should be the time for generativity according to Erikson's timetable. He meets his future wife at age 44 and gets married four years later. His generativity actually starts at Stage 6 when he financially assists his second elder brother who has four children. C does not have his own children until he adopts a son at age 55. Yet he is not satisfied with what he has done or produced and, therefore, more or less experiences a sense of stagnation.

In the final stage of life, C, after retirement, still hopes to be useful to society in an attempt to extend his sense of generativity. Because his adopted son is only 11 years old although he is already 66, C still can perform his function as a generator. On the other hand, C cannot avoid a feeling of despair as he regrets his ill fortune which was foretold at the beginning of his life cycle. He does not consider himself a man without talents but believes that there has been no opportunity to actualize his potentials. He is not contented with his career as an engineer, he thinks he should have been able to make a greater contribution to mankind in a different capacity. Rather than accepting the fact, as Erikson points out, that how one's life has been lived is one's own responsibility, C wishes that the things and people (with the exception of his mother and wife) had been different.

Case 5 (Y, female, age 64): Identity achievement without intimacy

Being the only child of her parents with a rational though strict mother, Y has developed more positively than negatively during the first five stages of life cycle. It is unusual in China that Y has attended church-operated schools from kindergarten through college. Her father's mental illness and the Japanese invasion plus the reading of translated Russian novels prompt her to develop occupational identity (as a psychologist) and ideological identity (as a Communist follower) respectively in the 5th psychosocial stage. Her cultural identity (filial piety) is formed even earlier when he has to look after both ill parents in early teens. Though she meets her man at age 23 and marries him at age 31, Y seldom experiences true intimacy as she has lived away from husband most of the time.

Y's adopted son is brought up by her mother. So Y's sense of generativity is achieved mainly in the teaching and guiding of her students in college. Her generativity spans both Stage 7 and 8 of life cycle as she is still teaching and publishing at age 64. Integrity is expected although she has just begun the final stage of psychosocial development. In retrospect, the only negative development is her apparent sense of isolation during Stage 6 but that does not affect her development otherwise in an appreciable measure.

Case 6 (F, female, age 66): An identity achieved the hard way

Being an unwanted child of her father, F's psychosocial development during the first five stages of life cycle has been hazardous. Her formal education does not start until the end of the 4th stage at age 12 but has learned some basics before that in father's private class. With a loving and understanding mother, however, F's development has been generally more positive than negative. Her sense of trust is later reflected in her candidness when interviewed by a visiting professor who is teaching and doing research in mainland China. Her autonomy and industry are demonstrated respectively in her insistence on going to school and her eagerness to learn in school. If initiative is the quality of playing and doing something for the sake of being active, as Erikson defines it, F may have lacked the opportunity to exercise it because her father was very restrictive and punitive.

At the beginning of the 5th stage of life when F starts to receive belated formal education, she has already set her mind on raising the socioeconomic status of her family and herself by becoming well educated. In doing so, she must integrate the identity elements (trust, autonomy, and industry) ascribed earlier to achieve her goal. Her determination to achieve her identity as an educated woman is fully demonstrated in her three trials at the college entrance exam and in her final success at the third trial. In addition to individualistic ambition, she has acquired in college a collectivistic responsibility--to serve her country.

F achieves identity as an educated woman for the good of herself, her family, and her country on graduation from college at age 25. She begins her intimate relationship with her man at about the same time and accomplishes the relationship when she gets married at age 30. Her occupational identity is well established at age 34 when she becomes a full-fledged college instructor.

Having conquered the psychosocial crisis of both identity and intimacy at about the same time, F fares well in the 7th stage of her life cycle. She achieves the sense of generativity by establishing and guiding the next generation--her two sons and numerous students. In the final stage of life after retirement, F reaches integrity as she is proud of her having received higher education while most of her former peers, rich or poor, have not. Although she has been unable to become a full professor as she has hoped, she is promoted to the rank of associate professor before retirement. At age 66 (about six years after retirement), she has adapted herself well to retirement and feels quite happy about the life she is living.

General Discussion

In Study 1 covering the first 6 stages of life span development of Hong Kong subjects, 14 female cases were analyzed in comparison with 14 male cases. At the first stage (age 0-1), the development of both sexes was almost identical with 12 male and 11 female cases positive, only two cases for each sex negative, and one female case mixed in the quality of development. Starting from the second stage (age 2-3) when the child becomes more resistant to disease and thus receives less careful and less even handling, the gender difference in development begins to show. The largest difference occurred at Stage 5 (adolescence) when 4 more boys than girls (6:

2) had successfully resolved identity crisis. One major reason for this sex difference is probably that the girls have to deal with intimacy (Stage 6) issues prior to identity (Stage 5) issues, which is a phenomenon not predicted by Erikson's theory.

Ochse and Plug (1986) suggested that the critical period in identity formation occurs well after adolescence. Erikson (1968) also said that identity formation is a lifelong process and not confined to adolescent years. That may explain why most of my Hong Kong subjects (20 out of 28 cases) failed to resolve identity crisis during adolescence. Worth noting are the first two mainland cases in Study 2. The two mainlanders were about the same age as the Hong Kong subjects in Study 1. Though living in a different political culture, their developmental trend was similar to that of their Hong Kong counterparts. For instance, they did not achieve their identity during adolescence either. In other words, they also experienced moratorium (Marcia, 1980) like the Hong Kong subjects.

Three out of 4 older mainlanders in Study 2, however, achieved identity at Stage 5. It is probably because the older people in China were born and raised in a period near the time when Erikson developed his theory in a world culture somewhat universally shared. The older Chinese might mature earlier psychosocially than the young generation. The young people in Chinese society and elsewhere, like my Hong Kong subjects and the two young mainlanders, may be late maturers in a psychosocial sense and, therefore, achieve identity at a later date than the older people.

The only older subject (Case 4 in Study 2) who failed to conquer the identity crisis at Stage 5 had a tyrannical father. This was unusual even in the average Chinese family half a century ago when the Chinese father was usually strict and controlling. That may account for the fact that the man in this exceptional case had great difficulty in identity formation. He did not marry and enjoy true intimacy until the 7th stage. Even at the final stage of his life in 1997, he still craves for emotional and social support from his old friend in Taiwan when he repeatedly asks for a 4th reunion after separation in 1949 although they already had three gatherings in the last 14 years.

In conclusion , we may say that the two studies lend support to Erikson's theory of personality development but with some reservations. The theory seems more applicable to men than women and to people of older generation born in the early part of the 20th century than those of the young generation born later. In addition to identity formation, generativity is a specific developmental task not confined to the period designated by Erikson. It often extends to the last stage of life so long as one is physically and psychologically capable of generating something. Three of the four aged mainlanders, all at their final stage of life, were still trying to strengthen their sense of generativity. To keep up with the changing world in which the modern men and women live, Erikson's theory seems to need some modifications, especially in its stagewise scheduling of developmental tasks for both genders.

✦   ✦   ✦

CHAPTER SIX

VALUES AND PERSONALITY

Values refer to orientations toward what is considered desirable or preferable by an individual or a group (Zavalloni, 1980). A value is a conception of the desirable "which influences the selection from available modes, means and ends of action" (Kluckhohn, 1951, p. 395). Values reflect culture and personality (Zavalloni, 1980). They interact with national development (Lasswell, Lerner, & Montgomery, 1976; Singha & Kao, 1988). Values and personality are closely related. The culture and personality school (Benedict, 1946; Mead, 1953) assumed that values are expression both of cultural institutions and of individual personality. According to Spranger (1923), personalities of men are best known through a study of their values. Rokeach (1973, p. 21) stated that personality as a cluster of traits "can be reformulated from an internal, phenomenological standpoint as a system of values." For example, Erikson's (1963, 1968) eight ego qualities (trust, autonomy, initiative, industry, identity, intimacy, generativity, integrity) are called values or virtues by some psychologists (e.g., Franz & White, 1985) as well as personality traits or dimensions by others (e.g., Ochse & Plug, 1986). Therefore, a study of a people's values should add to our understanding of their personality and a study of personality traits should help us gain a better insight into the underlying values. A value may denote a need or deficiency in culture or personality. For example, when tolerance

207

is desired or valued, it may indicate a need for tolerance. This assumption is in line with Rokeach's proposition that "values are the cognitive representation not only of individual needs but also of societal and institutional demands" (Rokeach, 1973, p. 20).

Human values have been widely investigated, mainly using the Rokeach Value Survey (RVS), a Western instrument (Braithwaite & Law, 1985). Hofstede (1980) described his empirical search for the value dimensions across which cultures vary. His survey of work-related values, however, may be culturally limited. He pointed out that "only others with different mental programs can help us find the limitations of our own' (Hofstede, 1980, p. 374). Bond and his colleagues developed the Chinese Value Survey (CVS) to study Chinese values around the world (Chinese Culture Connection, 1987; Bond, 1988). They found that three of their four factors of cultural valuing correlated at high levels with three of Hofstede's four (Chinese Culture Connection, 1987). Bond also compared the Rokeach and Chinese Value Surveys and found that the CVS contained a dimension of valuing not found in the RVS (Bond, 1988).

The present chapter supplements prior work by reporting six studies of Chinese values and personality using methods and instrument different from those used by previous researchers. Study 1 was a study of Chinese values extracted from the information provided by 120 male and female informants aged 19 to 91 in mainland China. Study 2 investigated with a questionnaire (MTPI as described in Chapter One) the personality dimensions of educated Chinese of both sexes and various ages in four regions or populations (mainland China, Taiwan, Hong Kong, and the United States). Study 3 examined with MTPI the personality traits, which also reflected the values, of the same groups of subjects as in Study 2. Study 4 explored the ambitions and aspirations, which are supposed to reflect personal or cultural values, of Chinese intellectuals, using information gathered from the same group of informants as in Study 1. Study 5 illustrated personality change with cases selected from the same 120 subjects as in Studies 1 and 4.

Study 6 was a preliminary study of mate preferences, which reflect cultural values, as reported by 29 unmarried college students in mainland China and Taiwan. The 1st, 4th and 5th studies were qualitative based on in-depth interviews. Study 2 and 3 were quantitative using the same questionnaire but varying in analysis of data. The 6th and last study applied simple statistical analyses to interview data. All the six studies were directly or indirectly related as they dealt with Chinese values, personality, and related variables.

STUDY 1
CULTURAL VALUES

The aim of this study was to explore the personal and social values in Chinese culture by inferring from related topics the informants talked about in interviews.

The subjects were the same 120 mainland Chinese men and women of various ages I interviewed as described in Chapter One.

I did not ask my informants any specific questions directly concerning values. The values were extracted from what they said about related topics, including their attitudes, preferences, personality traits; their hopes and wishes; their evaluative opinions about people; their parents' demands and expectations of them and what they required of their own children; and the way they treated people and were treated by others.

To categorize values, Rokeach's (1973) terms terminal and instrumental are borrowed. Instrumental values refer to desirable modes of conduct and terminal values refer to desirable end-states of existence. They are further classified as social and personal values. Personal values are self-centered or intrapersonal values and social values are society-centered or interpersonal values. The categorization is tentative, however, because clearcut distinction between instrumental and terminal values or between personal and social values is difficult, if not impossible,

From information provided by the 120 interviewees as informants, 17 terminal (7 social and 10 personal) values and 52 instrumental (32 social and 20 personal) values were extracted. This is in line with Rokeach's (1973, p. 11) estimation that "man possesses fewer terminal than instrumental values" although in his value survey he lists equal numbers of both terminal and instrumental values (18 of each). The 69 Chinese values I found are presented below with illustrations for each of them.

Terminal Social Values

1 **Harmony.**   Harmony is emphasized in interpersonal relations between and among friends, relatives, colleagues, and members of any group or organization. The Chinese proverb "Family prospers in harmony" applies to other groups including the nation. We can say, for example, that a nation prospers in harmony. Harmony implies peace. China needs peace as well as harmony for individual and national development. To achieve harmony, individualism is discouraged while collective effort is reinforced.

2. **Non-aggression**. Non-aggression is essential for harmony. Yet Chinese people are rather aggressive. Aggression or violence is rather common at home, in school, and in politics. Non-aggression or peace is very much needed in Chinese culture.

3. **Being respected by others**. In an authoritarian and hierarchical society like China, people are not duly respected until they reach adulthood or have a respectable job. Children are not equally respected as adults. Respect by others is, therefore, earnestly sought. It is a function of one's achievement, conduct, authority

or socioeconomic status.

4. **Surpassing others in achievement.** While collective effort is encouraged, individual achievement is still valued, especially when one surpasses others in achievement. Emulous parents often encourage their children to excel peers. It would be a shame to stay behind when compared with peers in academic achievement or in career advancement.

5. **Being useful to society.** A person must be useful to society in a meaningful way, or he or she will be looked down upon as a parasite. "Serve the people" is probably the most prevalent, though already trite, slogan in Communist China urging everybody to do something meaningful for the country and its people.

6. **Face. Miandzi or nien** (face)is a a well-known value in Chinese culture. It signifies dignity, identity, reputation, status, and authority. In a shame-oriented culture, Chinese are extremely face-conscious. They try hard to save, protect, and enhance face while preventing themselves from losing face.

7. **Democracy.** Democracy as a modern way of life and a viable political system is much preferred to authoritarianism, especially among the educated people. The Western idea of democracy was propagated in China during the May Fourth Movement in 1919 and re-emphasized during the June Fourth Incident in 1989.

Terminal Personal Values

1. **Safety.** Children are overprotected for safety early in life. For example, they are overclothed to prevent cold. They are not allowed to swim. Girls are not permitted to go out alone. Both boys and girls are warned not to make bad friends. That may explain why Chinese are less adventurous than some other races.

2. **Security.** Security is a broader value than safety; it implies freedom from fear, anxiety, danger, doubt, and want. For many centuries, civil and foreign wars and unstable economic and political conditions have made the Chinese people, especially

the older generation, feel insecure. The long history of insecurity has made security a foremost value.

3. **Fame.** It is the ambition of many educated young men to become famous in some specialty (e.g., to become a famous mathematician or writer). Although the desire for fame was once discouraged as an individualistic trait unfit for a collectivistic society, it is not so much suppressed today as before. Traditionally, fame (*min*) and profit (*li*) have often been cited as the primary motives of human endeavors.

4. **Wealth.** Wealth is a more popular value sought by more people than fame. In general, the educated people are more interested in fame than wealth while the reverse is true for the less educated. It would be ideal, however, to have both fame and wealth. Traditionally, wealth (*fu*) and nobility (*guei*) have often been cited as the foremost values in Chinese culture. In modern times, the nationwide aspiration of both the government and the masses is to build a rich and strong China, which connotes the values of wealth and power.

5. **High socioeconomic status.** This is a modern term for the Chinese character *guei* (nobility). Traditionally, *fu* (wealth) and *guei* (nobility or high social status) have been the twin values in Chinese culture. Although *guei* is mentioned less often today than before because of its feudalistic connotation, high socioeconomic status has become a substitute for it.

6. **Breakthrough in career.** Many people aspire to have a breakthrough in career, especially in midlife or around retirement. The Chinese term for retirement is *twei shiu* (withdrawing-resting). But it has often been heard that some people have *twei* (withdrawn) but not *shiu* (rested). Some of those who have withdrawn but not rested are even striving for a breakthrough in career.

7. **Self-sufficiency.** A person would gain self-esteem if he or she has the

necessary resources to get along without help. Self-sufficiency implies self-reliance and independence. While self-sufficiency is valued, especially among the educated people, most Chinese are in fact more dependent than independent or self-reliant. Independency training is not emphasized by Chinese parents, who expect, however, their children to be self-sufficient when grown up.

8. Moderation. Moderation is the Chinese golden mean. Excesses or extremes must be avoided. For instance, a person must not be too active or too passive, too extraverted or too introverted, too proud or too humble, too ambitious or too unambitious. Even a woman should not be too pretty because, as the saying goes, "Beautiful girls die young" (*hungyan baumin*).

9. Happy marriage. A happy marriage is the dream of many young people, especially young women. In traditional China, it was a dream not easy to come true through arranged marriage. Parental consent is necessary in most cases today when young people are free to date and court. The consent serves to protect the lovers against an unhappy union and increase the chance of building a happy family.

10. Non-divorce. If happy marriage is impossible, the wife or husband or both usually make every effort to avoid a divorce. Divorce would be a great shame or loss of face for a married couple, particularly for the wife. Under the Western impact, however, divorce rate is growing in China although non-divorce is valued.

Instrumental Social Values

1. Modesty. As the Chinese maxim says, "Pretension does harm while modesty does good." In a narcissistic society like China, a modest person will be more easily accepted by others than a pretentious person who often elicits disgust. The average Chinese, however, is modest outwardly but proud inwardly.

2. Non-assertiveness. To be humble and modest, one is not supposed to be self-assertive. An assertive person is very self-confident and very persistent in expressing himself or herself and in demanding recognition. Such a person is often frowned upon in an authoritarian society like China. One is supposed to work quietly and not to say anything about what is being done or what has been accomplished.

3. **Reciprocity.** To maintain good interpersonal relations, people are expected to make some sort of return for something done or given by others, such as exchange of gifts and visits. "Propriety rests on reciprocity" is a commonly heard Chinese proverb.

4. **Filial piety.** Although once deemphasized as a feudalistic value during the Cultural Revolution, filial piety is still valued today though not to the same extent as before. In traditional China, it was regarded as the most important of all virtues for the Chinese as the saying goes, "Filial piety comes first in a list of one hundred virtues."

5. **Repaying parents' nurturance.** This is a value related to both reciprocity and filial duty. It is an instance of reciprocity on the one hand and of filial piety on the other. Repaying parents' nurturance is a concrete way of showing gratitude for parental love and care. It is exercised by most sons and daughters as a moral obligation.

6. **Obedience.** To obey one's parents is essential for filial piety. Obedience to other authority figures is also necessary in Chinese society emphasizing hierarchical relationships. Almost all superiors like obedient subordinates. A popular saying is "obeying somebody is better than respecting him."

7. **Courtesy.** Courtesy or polite behavior is a traditional Chinese value but is not as much practiced in mainland China as in Taiwan and Hong Kong today probably because it was regarded as a feudalistic trait during the Cultural Revolution. Courtesy serves to maintain harmony with people and to make a good impression on others.

8. **Generosity.** Generosity is a sign of friendliness and hospitality. While most Chinese are thrifty, they are generous to friends and guests. To be generous is one way to protect face; to be stingy to others may cause one to lose face. Many people are found to be stingy to their folks but generous to their neighbors.

9. **Agreeableness.** Many Chinese are introverted and solemn-looking, but they pretend to be friendly and agreeable in order to make a good impression on others and maintain harmonious relations with people. Although many young people hate dissemblance, they find it at their disadvantage not to dissemble.

10. **Tolerance.** To ensure interpersonal harmony, tolerance is valued as a virtue. The legend of Chang Gung's one hundred tolerations sets an ideal model for a tolerant person.

11. **Self-control.** Self-control or self-restraint is a virtue on which some related traits or values are based. One must be self-controlled in order to be non-assertive, modest, obedient, tolerant, incorruptible, and observant of law and order. Self-control may be regarded as an inevitable condition for good social adjustment.

12. **Observance of law and order.** This is a value of any civilized society. Some Chinese argue that observance of law and order is possible in China only under an authoritarian government because Chinese people have been accustomed to authoritarianism. Others contend that a democratic political system is more effective in maintaining law and order in China. The debate remains to be settled.

13. **Incorruptibility.** For centuries, civil servants in China have been notoriously corrupt. Integrity or incorruptibility is, therefore, very much needed. It is a basic requirement of any public servant, who must be honest, upright, and does not take bribes.

14. **Honor.** Honor or glory is highly valued. Traditionally, the Chinese tried

to do something important or valuable (e.g., passing the civil service exam) in order to glorify ancestry and family. Now they are hailed for doing something significant or meaningful to win honor for their country, family, and/or themselves (e.g., winning a gold medal in Olympic games, entering a prestigious university).

15. **Loyalty.** Loyalty and filial piety used to be twin values in traditional China. Under the Communist rule today, loyalty to the country becomes more important than filial piety toward parents. In a fair sense, one must be loyal to one's boss, colleagues, friends, relatives, and spouse as well as to one's country.

16. **Patriotism.** Some intellectuals claim that they love their country as they love their mother. Patriotism is a value much emphasized by the government, the ruling party, and intellectuals. It is manifested by the compatriots in words and deeds. It is instrumental to solidarity of the people for the well-being of the nation.

17. **Solidarity.** This is a value often stressed by the ruling political party and government as China has long been confronted with threats of war and division from external and internal forces. It is also a common theme of many patriotic writers worried about self-centeredness of their compatriots. Sun Yat-sen, the founder of Republican China, was often quoted when he compared the Chinese people to a plate of loose sand, implying the urgent need for solidarity.

18. **Sense of justice.** While Chinese value justice and have a sense of justice, the Chinese in general do not have enough moral courage to do something about injustice which they hate.

19. **Sincerity.** A person must be sincere in order to be trusted. Chinese are not a very sincere people; there is much affectation in their social behavior. They fake good for self-protection. They promise more than they deliver. As a result, they do not always trust each other. Sincerity is much desired because there is a great need for it.

20. **Conscience.** **Liangshin** (conscience) is a general term in Chinese implying kindness, sympathy, and empathic concern. Literally, it simply means a "good heart." When a person is unkind or cruel, he or she will be described as having no conscience.

21. **Altruism.** To counteract egoism, altruism is valued in the collectivistic Chinese society, especially by the government and the Communist party. Yet in the minds of the masses, its value is declining.

22. **Human touch.** **Jenching** is a time-honored, widely practiced Chinese value without a commonly accepted translation. It is translated "human touch" here. It means a way or an act of dealing with people and handling interpersonal matters in a manner characterized by kindness, succor, sympathy, reciprocity, partiality, private favoring, and empathic concern. It also means a favor done, a gift presented, or a gesture of good will shown to somebody in interpersonal transaction. While *jenching* warms people's heart, it sometimes entails injustice.

23. **Deference to elders and superiors.** Deference to elders, superiors, and teachers is a traditional trait still valued in China, although it suffered a setback in the Cultural Revolution.

24. **Love of the young.** Chinese love the young, especially the young children, more than they respect the aged. Under the one-child family policy, the only child becomes the center of attention of two parents and four grandparents.

25. **Children's success.** Children's success is the parents' pride. Academic achievement is considered a predictor of future success in life. Many parents are so anxious to see their children succeed that they exert great pressure on their children in school urging them to do well in exams so that they can go on to a prestigious university.

26. **Yielding of elder siblings to younger ones.** In a dispute or squabble,

parents often tell their older children to yield to the younger ones. It is because the elder siblings are supposed to take good care of and set an example for their younger brothers and sisters. This sibling relationship is implied by the maxim, "Elder brothers are friendly and younger brothers are respectful."

27. **Male preference.** Male preference starts at home where sons are preferred to daughters, especially in the rural areas of China. This tradition is preserved more in the rural than urban areas mainly because male labor is in greater demand than female labor for farming. Male preference persists in spite of the Socialist slogan, "Women share half of the sky with men."

28. **Being a good wife and mother.** This is a traditional value for Chinese women, though not as much emphasized as before. Although modernized women may not like it, a good wife-mother is still an image of woman preferred by the average Chinese.

29. **Authority.** Authority is the power or right to give commands, influence others, or make final decisions. A person with authority or greater authority is respected more than one without authority or with lesser authority. Other things being equal, the older generation usually has greater authority than the young and middle-aged generations.

30. **Power.** Power, like authority, is much desired in Chinese society, especially by those who are interested in controlling and influencing others. People in power are often the targets of flattery. Although in the first few years after the Cultural Revolution, many people, especially the intellectuals, shun authority and power for fear of persecution, this fear has gradually diminished in recent years.

31. **Leadership.** A leader has authority and power. Since authority and power are valued, so is leadership. Unfortunately, there are more Chinese people, particularly men, desiring to be leaders than those who are willing to be led. The

Chinese, especially the educated, would rather be leaders than followers. They tend to think that they are no less capable of being leaders than their leaders.

32. **Personal connection.** **Guanshi** (connection or relationship) is highly valued in China. It means one's personal connection with somebody who has the influence, authority, or power to get things done in one's favor. In a society which has no well-enforced public law, people are customed to depend on *guanshi* to meet their personal needs. Relying on *guanshi* to get things done is said to be "going through the back door" in Chinese.

Instrumental Personal Values

1. **Health.** Health is a basic value, especially for the aged. It is instrumental to many other values. Without good health no one can expect to achieve any major life goal. Health as a value of great importance is demonstrated by the fact that all forms of exercise, including the Chinese *chigong* and the Western jogging, are popular in China. Health is related to longevity, a traditional Chinese value. " Health and long life" is a common wish in letters addressed to aged relatives.

2. **Self-protection.** Chinese tend to mistrust people. Children are taught to protect themselves early in life. Strict discipline by parents also leads to self-protection by children. As a result, Chinese become a cautious people.

3. **Sense of shame.** The Chinese culture may be considered a shame culture, which is shame oriented. In such a culture people generally have a sense of shame without which one would be humiliated as "wanting no face" (*buyau nien*). A sense of shame is a combination of conscience and self-respect. It guards people against wrongdoing.

4. **Moral character.** Morality or moral character is one of the three determinants for a student of "three goodnesses" in school and college. The other two goodnesses are academic achievement and physical fitness. Although moral

character, which is hard to assess, comes first in the trio, the second goodness (academic achievement) is actually given more weight than the first one.

5. **Education.** Education has long been valued in China. It used to be a key to *fu* (wealth) and *guei* (nobility). In modern China, more and more students are not contented with a domestic education; further education in an advanced foreign country is sought by an increasing number of them. A higher academic degree, especially one earned in an advanced Western country, increases the probability of getting a good job.

6. **Knowledge.** Knowledge gained through education is a status symbol. That is why knowledgeable people (the educated) are respected more than the less educated in Chinese society.

7. **Academic degree or diploma.** The academic degree or diploma stands for the knowledge or education one has received. With a degree or diploma, one finds it much easier to get a desired job. The Communist regime has once abolished the conferment of academic degrees but has resumed it since 1980.

8. **Science and technology as profession.** Science and technology attract more talented students in schools and colleges than other fields of study because scientists and engineers enjoy higher social status and a more stable career than other professionals.

9. **Working in a big city.** Working in a big city like Shanghai and Peking has many advantages (e.g., better living conditions). A city job is also a status symbol.

10. **Material possessions.** Any costly material possession is a status symbol (e.g., a refrigerator or TV set before it became a common commodity). It is not only necessary for a comfortable life but also has a psychic value.

11. **Matching socioeconomic status for marriage partners.** For

prospective married couples, matched socioeconomic status is an important condition for happy marriage or successful matrimony. This condition is heeded in most cases today, though to a lesser extent than it used to be.

12. **Having sons and grandsons.** This value is related to male preference. Having sons and grandsons is a means to the end of gaining pride and happiness in later life. Sons and grandsons are considered the parents' and grandparents' fortune while daughters and granddaughters are to be possessions of other families. The former are entitled to perpetuate the ancestral lineage while the latter are not.

13. **Seniority.** Seniority is an important determinant of career development. The older colleagues are usually entitled to priority in promotion and wage raise although the respect they command may not be proportionate to their age. This has an effect of reducing competition and increasing harmony among colleagues.

14. **Diligence.** "Diligence can compensate for dullness" is a Chinese proverb indicating the importance of industry in study and work. In other words, steady effort is valued more than ability or intelligence.

15. **Thrift.** Thrift used to be stressed along with diligence as in the Chinese maxim "Manage your home with diligence and thrift." There is also a precept for civil servants against corruption embodied in the old saying, "Cultivate integrity by thrift."

16. **Beauty in woman.** Beauty in woman was once deemphasized as a feudalistic value in Communist China but has resumed its desirability after the Cultural Revolution, particularly for the young generation.

17. **Talent in man.** Talent is to man what beauty is to woman. That is why a talented man and a beautiful woman are considered an ideal couple in China. The Chinese word *tsai* (talent), however, has enlarged its connotation in recent years to imply wealth, status, and power.

18. **Quietude in woman.** A woman is not supposed to be talkative. Chinese men prefer quiet women.

19. **Tenderness in woman.** A woman is supposed to be soft and gentle. Chinese men prefer tender women.

20. **Toughness in man.** In Chinese culture men and women are stereotyped: men are supposed to be tough and strong while women are supposed to be soft and tender (*nangang niuzou*).

STUDY 2
PERSONALITY DIMENSIONS

The purpose of this study was to compare the personality of the various age groups of the four Chinese samples presumably representing the four Chinese populations. They were compared in terms of the nine factors or dimensions of personality as yielded by factor analysis of the responses to the 122 items of MTPI.

The subjects were the four samples of Chinese men and women as described in Chapter One. They were divided into 21 age groups: 12 male groups (4 ML, 4 TW, 2 HK, and 2 US) and 9 female groups (3 ML, 2 TW, 2 HK, and 2 US). We did not have four age groups for both sexes in all the four samples because of insufficient numbers of older subjects.

All the subjects were administered the 122-item questionnaire MTPI as described in Chapter One. The responses to the MTPI were subjected to principal-components factor analyses with oblimin rotation, which yielded nine factors or dimensions of personality. The mean score of each age group was first compared with mean score (s) of other group (s) of the same sex in the same sample and then with the mean of all other 20 age groups of the four samples by analysis of variance (ANOVA) , Scheffe test or *t* test whenever appropriate. For example, the four ML male groups were compared by ANOVA and then by Scheffe test if necessary. The mean of each group was compared with the mean of other 20 groups by *t* test. To reduce Type I errors, the alpha level for significance was set at .01.

The results of statistical analyses are shown in Table 1. The following differences and commonalities were found:

1. On the personality dimension E (Extraversion), the ML male Group 1 (aged 19-30 with a mean of 3.95) is more extraverted than not only ML male Groups 2 (aged 31-40) and 4 (aged 51-65), but its mean is larger than the mean of all other 20 groups. All the 21 groups score, however, only slightly higher than the midpoint (3.50) of the 6-point scale, indicating that they are somewhat midway between introverted and extraverted or that they are neither very introverted nor very extraverted.

2. On the personality dimension D (Self-Discipline), all the 21 groups score higher than the scale midpoint (3.50), indicating that they all perceive themselves as fairly self-disciplined. The most self-disciplined groups are ML male 4, ML female 2, TW male 2 and 3, and TW female 2. Relatively, the least self-disciplined groups are TW male 1 and female 1, and HK male 1 and female 1.

3. On the dimension A (Authoritarianism),none of the 21 groups perceive themselves as authoritarian as their mean scores all fall below the scale midpoint.

4. On the dimension S (Submission), all except three groups (ML male 1 and female 1, and TW male 1) score only slightly higher than the scale midpoint, indicating that they are somewhat halfway between dominant and submissive or that they are neither very dominant nor very submissive. In comparison, the most submissive groups are ML male 2 and 3, and TW male 2 and 3. The least submissive groups are ML male 1 and female 1.

5. On C (Cautiousness), almost half (10) of the 21 groups score slightly higher than the scale midpoint and the other half (11 groups) do not.

6. On O (Other-Orientation), all groups perceive themselves as fairly other-oriented, especially the seven ML groups.

7. On I (Independency), the four ML male groups, the three of the four TW male groups (except Group 1), and one of the US groups (male 2) are relatively independent while the two HK female groups and one US female group (the younger one) are less independent.

8. On M (Modernism), all groups perceive themselves as modern, especially ML male 1 with highest mean of 4.69 significantly larger than the means of other three ML male groups and the mean of the other 20 groups.

9. All group means on N (Neuroticism) are slightly below the scale midpoint, indicating that all groups are midway between healthy and neurotic.

10. As the group means show, although they are not all significantly different from some other group mean (s), the youngest groups of both sexes in the four samples are all less self-disciplined, submissive, and other-oriented but more modern than the older groups. This commonality in personality of educated young people (aged 19-30) reflect probably at once their common psychological development and social change as they were all born and raised in times of gradual modernization though in three different Chinese societies (the US subjects came from ML, TW, or HK although received further education in the US).

11. The fact that all ML groups are relatively more other-oriented than other groups is probably due to cultural disparity because Communist China is a collectivist society while Chinese in TW, HK, and US are becoming individualistic under Western influence.

12. In the personality dimension of independency, the group means indicate that in each of the four samples independency is a function of age--the higher the group mean the older the age, regardless of sex. In other words, Chinese men and

women become more and more independent as they grow and mature.

13. In modernism, the group means in general imply the negative relationship between age and modernism--the older the age the less modern or more traditional are the Chinese. Generally, men are more modern than women when men and women are compared with the same or similar age groups in the same sample.

14. In neuroticism, while all groups perceive themselves as fairly healthy, women are generally more neurotic than men when compared within the same or similar age groups in the same sample. Although the youngest ML group is healthier than the older groups of the same sex, this is not the case for the other three samples. This difference may imply that ML young people experienced less stress and pressure than not only their older compatriots but also their counterparts in the other three societies.

Table 1
Personality of 21 Age groups in Four Chinese Populations Compared on the Nine Personality Dimensions
(See Notes next page.)

Popula-tion	Sex	Group	Age	n	Personality Dimension								
					E	D	A	S	C	O	I	M	N
ML	M	1	19-30	240	3.95+++	4.43*	3.00	3.38***	3.30**	4.30++	3.97++	4.69+++	2.93**
		2	31-40	153	3.75*	4.55++	2.88**	3.71+++	3.46	4.34++	3.99++	4.46*	3.08
		3	41-50	173	3.78	4.48	2.97	3.72+++	3.46	4.41++	4.00++	4.42*	3.06
		4	51-65	86	3.72*	4.62+++	2.89	3.74+	3.42	4.42++	4.03++	4.40*	3.08
	F	1	19-30	128	3.80	4.43*	3.04	3.43***	3.47*	4.40++	3.68	4.52++	3.08*
		2	31-40	52	3.85	4.70+++	2.94	3.71+	3.35***	4.57++	3.75	4.37	3.21
		3	41-58	68	3.92	4.53	3.03	3.75*	3.38***	4.45++	3.82	4.35	3.31+++
TW	M	1	20-30	105	3.82	4.23***	3.00+	3.50*	3.63	3.89***	3.67*	4.44	3.12
		2	31-40	144	3.78	4.54++	2.86*	3.71+++	3.68++	4.16*	3.85++	4.31	2.94**
		3	41-50	96	3.77	4.60+++	2.75***	3.79+++	3.67	4.23*	3.91++	4.23	3.07
		4	51-65	51	3.72	4.57+	2.80*	3.65	3.49	4.25*	4.03+++	4.27	3.00
	F	1	20-30	157	3.83	4.31***	3.02	3.52*	3.54	4.07+	3.56	4.39+	3.15
		2	31-55	87	3.87	4.56+++	2.93	3.75*	3.62	4.27*	3.68	4.16***	3.17
HK	M	1	20-30	326	3.86	4.24**	3.08++	3.58	3.63	3.86**	3.73	4.34	3.02
		2	31-53	103	3.79	4.36	3.03	3.59	3.61	3.90**	3.78	4.32	3.05
	F	1	20-30	290	3.73	4.33**	3.05++	3.61	3.57	3.99**	3.34**	4.15**	3.35++
		2	31-42	50	3.81	4.39	3.04	3.73	3.49	4.04	3.40*	4.04**	3.27
US	M	1	20-30	65	3.83	4.36	2.98	3.52	3.50	3.89**	3.80	4.41	2.95
		2	31-58	105	3.90	4.47	2.99	3.54	3.40	4.02	3.91++	4.50	2.98
	F	1	20-30	48	3.91	4.35	2.91	3.64	3.52	4.00	3.36*	4.41	3.15
		2	31-45	44	3.85	4.52	3.01	3.71	3.58	4.17	3.57	4.19	3.06
Mean					3.82	4.42	2.99	3.61	3.52	4.13	3.75	4.34	3.10

Table 1 Note.
E=Extraversion, D=Self-Discipline,
A=Authoritarianism, S=Submission,
C=Cautiousness, O=Other-Orientation,
I=Independency, M=Modernism, N=Neuroticism.
$^+$ denotes that the group mean is significantly larger than the group mean (s) indicated by * in the same sample of the same sex. $^{++}$ indicates that the group mean is significantly larger than the mean of the other 20 groups in the four samples. $^{+++}$ denotes the combined results indicated by both $^+$ and $^{++}$.
*denotes that the group mean is significantly smaller than the group mean (s) indicated by $^+$ in the same sample of the same sex. ** indicates that the group mean is significantly smaller than the mean of other 20 groups in the four samples. *** denotes the combined results indicated by both * and **.

STUDY 3

SALIENT PERSONALITY TRAITS

Study 2 compared the 21 age groups in four populations according to the nine personality factors, which depict the broad aspects or dimensions of personality. The intent of the present study was to go into the depth or specific aspects of Chinese personality by examining the salient variables or traits of the nine personality factors or dimensions. It was hypothesized that the specific salient traits reflect the values more explicitly than the personality dimensions.

The subjects and instrument were the same as in Study 2. We used 2.50 and 4.50 as cut-off points on the 6-point scale to single out the salient traits of the subjects in the 21 age groups of the four samples. Because the 122 items of the MTPI representing personality traits are bipolar, there is one descriptor on each side of the continuum measured by a 6-point scale. Any item with a score less than 2.50 or more than 4.50 is considered a salient trait indicated by the descriptor at the left or right pole of the continuum respectively. Due to the effect of narcissism and/or social desirability, a salient trait may well represent a preferred personality characteristic and/or socially desired value. Therefore, a salient trait may well be a prominent personality characteristic on the one hand and an important personal or social value on the other hand.

Listed in Table 1 are the salient traits and/or values characterizing at least one age group of one sample. There are 47 of them in all. The number of traits or values associated with each of the nine bipolar personality dimensions varies: there are 3 with Introversion--Extraversion, 13 with Negligence--Self-Discipline, 6 with Democratism-- Authoritarianism, none with Dominance--Submission, one with Adventurousness-- Cautiousness, 11 with Self-Orientation--Other-Orientation, 5 with Dependency-- Independency, 3 with Traditionalism--Modernism, and 5 with Healthiness--Neuroticism.

Of the 47 salient traits only three are salient in all 21 age groups of the four samples; namely, responsible, faithful in love, and sincere. The first two of the three traits are associated with Self-Discipline and the last one with Other-Orientation. Besides Self-Discipline which has 13 components as salient traits, Other-Orientation is the second most robust source trait with 11 components as salient traits, three of which (opposes premarital sex, unsnobbish, and sincere) being salient in 14, 17, and 21 age groups respectively. The two robust source or general traits (Self-Discipline and Other-Orientation) may be regarded also as two most important terminal values while the three common specific traits (sincere, responsible, and faithful in love) as three most important instrumental values.

Table 1
Salient Traits/Values of 21 Male and Female Age Groups of Educated Chinese in Four Populations

Salient Trait/Value (under each dimension)	Mainland M 1	2	3	4	Mainland F 1	2	3	Taiwan M 1	2	3	4	Taiwan F 1	2	Hong Kong M 1	2	Hong Kong F 1	2	United States M 1	2	United States F 1	2
EXTRAVERSION (3 traits)																					
1 Amiable																					S
2 Has many friends							S												S	S	S
3 Sociable	S	S	S	S	S	S	S	S	S	S	S		S					S	S	S	S
SELF-DISCIPLINE (13 traits)																					
4 Is a person of deed		S	S	S		S	S	S	S	S	S		S								S
5 Principled		S					S		S	S			S								
6. High in need for achievement										S											
7 Realistic				S		S	S	S	S	S	S		S			S	S				S
8 Responsible	S	S	S	S	S	S	S	S	S	S	S	S	S	S	S	S	S	S	S	S	S
9 Adheres to what is right			S	S		S	S		S	S	S		S		S		S	S	S		
10 Works quietly			S	S		S	S	S		S	S										
11 Concentrates on work		S	S	S		S	S				S	S									
12 Consistent in word & deed	S	S	S	S	S	S	S	S	S	S	S		S					S	S		S
13 Self-controlled		S	S							S	S										
14 Values virginity	S	S	S	S	S	S	S	S	S	S	S	S	S	S	S	S	S			S	S
15 Faithful in love	S	S	S	S	S	S	S	S	S	S	S	S	S	S	S	S	S	S	S	S	S
16 Has self-knowledge	S	S	S	S	S	S	S				S		S					S	S	S	S

Table 1 (Continued)

Salient Traits/Values of 21 Male and Female Age Groups of Educated Chinese in Four Populations

Salient Trait/Value (under each dimension)	Mainland M 1	M 2	M 3	M 4	F 1	F 2	F 3	Taiwan M 1	M 2	M 3	M 4	F 1	F 2	Hong Kong M 1	M 2	F 1	F 2	United States M 1	M 2	F 1	F 2
DEMOCRATISM (6 trails)																					
17 Democratic			S					S	S	S		S								S	
18 Respects others	S	S			S	S		S	S	S		S	S		S			S		S	S
19 Disinclined to boast						S	S							S							
20 Trustful				S					S	S											
21 Forgiving									S												
22 Tolerant of different opinions									S	S											
SUBMISSION (0 trait)																					
CAUTIOUSNESS (1 trait)																					
23 Moderate										S	S										
OTHER-ORIENTATION (11 traits)																					
24 Sincere	S	S	S	S	S	S	S	S	S	S	S	S	S	S	S	S	S	S	S	S	
25 Prefers things native										S	S										
26 Helpful to colleagues					S																
27 Champions justice bravely						S															

Table 1 (Continued)

Salient Traits/Values of 21 Male and Female Age Groups of Educated Chinese in Four Populations

	Mainland							Taiwan						Hong Kong				United States			
	M				F			M				F		M		F		M		F	
Salient Trait/Value (under each dimension)	1	2	3	4	1	2	3	1	2	3	4	1	2	1	2	1	2	1	2	1	2
28 Thoughtful to others						S				S	S								S	S	S
29 Unsnobbish	S	S	S	S	S	S	S		S	S	S	S	S			S	S	S	S	S	S
30 Has no desire for power		S		S		S	S														
31 Considers group first						S															
32 Spiritual	S				S							S									
33 Interested in opposite sex														S				S			
34 Opposes premarital sex	S	S	S	S	S	S	S			S		S	S			S	S			S	S
35 Independent	S	S	S	S	S			S	S	S	S								S	S	
36 Faces reality									S	S											S
37 Does not believe in the existance of any god	S	S	S	S	S																
38 Empirical (relying on facts)											S										
39 Easily moved to tears by touching stories							S					S				S				S	S

INDEPENDENCY (5 traits)

Table 1 (Continued)
Salient Traits/Values of 21 Male and Female Age Groups of Educated Chinese in Four Populations

Salient Trait/Value	Mainland							Taiwan						Hong Kong				United States			
	M				F			M				F		M		F		M		F	
(under each dimension)	1	2	3	4	1	2	3	1	2	3	4	1	2	1	2	1	2	1	2	1	2
MODERNISM (3 traits)																					
40 Imaginative	S																				
41 Self-effacing			S			S															
42 Accepts new things easily	S	S			S					S											
HEALTHINESS (5 traits)																					
43 Generous	S				S	S	S					S									
44 Sleeps well	S	S	S	S	S	S	S		S	S								S			
45 Sane												S						S	S		
46 Adaptable													S					S	S	S	S
47 Physically healthy	S																	S	S	S	S

Note. The group marked by S perceived the trait or value as salient. The age of each group is the same as in Table 1 of Study 2.

As indicated in Table 1 and by the actual scores not presented here, the following observations are worth mentioning. The salient traits are numbered in the table for easy identification.

1. The HK groups are less sociable (Trait 3) than most other groups.

2. The youngest groups (aged 19-30) of both sexes in ML and TW, along with all HK and US groups except the older US female group, do not perceive being a person of deed (Trait 4) as a salient trait. In other words, they probably talk more and act less than other groups.

3. The youngest groups of both sexes are all less inclined to concentrate on work (Trait 11) than the older groups.

4. Although all ML groups highly value virginity (Trait 14), the male groups of other three samples do not do so as the female groups do. This indicates that ML Chinese of both sexes, along with Chinese women in HK, TW, and US, are more conservative on heterosexual relationships than Chinese men in HK, TW, and US.

5. Five of the six TW groups are saliently democratic (Trait 17) while only the oldest ML male group (aged 51-65) and the younger US female group (aged 20-30) perceive themselves as saliently democratic.

6. Tolerance (Trait 22), a traditional Chinese virtue, and moderation (Trait 23), a traditional Confucian value, are both perceived salient only by two older TW male groups (aged 41-65).

7. Only the three ML female groups and the oldest ML male group have no desire for power (Trait 30).

8. Although all ML groups of both sexes and all female groups of other three samples oppose premarital sex (Trait 34), almost all male groups of other three samples do not perceive it as a salient trait or value.

9. All ML groups but no other groups tend to doubt the existence of any god

(Trait 37).

10. Although moderation is no longer a salient trait as perceived by the majority of Chinese sampled in the present study, our subjects are generally moderate in personality as indicated by the fact that in most (the 75 traits not found in Table 1 because they were not salient) of the MTPI's 122 bipolar traits none of the 21 groups in the four populations reached the point of saliency. For example, they are neither very subjective nor very objective, neither very talkative nor very quiet, ·neither very planful nor very unplanful, neither very humble nor very arrogant, neither very competitive nor very cooperative, neither very obedient nor very rebellious, neither very impulsive nor very calm, neither very optimistic nor very pessimistic, etc. They are probably moderate unknowingly. This is of course the result based on group means. The personality of people near the end or extreme of the bipolar scale was obscured by statistical analyses.

STUDY 4

AMBITIONS AND ASPIRATIONS

The terms ambitions and aspirations are often used interchangeably. Aspiration is strong desire or ambition, or the thing so desired. Ambition is strong desire to gain a particular objective or the desire to gain fame, power, wealth, etc. Ambition may also mean the objective strongly desired. A person's ambition or aspiration not only reflects his or her personality, but also his or her personal or cultural values (Hurlock, 1967).

For many centuries. educated Chinese as a group have had a sense of mission. A sense of social obligation has remained a dominant motive of modern Chinese intellectual life (Grieder, 1981). Besides taking care of their families, the Chinese intellectuals aspire to do something significant for their country and the world. This study investigated the ambitions and aspirations of the educated people in mainland

China today, by which we hope to gain a better insight into the personality and values of the Chinese people.

The subjects were the same 120 educated Chinese of both sexes and various ages as described in Chapter One. They served as interviewees or informants.

I asked my interviewees what were or had been their ambitions, aspirations, wishes, or life goals. They were free to say what they had in mind or remembered in response to my questions. The answers were recorded and categorized.

In present-day China, many intellectuals aim at self-actualization so that they can serve their country and improve their society although the Cultural Revolution (1966-1976) had some inhibitive effect on their ambitions. While the aspirations of some educated people are moderate, the aspirations of others are unrealistically high. Their hopes and aspirations or ambitions include:

1. China will improve economically and politically.

2. Life will get better.

3. People will be less selfish.

4. Have a good status in society and be respected by others.

5. Have a good job.

6. Have a successful career.

7. Gain fame in a profession (e.g., be a famous writer, scientist, or educator).

8. Have a happy family and a successful husband (aspired by women).

9. Follow father's career (e.g., as a professor).

10. Do something significant for the country and people.

11. Work for the well-being of society.

12. Woman's status will be uplifted (aspired by female intellectuals).

13. Do my best but not necessarily to excel.

14. Be a useful person.

15. Be realistic and satisfied with status quo.

16. Go abroad for further education (aspired by many college graduates of both sexes).

For illustrations, some specific examples are presented below.

1. Graduate student, male, age 26: "I once aspired to reform China and the world. Now I know it is impossible."

2. Mathematician, male, age 44: "I aspired as a college student to be a famous mathematician or scientist."

3. College instructor, male, age 31: "I once aspired to be a great educator."

4. Teaching assistant, male, age 25: "I hope to go abroad for advanced study."

5. Teaching assistant, male, age 24: " I hope to improve my English and get a higher degree. I aspire to be a full professor."

6. Research assistant, male, age 25: "I aspire to create a theory of economics suited for China."

7. College senior, male, age 20: "Many of us young people wish to excel in learning and work but few of us really do it. I am one of the few who don't just wish it, but do it."

8. College junior, male, age 22: "I hope to enter the graduate school. I aspire to be a scholar devoted to research."

Many college students failed to enter the departments of their choice, they had to pursue a career of lesser interest such as a liberal arts graduate student who admitted, "I aspired in high school to study science and technology in college but failure in the college entrance exam forced me to change my specialty." To study science and technology as an aspiration of many young people is more highly valued in China than to study humanities or social sciences. The competition for college admission is, therefore, keener in the former than the latter.

While many female graduate students have fear of success and are, therefore, worried about being unable to find the right mate, an attractive college senior aspiring to enter the graduate school does not think it will be difficult for her to marry the right man.

Many middle-aged intellectuals become disillusioned about unrealistic aspirations and settled for less--they only hope that they don't have to worry about livelihood and that their children will fare well. For example, a middle-aged man says that he once aspired to be a scholar and now doesn't think his personality fits his aspiration. Being a scholar is much more valued in China than just being a teacher.

Before or after retirement, some old intellectuals still aspire to have a breakthrough in career. For example, a retired school teacher and calligrapher invented a new way of writing Chinese with a fountain pen. He tries to popularize it at home and abroad. He asked me to give him a helping hand.

A 60-year-old female professor spent one year at a prestigious American university as visiting scholar. She afterwards translated a book by a well-known American professor and had it published in China. Like the retired school teacher just mentioned, she aspired to have a breakthrough in career before retirement.

Another retiring man, however, says that he aspired as a college student to make a contribution to his country but has no more ambition now on the eve of retirement.

STUDY 5

PERSONALITY AND VALUE CHANGE

There are both continuity and change in personality. Since personality traits sometimes reflect values, change in personality may also reflect change in personal or cultural values. The aim of this study was to explore how stable personality is and what, how, when, and why change occurs in personality.

The subjects were the same 120 educated Chinese as described in Chapter One. I asked my subjects whether there was any change in their personality as they remembered it. If there was, I then asked them what change it was and when, how, and why it occurred.

Although Western data support the position that personality is stable after age 30 (Costa, Jr. & McCrae, 1988), my interview data collected from mainland China demonstrate that personality becomes stabilized in late adolescence (age 16-19) or early adulthood (age 20-25). When any change occurs after that, it is temporary or permanent but not fundamental. It usually occurs in a certain aspect or trait of personality. It often results from change in environment (family, school, or society), in life experience, in human relations, in health, or in cognition. It may also result from success or failure to meet one's expectations.

The following are 17 (13 male and 4 female) cases illustrating personality change. Some of the cases also reflect value change. Possible causes of change are indicated in parentheses at the end of each case.

1. College senior, male, age 21: Enjoy literature but major in engineering as demanded by father. Become realistic and ready to accept the career as engineer after having a girl friend in sophomore year. "Girl friend's realism changed my idealism." (Girl friend's attitude)

2. College senior, male, age 20: Active and naughty in grade school. Became quiet in high school under pressure of college entrance exam. Still quiet in college. (Academic pressure)

3. Engineer, male, age 52: Ambitious in college aspiring to make a contribution to country. Frustrated by reality and gradually become ambitionless.

(Frustration)

4. Professor, male, age 65: Enjoyed singing, playing volley ball, chatting, going to movies as student in college and high school before 1949. Married in 1948. Turned quiet after 1949 when Communists seized power. (Marriage and change in social environment)

5. Engineer, male, age 43: Identified since high school with elder brother who was hardworking as a student and conscientious as an engineer and never complained. Have become less hardworking and conscientious but more outspoken since learning a lesson three years ago from elder brother's death due to mental breakdown. (Learning from brother's death)

6. Doctor, male, age 35: Become more cautious in making diagnosis and promises after ten years' practical experience as a surgeon. (Professional experience)

7. Teaching assistant, male, age 23: Lost confidence and felt inferior as a college student because of ill health. Feel unable to catch up on work and confused. (Poor health)

8. College senior, male, age 22: Acquiescent to parents regardless of generation gap during high school years. Became assertive and outspoken to parents and less egocentric to peers after entering college. (Change in status and cognition)

9. College senior, male, age 22: Extraverted before age 10. Turned introverted later due to unpleasant experiences in home and school until age 18 when peer relations and family conditions improved. Became cheerful and outgoing again after entering college at age 19. (Change of school and home environment)

10. Teaching assistant, male, age 23: Introverted before entering college. Become extraverted later realizing that being extraverted has more advantages than disadvantages. (Change in cognition)

11. College instructor, male, age 28: No longer aspired to surpass others since senior year in college. Feel happy now "so long as I perceive myself as achieving and useful to society." Changed philosophy of life after reading many books on life. (Learning from reading)

12. Deputy department head, male, age 57: Extremely introverted before age 31. Become less timid and introverted after serving as deputy department head for 26 years. (Administrative experience)

13. Department head, male, age 52: Timid and introverted as student. Gradually turned extraverted with experience as educator. (Learning from experience)

14. Graduate student, female, age 27: Have felt less inferior and more confident since having boy friend at age 20. Become cheerful and enjoy better health after getting married at age 25. "Husband takes good care of me." (Good heterosexual relations)

15. Graduate student, female, age 26: Very active during the first three years in grade school and often selected to participate in children's show. Then the Cultural Revolution broke out and father, being a businessman, brought disgrace to the whole family. "I feel inferior and have shunned public attention since then." (Political influence)

16. School teacher, female, age 48: Became less active and quieter in college in order to concentrate on studies. Active again after joining the teaching profession. (Change of life situation)

17. Psychologist, female, age 63: Introverted before age 32. Sent down to the countryside in 1960s (after age 32) for rustication (re-education by the peasants) and hence had more contact with people. In early 1970s taught three years in grade and high schools and had more chance to talk to people. Have become less introverted

since then. (Social interaction)

STUDY 6

MATE PREFERENCES

The study of mate preferences or preferences in selecting mates has received increasing attention in recent years (Bateson, 1983; Buss and 49 collaborators, 1990; Sprecher, Sullivan, & Hatfield, 1994)). According to Buss et al (1990), mate preference has been important in evolutionary biology since Darwin's classic 1871 treatise *The Descent of Man and Selection in Relation to Sex*. Darwin's sexual selection has two pivotal components: intersexual selection and intrasexual selection. The former refers to the preferential choice of some mating partners over others. The latter indicates competition between members of the same sex for access to members of the opposite sex.

Interest in sexual selection, however, transcends the boundaries of scientific disciplines. Mate preference has been studied by social and behavioral scientists as well as by biologists. The largest research project has been undertaken by Buss and 49 collaborators (1990) from 33 countries. They investigated mate characteristics in 37 cultures. Although they admitted that their samples were not representative, they have found some significant effects of culture and sex on mate preferences.

A face-loving people like the Chinese are very sensitive to the problem of finding the right mate because failing to find one would mean losing face. Friends and relatives are interested in knowing whether their unmarried friend or relative has a girl or boy friend and/or when he or she is going to get married.

This study should be taken as a preliminary one because the sample was too small to be representative. The findings, however, seem to be interesting when compared with Buss et al's (1990) and Sprecher et al's (1994) results. Hopefully, this study may shed some light on mate preferences for future researchers. Mate preferences reflect cultural values because values refer to what is preferred by an individual or a group in a culture and a value "influences the selection from available modes, means, and ends of action" (Kluckholm, 1951, p. 395).

In addition to a personality inventory administered to more than 2600 educated Chinese, I interviewed about 200 Chinese in mainland China and Taiwan for my project on Chinese personality. For time was restricted and my questions were numerous, I had to distinguish between general and specific questions. I asked all my interviewees every general question and some of them some specific questions. As specific questions, I asked my subjects what conditions or characterisitics they preferred for their future mates and what conditions or characteristics which they thought men and women in general would value for their potential spouses. My subjects who were asked these specific questions totaled 29 in number. They were 7 men and 11 women (mostly college students) in mainland China , and 5 men and 6 women (mostly college graduates) in Taiwan. They were unmarried and about 30 years old or younger.

Each subject emits responses (mate conditions or characteristics) in his or her own order, which stands for the relative importance of the response--the early emitted responses are assumed to be more important than the later ones. The first to fifth responses are assigned 5 points to 1 point (the first response is considered the most important and given 5 points; the fifth and later responses are given 1 point), which may be called the order score. This order score is multiplied by the number of times the same condition or characteristic is mentioned by the interviewees to yield a cumulative score for each condition or characteristic. The cumulative score is thus indicative of the total value or importance of each condition or characteristic for the potential mate. A special case is compatible personality (CP) as a preferred mate condition or characteristic. Instead of or in addition to pointing out CP (*geshing shiangtou*) as desirable, the subject may mention one or several personality traits (e.g., considerate, respects wife) that would contribute to compatibility or happy marriage. The sum of the cumulative scores of CP along with its traits then becomes the total cumulative score of CP as a valued or preferred mate condition or characteristic. The subject may just give his or her own answer if he or she does not know what answers might be given by men and women in general to the same question. The number of responses each subject may emit is not restricted.

Although the number of responses was not restricted, most interviewees gave not more than five mate conditions or characteristics. The results are shown in Tables 1 and 2. For the sake of comparison, Buss et al's Chinese (mainland China and Taiwan) rank ordering of rated variables is presented in Table 3.

Table 1
Mate Characteristics Preferred by Unmarried Chinese Young Men and Women in Mainland China and Taiwan

Mate Characteristics	Rank Order[a]				Cumulative Score			
	China		Taiwan		China		Taiwan	
	M	F	M	F	M	F	M	F
1. Compatible personality[b]	1	1	1	1	72	53	61	35
2. Good looks	2	11	2	4	45	2	16	9
3. Good character	3	3		5	11	22		8
4. Intelligence and talents[c]	4	2		6	7	38		6
5. Education[d]	5	7	3	10	6	8	10	2
6. Parents' socioeconomic status[e]	5	8	7		6	7	1	
7. Mutual love	6	10	4	7	5	5	5	5
8. Height and weight	6	6		8	5	12		4
9. Good housekeeper	7		6		4		3	
10. Manners and culture	8				3			
11. Ambition	9	4			2	21		
12. Age[f]	10	12	7	9	1	1	1	3
13. Health			5	7			4	5
14. Sex appeal			5				4	
15. Occupation		10	6	3		5	3	14

Table 1 (Continued)
Mate Characteristics Preferred by Unmarried Chinese Young Men and
Women in Mainland China and Taiwan

Mate Characteristics	Rank Order[a] China M	F	Taiwan M	F	Cumulative Score China M	F	Taiwan M	F
16. Economic conditions or earning capacity				2				18
17. Posture		5				13		
18. Individuality				7				5
19. Masculinity		9				6		
Total number of items mentioned:	12	13	10	12				
Mean of cumulative scores[g]:					24	18	22	19

[a] The rank order is based on the cumulative score, the greater the score the higher the rank.

[b] See Table 2 for its traits.

[c] Wife should not surpass husband in this characteristic.

[d] Wife should not surpass husband in educational level.

[e] The husband's and the wife's parental socioeconomic status should match; the wife's side should not surpass the husband's side.

[f] Wife should be a little younger than husband.

[g] The mean is derived from dividing the total cumulative score by the number of interviewees.

Table 2
Traits of Compatible Personality Valued by
Unmarried Chinese Men and Women

Mainland Trait	CS[c]	Taiwan Trait	CS	Both[a] Trait	CS
Kindhearted	5	Submissive	5	Warm and tender	20
Loyal	5	Independent	5	Mature (affectively and	
Honest	5	Emotionally stable	4	cognitively)	17
Understanding	4	Has similar views	3	Can carry on a dialogue	
Is a good wife and				in harmony	13
good mother	4			Considerate	12
Diligent	3			Docile	9
Tolerant	3			Has similar interests	6
Cheerful	3			Gentle and quiet	5
Autonomous	2				

Mate Traits Valued by Men

Table 2 (Continued)
Traits of Compatible Personality Valued by
Unmarried Chinese Men and Women

Mainland		Mate Traits Valued by Women Taiwan		Both[b]	
Trait	CS[c]	Trait	CS	Trait	CS
Kindhearted	8	Can carry on a dialogue		Faithful and honest	22
Playful	4	in harmony	7	Autonomous	9
Active	3	Mature (affectively		Considerate	8
Sociable	3	and cognitively)	3	Emotionally stable	6
Sentimental	3	Patient	2	Respects wife	6
Self-effacing	2	Realistic	1		
Has a sense of humor	1				

[a] These traits are valued by men in both mainland China and Taiwan. [b]These traits are valued by women in both mainland China and Taiwan. [c]CS=cumulative score.

Table 3
Buss et al's Chinese (Mainland China and Taiwan) Male and Female Rank
Ordering of Rated Variables

Mate Characteristics	Mainland		Taiwan	
	M	F	M	F
1. Mutual attraction--love	4	8	1	2
2. Dependable character	6	7	2	1
3 .Emotional stability and maturity	5	1	5	3
4. Pleasing disposition	13	16	3	7
5. Education and intelligence	8	4	6	5
6. Good health	1	3	4	6
7. Sociability	12	9	14	13
8. Desire for home and children	2	2	11	9
9. Refinement, neatness	7	10	9	12
10. Ambition and industrious	10	5	10	4
11. Good looks	11	15	13	16
12. Similar education	15	12	12	8
13. Good financial prospect	16	14	15	10
14. Good cook and housekeeper	9	11	8	15
15. Favorable social status or rating	14	13	16	14
16. Similar religious background	18	18	17	18
17. Chastity (no previous experience in sexual intercourse)	3	6	7	11
18. Similar political background	17	17	18	17

Source: Buss et al (1990), p. 24.

The results of this study indicate that the most desirable condition or characteristic in Chinese mate preferences is compatible personality (CP), which is ranked 1 by both mainland (ML) and Taiwan (TW) men and women. This confirms the opinion of several elderly people with whom I have discussed mate preferences that CP is the most desirable factor of happy marriage. CP comprises many traits mentioned by the interviewees as listed in Table 2. Some traits are identical or similar to several items or variables of Buss et al's (1990) 18-characteristic instrument including emotional stability and maturity. pleasing disposition, and sociability (see Table 3). The trait "good wife and good mother" may be related to their "desire for home and children." In other items, their "good financial prospect" is similar to my "economic abilities or earning capacity;" their "chastity" and "dependable character" are implied in my "good character"; their "favorable social status or rating" is related to my "occupation;" and their "similar education" and "refinement, neatness" may be included in my "education" and "manners and culture" respectively. "Similar religious background" and "similar political background," the two items ranked the lowest (17 or 18) among their 18 mate characteristics, were not mentioned by my subjects.

Another instrument Buss et al (1990) used has 13 characteristics, most of which are similar to those in the other instrument mentioned above except two--"good heredity" and "creative and artistic." These two items are related to my "parents' socioeconomic status" and "intelligence and talents" respectively.

The traditional Chinese conception of an ideal couple is a talented man plus an attractive woman. This criterion is met by my findings as reflected by the rank ordering of the mate's intelligence and talents preferred by ML Chinese women and economic abilities or earning capacity valued by TW Chinese women, both rank 2; and by the ranking of mate's good looks desired by both ML and TW men, which also ranks 2. This is in line with Sprecher et al's (1994) study on gender differences in mate selection preferences examined in a national sample. It is also consistent with Buss et al's (1990) finding for the entire Asian sample which demonstrates the typical sex difference in preference for female's physical appearance and male's earning capacity. Buss et al's Chinese samples (ML and TW), however, depart from the Asian norm in placing less value on physical appearance (good looks).

The tendency to place great value on mutual love (or mutual attraction--love), an ideal condition for a happy couple, is similar for both Buss et al's (1990) study and mine, but Buss et al's samples, especially TW males and females, value it even more. While the ML samples of our two studies and their TW sample show almost identical mate preference for ambition (or "ambition and industrious' in their term), my TW subjects of both sexes ignore it. On the other hand, the TW samples of both studies place almost the same value on health (or good health) , but my ML sample of both sexes ignore it or just take it for granted.

An important difference between the two sides of the Taiwan Strait is that my TW subjects, especially female, pay less or no attention to such abstract or remote condition as ambition and place greater value on such concrete or immediate characteristics as occupation and economic abilities or earning capacity, while my ML subjects demonstrate the contrary tendencies. Another notable difference lies in female preferences that the ML women highly value intelligence and talents, a relatively abstract and traditional mate characteristic, while their TW counterparts greatly value economic abilities or earning capacity, a more concrete and modern condition for potential mate. These differences obviously reflect a contrast in social and economic situations of the two Chinese societies. These differences, however, were not detected by Buss et al's (1990) study.

The most interesting finding of this preliminary study is CP *(geshing shiangtou)*, the mate condition or characteristic overwhelmingly valued by my subjects, especially male, in the two Chinese societies as indicated by the cumulative scores. Buss et al's (1990) instruments also include some characteristics (pleasing disposition, sociability, emotional stability and maturity, kind and understanding, exciting personality, easygoing) resembling some of my CP traits. Their "emotional stability and maturity" is ranked 1 and 3 by ML and TW females respectively, while "emotionally stable" is a desirable CP trait preferred by my female subjects in both Chinese societies. Of all the CP traits "warm and tender" (*wen zou*) in future wife is most preferred by men and "faithful and honest" (*dzong cheng*) in potential husband is given the highest value by women, which was not detected either by Buss et al (1990) or Sprecher et al (1994).

While the numbers of items (mate conditions or characteristics) mentioned by the four groups of my interviewees are similar (from 10 to 13), some items are chosen by more groups than other items. Of the 19 items five (CP, good looks, education, mutual love, and age) are desired by all the four groups, other five (good character, intelligence and talents, parents' socioeconomic status, height and weight, and occupation) are preferred by three groups, and the remaining nine items are valued by one or two groups. The cumulative score (CS) reflects the relative importance or value given to an item. The means (*M*s) of CSs indicate that, relative to female interviewees, male subjects mention fewer items but give greater weight or value to the items mentioned, so the *M*s are larger for men (ML=24, TW=22) than for women (ML=18, TW=19). As the CSs indicate, the values given by men to the first two items (CP and good looks) are much greater (ML=72 and 45, TW=61 and 16) than the values given by women (ML=53 and 2, TW=35 and 9), although there are more female than male subjects in my sample. On the other hand, much greater weight or importance is given to good character (CS=22), intelligence and talents

(CS=38) and ambition (CS=21) by ML women than men; and to occupation (CS=14) and economic abilities or earning capacity (CS=18) by TW women than men.

In sum, the preferred mate characteristics found in the present study reflect Chinese cultural values, some of which (e.g., education, health, CP traits) are identical or similar to some of the values and personality traits found in Study 1 through 4. Buss et al's mate characteristics and mine are similar in many ways, but my findings seem to be closer to reality than theirs although my sample was small. As Buss et al (1990) recognized, their instruments "originated within the United States" and "carry cultural limitations" (p. 11). Because my mate conditions or characteristics were emitted spontaneously by the subjects, they were not confined to the predetermined items as in Buss et al' instruments. Some of my items (such as parents' socioeconomic status, height and weight, age, sex appeal, posture, individuality, and masculinity), as a result, were not included in their instruments. Future researchers need to administer instruments containing more diverse items to more representative samples. Open-ended questions may be asked to tap potential mate conditions or characteristics in various cultures for both sexes.

General Discussion

In order to compare the 69 Chinese values I found in Study 1 with other lists of values (see Table 1 below), I tried to match the full and partial equivalents in five value lists. The other four lists were proposed by Bond (Chinese Culture Connection, 1987), Rokeach (1973), Kahle (1983), and Lasswell (Lasswell & Kaplan 1965; Lasswell, Lerner, & Montgomery, 1976). Bond's 40 values are contained in his Chinese Value Survey (CVS), Rokeach's 36 values in his Rokeach Value Survey (RVS), Kahle's 9 values in his List of Values (LOV), and Lasswell's 8 values are his basic values for modernization and national development.

Table 1
A Comparison of Five Lists of Values by Matching the Full and Partial Equivalents

Lew's Chinese Values[a]	Bond's Chinese Values[a]	Rokeach's Values[b]	Kahle's Values	Lasswell's Values
Terminal social values				
1 Harmony	Harmony with others	A world at peace		
2 Non-aggression	Harmony with others, Non-competitiveness	A world at peace		
3 Being respected by others	Protecting your "face"	Social recognition	Being well-respected	Respect
4 Surpassing others in achievement		Ambitious, A sense of accomplishment	A sense of accomplishment	
5 Being useful to society		Self-respect	Self-respect	
6 Face	Protecting your "face"	Social recognition, Self-respect	Being well-respected, Self-respect	Respect
7 Democracy		Equality, Freedom	Self-fulfillment	Well-being
Terminal personal values				
8 Safety				Well-being
9 Security		Family security, National security	Security	Well-being
10 Fame		Social recognition		Respect
11 Wealth	Wealth	A comfortable life		Wealth
12 High socioeconomic status		Social recognition		Respect
13 Breakthrough in career		Ambitious, A sense of accomplishment	A sense of accomplishment	

Table 1 (Continued)
A Comparison of Five Lists of Values by Matching the Full and Partial Equivalents

Lew's Chinese Values[a]	Bond's Chinese Values[a]	Rokeach's Values[b]	Kahle's Values	Lasswell's Values
14 Self-sufficiency		Self-respect, Independent	Self-respect	
15 Moderation*	Moderation, following the middle way			
16 Happy marriage		Happiness, mature love		Well-being
17 Non-divorce*	Protecting your "face"			
Instrumental social values				
18 Modesty*	Humbleness			
19 Non-assertiveness*	Humbleness			
20 Reciprocity	Reciprocation of greetings, favors, and gifts		Warm relationships with others	
21 Filial piety*	Filial piety			
22 Repaying parents' nurturance*	Filial piety			
23 Obedience		Obedient		
24 Courtesy	Courtesy	Polite		
25 Generosity*	Courtesy, Protecting your "face"			
26 Agreeableness	Kindness (Forgiveness, Compassion)	Forgiving		
27 Tolerance	Tolerance of others	Broadminded		
28 Self-control	Self-cultivation	Self-controlled		Rectitude
29 Observance of law and order		Self-controlled	Security	Well-being

Table 1 (Continued)
A Comparison of Five Lists of Values by Matching the Full and Partial Equivalents

Lew's Chinese Values[a]	Bond's Chinese Values[a]	Rokeach's Values[b]	Kahle's Values	Lasswell's Values
30 Incorruptibility	Resistance to corruption	Honest, Responsible		Rectitude
31 Honor		Social recognition	Being well-respected	Respect
32 Loyalty	Loyalty to superiors	Loving	Warm relationships with others	Affection
33 Patriotism	Patriotism	Loving	A sense of belonging	Affection
34 Solidarity	Solidarity with others	Family security, National security	A sense of belonging	Affection
35 A sense of justice	A sense of righteousness	Courageous		
36 Sincerity	Sincerity	Honest		Rectitude
37 Conscience	Kindness (Forgiveness, Compassion)	Inner harmony		Affection
38 Altruism		Helpful		
39 Human touch	Kindness, reciprocation of greetings, favors, and gifts	Forgiving	Warm relationships	Affection with others
40 Deference to elders and superiors*	Ordering relationships by status and observing this order			
41 Love of the young	Kindness (Forgiveness, compassion)	Loving	Warm relationships with others	Affection
42 Children's success	Protecting your "face"	A sense of accomplishment	A sense of accomplishment	Respect

Table 1 (Continued)
A Comparison of Five Lists of Values by Matching the Full and Partial Equivalents

Lew's Chinese Values[a]	Bond's Chinese Values[a]	Rokeach's Values[b]	Kahle's Values	Lasswell's Values
43 Yielding of elder siblings to the younger ones	Kindness (Forgiveness, compassion)	Loving	Warm relationships with others	Affection
44 Male preference*	Respect for tradition			
45 Being a good wife mother	Respect for tradition	Loving, Responsible	Warm relationships with others	Affection, Rectitude
46 Authority	Benevolent authority			Power
47 Power				Power
48 Leadership				Power
49 Personal connection	Solidarity with others		A sense of belonging	Affection
Instrumental personal values				
50 Health	Having few desires	Inner harmony	Self-fulfillment	Well-being
51 Self-protection	Protecting your "Face"	Self-respect	Security, Self-respect	Respect
52 A sense of shame	Having a sense of shame	Self-respect	Self-respect	Respect
53 Moral character	Self-cultivation	Inner harmony	Self-fulfillment	Rectitude
54 Education	Knowledge (Education)	Intellectual	Self-fulfillment	Enlightenment, Skill
55 Knowledge	Knowledge (Education)	Intellectual, Wisdom	Self-fulfillment	Enlightenment
56 Academic degree or diploma		A sense of accomplishment	A sense of accomplishment	Respect
57 Science and technology as profession		Social recognition	Being well-respected	Respect
58 Working in a big city		Social recognition	Being well-respected	Respect
59 Material possessions	Wealth	A comfortable life		Wealth

Table 1 (Continued)
A Comparison of Five Lists of Values by Matching the Full and Partial Equivalents

Lew's Chinese Values[a]	Bond's Chinese Values[a]	Rokeach's Values[b]	Kahle's Values	Lasswell's Values
60 Matching SES for marriage partners*	Respect for tradition			
61 Having sons and grandsons*	Respect for tradition			
62 Seniority*	Respect for tradition			Rectitude
63 Diligence	Industry (Working hard)			Rectitude
64 Thrift	Thrift			
65 Beauty in women		A world of beauty		
66 Talent in men	Knowledge (Education)	Capable		Enlightenment, Skill
67 Quietitude in women*				
68 Tenderness in women		Loving		Affection
69 Toughness in men*				
Observation of rites and social rituals*				
Personal steadiness and stability*				
Keeping oneself disinterested and pure				
Persistence (Perseverance)*				
Patience*				Rectitude
Repayment of the good or the evil that another person has caused you*				

Table 1 (Continued)

A Comparison of Five Lists of Values by Matching the Full and Partial Equivalents

Lew's Chinese Values[a]	Bond's Chinese Values[a]	Rokeach's Values[b]	Kahle's Values	Lasswell's Values
	A sense of cultural superiority*			
	Adaptability*			
	Prudence (Carefulness)*			
	Trustworthiness	Honest, Responsible		Rectitude
	Contentedness with one's position in life	Happiness, Inner harmony		
	Being conservative*			
	A close, intimate friend	True friendship	Warm relationships with others	Affection
	Chastity in women*			
		An exciting life	Excitement	
		Pleasure	Fun and enjoyment in life	Well-being
		Salvation		
		Cheerful		
		Clean		
		Imaginative		
		Logical		

Notes: [a]The value indicated by an asterisk in the Lew and Bond lists has no equivalent, full or partial, in the three Western lists (Rokeach, Kahle, and Lasswell) and in all other four lists respectively. [b]The nouns or noun phrases in Rokeach's list indicate terminal values while the adjectives denote instrumental values.

As we note from Table 1 in this section, 14 values in the Lew list find no equivalents, full or partial, in the three Western lists (Rokeach, Kahle, and Lasswell). Twelve of the 14 values have full or partial equivalents in the Bond list. These 12 values may be regarded as relatively unique in the Chinese culture. Ten items in the Bond list find no equivalents not only in the Western lists but also in the Lew List. Most of these 10 items are traditional values which may be considered more important by Bond and his associates (Chinese Culture Connection, 1987) than by the Chinese people in general who are much less traditional today than they were over 40 years ago.

The fact that all items in the Lasswell list and most items in the Kahle (6 out of 8) and Rokeach (29 out of 36) lists find full or partial equivalents in the Lew list demonstrates that Chinese share most values with Westerners. Two Kahle values (excitement, fun and enjoyment in life) and seven Rokeach values (an exciting life, pleasure, salvation, cheerful, clean, imaginative, logical) are not equivalent, fully or partially, to any item in the two Chinese lists (Bond and Lew). The seven Rokeach values (Kahle's "excitement" and "fun and enjoyment in life" are similar to Rokeach's "an exciting life" and "pleasure" respectively), the first three being terminal and the last four instrumental, can be regarded as unique in the Western culture. This does not mean, however, that the Chinese would reject these seven Western values. It simply signifies that the Chinese do not consider them as important and popular as the 69 Chinese values in the Lew list.

Out of the 69 Chinese values found by Lew, 43 are equivalent to or associated with Lasswell's 8 basic values for modernization and national development. Eleven of these 43 values are related to respect, 10 to affection, 6 to rectitude, 6 to well-being, 3 to enlightenment, 3 to power, 2 to wealth, and 2 to skill. From these figures it may be inferred that for modernization or national development the Chinese desire or need respect, affection, rectitude, and well-being most. The next basic values they consider most important for China's modernization or national development are enlightenment, power, wealth, and skill.

I also interviewed 57 (42 male and 15 female) intellectuals across a wide age range in Taiwan asking them the same questions as I did the ML interviewees. Meanwhile, 651 (398 male and 253 female) educated people of various ages in Taiwan were administered the same questionnaire (MTPI). The results were nearly identical except that (1)the TW Chinese value security (family security and national security), democracy, power, and wealth more than their ML counterparts; (2)thrift is not as much valued among the younger people in Taiwan; and (3)happy marriage is not as much valued in Taiwan as on the mainland because the TW Chinese are less traditional in heterosexual relations (for instance, the TW Chinese value virginity and oppose premarital sex to a lesser extent than their ML counterparts--see Traits 14 and 34 in Table 1 of Study 3).

In general, since Taiwan surpasses the mainland in affluence, urbanism, social mobility, and exposure to modern mass media, which are antecedents of individualism (Triandis et al, 1990), Taiwan is somewhat more individualistic and less collectivistic than the mainland. This observation about Taiwan applies to Hong Kong and the Chinese community in the United States. The concern of the Chinese people everywhere for collective interests, however, does not extend beyond their in-group.

Schwartz (1992) proposed ten universal value types based on a study of 20 countries. While 14 of my 69 Chinese values fail to find equivalents in Rokeach list (see Table 1 in this section), all my Chinese values can be covered by Schwartz's ten universal value types. In consultation with him (Shalom Schwartz, personal communication, November 21, 1994), I categorized my 69 Chinese values (see Table 2 in this section).

Table 2
Lew's Chinese Values as Categorized by
Schwartz's Ten Universal Value Types

Schwartz's Value Types	Chinese Values as Numbered in Lew List
Individual types (serving individual interests)	
Power: Status, prestige, authority , wealth, control or dominance over people and resources	3, 4, 6, 10, 11, 12, 17, 31, 46, 47, 48, 49, 51, 56, 57, 58, 59, 65, 66, 69
Achievement: Personal success for social approval	13, 42, 54, 55, 56, 57, 65, 66
Hedonism: Pleasure, sensual gratification	None
Stimulation: Excitement, novelty, and challenge	None
Self-direction: Independent thought and action	14, 63, 54, 55
Collective types (serving collective interests)	
Benevolence: Concern for the welfare of close others	17, 20, 24, 25, 26, 36, 37, 38, 39, 41, 42, 43, 45, 53, 68
Conformity: Restraint of actions and impulses	15, 17,18, 19, 23, 24, 26, 27, 28, 30, 37, 40, 43, 52, 53, 64
Tradition: Acceptance of traditional customs and ideas	15, 21, 22, 40, 43, 44, 45, 60, 61, 62, 67, 68, 69
Mixed types (serving both individual and collective interests)	
Security: Safety, harmony, and stability of self, society, and relationships	1, 2, 8, 9, 16, 20, 24, 26, 29, 32, 33, 34, 40, 43, 50, 51
Universalism: Concern for the welfare of all people and protection of the natural environment	5, 7, 27, 35

I found that 32, 44, and 20 values in Lew list (see Table 1 in this section) belong to Schwartz's individual, collective, and mixed value types respectively. A few values in Lew list can be placed under more than one Schwartz's value types.

From this categorization as shown in Table 2 of this section, we may speculate that Chinese culture is 44/ (32+44) or 58% collectivist and 32/ (32+44) or 42% individualist, assuming that all Chinese values in Lew list are equally important and that individual value types serve individualist interests and collective value types serve collectivist interests The ratio of collectivism and individualism is then about 6 : 4 in Chinese culture with some geographical variation.

As we can infer from the number of Chinese values associated with each of the ten universal value types proposed by Schwartz (see Table 2), the six salient value types in Chinese culture are power (20 values), security (16 values), conformity (16 values), benevolence (15 values), tradition (13 values), and achievement (8 values) while the less salient value types in Chinese culture are hedonism (0 value), stimulation (0 value), self-direction (4 values), and universalism (4 values).

As I have observed in Study 3 of Chapter Four, the Chinese are authority-directed. This is further borne out by the result of categorizing the Chinese values that power is the most salient value type because it is characterized by authority and power or dominance over other people and resources. Another salient value type achievement is instrumental to power because achievement or personal success raises one's status and prestige and in turn one's authority. In Chinese society, the superior or person with greater authority is respected to a greater degree than the inferior or person with lesser authority.

Values reflect personality. As a matter of fact, Rokeach selected his instrumental values from a list of personality trait words (Braithwaite & Law, 1985). When a person takes "ambitious" in Rokeach list as a value, for example, it implies one or two of his or her personality traits: he or she either is ambitious or thinks that a person should be ambitious, or both. Even terminal values reflect personality.

When one takes "a comfortable life" in Rokeach list as a terminal value, it implies either that he or she leads a comfortable life or that he or she aspires to lead a comfortable life.

Values and personality traits are sometimes semantically overlapping. A function of values, as stated by Rokeach (1973. p. 13), is that values are standards employed to *evaluate* ourselves and others. This coincides with Borkenau's (1990) finding that the main purpose of trait terms is not so much to describe but rather to *evaluate* people. Borkenau (1990) suggests that the five major factors of personality or source traits (the Big Five: extraversion, agreeableness, conscientiousness, emotional stability, and intellect-culture-openness) are the most important attributes that qualify people for personal or societal goals. He (Borkenau, 1990) conceives traits as ideal-based and goal-derived categories. The Big Five are, in this sense, five basic values as well as five fundamental traits.

The results of Study 2 through 6 all lend support to the findings in Study 1. Democracy as a value in Study 1, for example, is supported by the finding in Study 2 that none of the 21 Chinese groups perceive themselves as authoritarian (the opposite of democratic), which reflects the value of democracy. Self-discipline, a fundamental trait as demonstrated in Study 2, is similar to self-control as found in Study 1 (see Lew list) and can be considered a basic value as well equivalent to Lasswell's rectitude.

Values and traits are, however, not identical. While they mirror each other, they cannot be equated with each other. The self-report, like the response to an item in the MTPI, can be interpreted in several ways. When a person or group self-reports possessing a trait like a salient trait in Table 1 of Study 3, there are three possible interpretations:

1. The person or group values the trait (i.e., takes it as a value) and possesses

it simultaneously.

2. The person or group values the trait but does not actually possess it.

3. The person or group possesses the trait but does not value it.

The following findings correspond to the foregoing three interpretations respectively:

1. As Table 1 in Study 3 shows, all the 21 groups perceived themselves as sincere (i.e., they self-reported possessing the trait), whereas sincerity is also an instrumental social value as found in Study 1 and listed in Table 1 in this section (see the Lew list). These two findings indicate that the Chinese value and possess the same trait simultaneously.

2. While tolerance is a value as found in Study 1 and listed in Table 1 above (see the Lew list), in Study 3 only two groups self-reported possessing "tolerant of different opinions" as a salient trait (see Table 1 in Study 3) and the other 19 groups did not. These two findings demonstrate that the Chinese value tolerance but the majority of them do not possess it as a salient trait.

3. The majority (15) of the 21 groups in Study 3 self-reported possessing "respects others" as a salient trait (see Table 1 in Study 3), but respecting others is not a value in the Lew list as found in Study 1 (see Table 1 above). These two findings may testify that the majority of Chinese claim to possess the trait but do not value or practice it. It is probably because the Chinese value or desire being respected by others (a terminal social value found in Study 1) far more than respecting others.

From Study 4 on ambitions and aspirations, we learn that educated Chinese are ambitious and patriotic. They desire to be respected by others. Some older intellectuals are even anxious to have a breakthrough in career before or after retirement so that they will enjoy greater authority or social power. If we try to match the ambitions or aspirations in Study 4 with the relevant results in Study 1, 2, 3, and

6, we will find the former very consistent with the latter.

In Study 5 on personality and value change, we note that change in some aspects or traits of personality reflects change in valuing. For example, young people in China are generally ambitious. Ambition or being ambitious is almost a universal value and/or trait in youth and early adulthood. Yet the saliency of the trait "ambitious" and the popularity of the value "ambitious" both decrease with age, especially after one has experienced failures or frustrations before or during mid-life. Another example is that one may become extraverted as a result of valuing extraversion like the male teaching assistant in Case 10 of Study 5. On the other hand, change in valuing may also lead to personality change. In Taiwan, for example, family security (security of family members) becomes the top value (The 21st Century Foundation, 1991) due to deteriorating societal harmony and increasing crime rate in the process of democratization. Hence the people, especially women and children, tend to be more cautious than before when they go out in order to avoid any possible danger or unsafety.

Change may occur in any trait or value at any time during the life course. As a rule, however, no fundamental change takes place after age 25. The change may take place gradually over several years, in a short period of time, or suddenly (like a one-trial learning). The causes of change are numerous as illustrated by the 17 cases in Study 5. They may be personal (e.g., health), interpersonal (e.g., marriage), educational (e.g., academic pressure), occupational (e.g., work experience), intellectual (e.g., changed cognition), political (e.g., change in political environment), etc.

As for Study 6 on mate preferences, the preferred mate characteristics reflect cultural values in mainland China and Taiwan, some of which (e.g., education, health, occupation, good looks, good character) have their equivalents in the findings of Study 1 through 4. All the six studies in this chapter examined directly or indirectly Chinese values and personality traits with an emphasis on the relationship between them. It is hoped that this chapter will contribute to a fuller understanding of Chinese values and personality. Any limitation one may find in the six studies should be seen as a problem for future researchers to solve. For example, the sample of Study 6 was too small and restricted to unmarried college students, a larger representative sample is therefore needed for future research on mate preferences in Chinese society.

✦　✦　✦

CHAPTER SEVEN

MORALITY AND INTERPERSONAL RELATIONSHIPS

Morality and human relations are two features of great importance in Chinese culture. This chapter will present two major studies and one minor study concerning the two features. One major study (Study 1) was on moral judgment and moral development in three Chinese societies (Mainland China, Taiwan, and Hong Kong), the other major study (Study 2) was on interpersonal relationships in mainland China. The minor study (Study 3) dealt with supportive relationships in the three Chinese societies plus the Chinese community in the United States. The relation between the two features or spheres in Chinese culture will be discussed.

In speeches and writings when the major components of formal education are mentioned or discussed in mainland China, Hong Kong, or Taiwan, moral education is always named first followed by intellectual education and physical education as the second and third components. Aesthetic education is sometimes added as the fourth component in mainland China, while social education and aesthetic education are often added as the fourth and fifth components in Hong Kong and Taiwan. Wilson (1981, p. 1) is right when he says:

> Scholars of both traditional and modern China are aware that Chinese speech and writings are infused with exhortation for moral behavior. The ubiquity of this characteristic seems especially pronounced when compared with the more muted way that issues regarding morality are dealt with in many other societies.

The main theme of Chinese philosophy, as Hsieh (1967) points out, has centered around ethics. Ethics for Confucians is not only the study of standards of conduct and moral judgment but also a way of life. Mei (1967, p. 150) listed the first three tenets of ethics in Chinese philosophy as follows:

> 1. Running through life and the universe is one all -pervading principle, rational and ethical in nature.
> 2. Man's duty is to follow this principle, which brings him into harmony with society and in tune with the universe.
> 3. Evil results when there is deviation from this path.

Yet, moral fervor in traditional and modern Chinese society notwithstanding, empirical study of Chinese morality did not attract much scholarly attention until recently. Inspired by Kohlberg's (1969, 1976, 1981, 1984) theory of moral development, a number of studies have been conducted in Hong Kong, Taiwan, and mainland China (Hau & Lew, 1989; Lei, 1984 ; Lei & Cheng, 1984; Ma, 1988a, 1988b; Walker & Moran, 1991). These studies have mainly dealt with moral judgment in the three Chinese societies and used Kohlberg's (1969) Moral Judgment Interview (MJI) or Rest's (1975, 1976) Defining Issues Test (DIT). As Kohlberg's (1976, 1984) theory of moral development will be applied in the present chapter, a description of it is in order (Bee & Mitchell, 1980; Ingersoll, 1989; Lefrancois, 1990).

In studying moral judgment, Kohlberg has devised a number of moral "dilemmas," which he presents to his subjects, such as the story of Heinz (a man whose wife is dying but might be saved if given a drug that was discovered by a local pharmacist who charges such an exorbitant price that Heinz can't pay. Should Heinz steal the drug to save his wife's life? Why or why not?) After analyzing the responses to these dilemmas given by his subjects of various ages, Kohlberg has reached the conclusion that there are three distinct levels (preconventional, conventional, and postconventional) of moral reasoning or judgment, each with two separate stages. Moral development moves through the six stages from the preconventional level to the postconventional level. A child's moral judgment starts at Stage 1 and gradually progresses upward till adulthood. Few people, however, reach Stages 5 and 6. Many adults stay at Stage 2, 3, or 4 without further development. The three levels and six stages are described below.

Level One: The Preconventional Level

At this level an individual does not think of the rightness or wrongness of an act. Rather, the individual is motivated toward serving him- or herself.

Stage 1: The punishment-obedience orientation. In this stage moral judgment is motivated by a desire to avoid punishment or possible unpleasant consequences. A person in this orientation obeys authority figures or those in power not because they are right in an abstract sense but because they have superior authority or power (physical or other power). Stage 1 morality justifies nearly any behavior as long as there is no threat of punishment.

Stage 2: The instrumental-relativist orientation. A person's primary motivation in this stage is the satisfaction of personal, social, or physical needs or interests. When the person interacts with others, his or her moral judgment is based on a trade-off model ("what's in it for me?"). He or she may sometimes think of other people's needs or interests, but only in a reciprocal sense: "If you help me, I will help you."

Level Two: The Conventional Level

At this level of moral judgment, an individual's moral reasoning has shifted from the consequences of behavior to the norms and expectations of the group (the family, friends, the society, or the nation).

Stage 3: The good boy/nice girl orientation. People in this stage believe that good behavior is whatever pleases other people. The Stage 3 morality is designed to maintain good relations with an immediate group of significant people (peers, teachers, bosses, family members, etc.). Being good means having good motives, showing concern about others, believing in the Golden Rule.

Stage 4: The law and order orientation. People in this stage think it right to uphold laws and maintain the social order. The reason for doing so is to keep the institution going as a whole and to avoid a breakdown in the system. They take the point of view of the system that defines values and rules. They consider individual relations in terms of place in the system.

Level Three: The Postconventional Level

At this highest level of moral reasoning, a person views morality in terms of individual rights and personal standards of behavior.

Stage 5: The social contract or legalistic orientation. People who reason in the orientation of this stage recognize that laws may be arbitrary, but they work within the system to change those laws rather than ignoring them or breaking them. They no longer see values and rules as absolutes; they assess morality in relative terms. The relative rules should usually be upheld, however, because they are the social contract.

Stage 6: The universal ethical principle orientation. People who reason in this final stage assume personal responsibility for their own actions. They follow self-chosen ethical principles which are universally applicable. When laws violate these principles, the Stage 6 people act in accordance with the principle. These people believe in the universal moral principle of justice: the equality of human rights and respect for the dignity of human beings. They believe that individual persons are ends in themselves and must be treated as such.

STUDY 1

MORAL JUDGMENT AND MORAL DEVELOPMENT

The purpose of this study of Chinese morality was to find (1) the common stages of moral judgment of the Chinese people; (2) the differences, if any, in moral judgment between the educated and the less educated Chinese; (3) the differences, if any, in moral judgment among upper, middle, and lower social classes in Chinese society; (4) the degree of inconsistency between moral judgment (cognition) and moral behavior (action); and (5) the relative influence of the family, school, and society at large on moral development of the individual.

The students in a Developmental Psychology class I taught at two universities in mainland China, one university in Hong Kong, and one university in Taiwan served as informants in the three Chinese societies. They were 106 juniors, seniors, and graduate students at the two mainland institutions, 77 graduate students at the Hong Kong university, and 64 graduate students at the Taiwan university.

The questions to be answered by the informants were: (1) What are the people's most common stages of moral judgment in mainland China (Hong Kong, or Taiwan)? Illustrate by real-life examples of what you have heard people talk and seen people do. (2) Are there any differences in moral judgment between the educated (those who have received higher education) and the less educated (those who have received no more than nine years of education)? (3) What are the differences, if any, in moral judgment among the upper (e.g., high-ranking government officials), middle (e.g., school teachers), and lower (e.g., laborers) social classes? (4) Are the above Chinese people's moral judgment in hypothetical situations (like Kohlberg's moral dilemmas) and their motives or reasons for their moral behaviors in real-life situations consistent? List the distance or degree of inconsistency , if any, in descending order between moral judgment (as expressed in hypothetical situations) and moral behavior (as reflected by the motives for their own actions in real-life situations) of the above Chinese people. (5) Which has the greatest influence on moral development of the Chinese people--family, school, or society at large?

The students as informants were divided into discussion groups with five or six members in each group. There were 18 groups at the two mainland universities, 15 groups at the Hong Kong university, and 12 groups at the Taiwan university. Each group discussed the above five questions for two hours and tried to reach a consensus on each question. Each group was required to submit a written report on the discussions. The contents of the 18 mainland reports, 15 Hong Kong reports, and 12 Taiwan reports were analyzed and the following results were yielded.

The most common stages

As regards our first question, while all the six stages were observed, some groups saw one stage as the most common and other groups observed two or three stages as equally common. As shown in Table 1, 13 (72.2%) out of the 18 groups of mainland informants perceived Stage 4 as the most common stage of moral judgment in mainland Chinese society, which was followed by Stage 3 and Stage 2 perceived by 6 (33.3%) and 3 (16.7%) of the mainland groups respectively as the most common stages. Most (12 or 80%) of the 15 Hong Kong groups, however, saw Stage 2 as the most commonly found, followed by Stage 3 and Stage 4 observed by 9 (60%) and 6 (40%) of the Hong Kong groups respectively as the most common stages. In Taiwan, both Stages 2 and 3/4 (a transition stage between Stages 3 and 4) were observed by 50% of the groups as the most common stages while Stages 3 and 4 by 16.7% of the groups as the most common stages. If we add all the groups of informants in the three Chinese societies, Stages 2 and 4 were equally common (46.7% of the 45 groups perceived these two stages as the most common ones). The real-life examples are presented in Table 2.

Table 1

Number and Percentage of Groups of Informants who Perceived the Most Common Stages of Moral Judgment in three Chinese Societies

	Mainland (n=18)		Hong Kong (n=15)		Taiwan (n=12)		Total (n=45)	
	No.	%	No.	%	No.	%	No.	%
2	3	16.7	12	80	6	50	21	46.7
3	6	33.3	9	60	2	16.7	17	37.8
3/4	0	0	0	0	6	50	6	13.3
4	13	72.2	6	40	2	16.7	21	46.7

Table 2

Real-Life Examples of Common Stages of Moral Judgment as Observed by Groups of Informants in Three Chinese Societies

Stage	Society	Behavior	Motive or Reason
2	Mainland	Satisfying own needs	"Most people are selfish."
		Exchanging favors	"If you are nice to me, I'll be nice to you."
	Hong Kong	Deliberating before acting	"See if the action will do me good."
		Exchanging gifts	Return favor for favor received
	Taiwan	Trading votes for money in general election	Meet the needs and interests of both candidates and voters
3	Mainland	Being reluctant to act differently from others	Avoid appearing strange or being frowned upon
		"Reducing a big problem to a small one and the small one to nothing."	Maintain interpersonal harmony
	Hong Kong	Being filial to parents and helpful to siblings	Maintain good family relations
		Queuing up for bus	Live up to what is expected by others
	Taiwan	For good or for evil, acting as the others do	Conform to the group norm
3/4	Taiwan	Being a good child, student, and citizen	Maintain interpersonal and social accord

Table 2 (Continued)
Real-Life Examples of Common Stages of Moral Judgment as Observed by
Groups of Informants in Three Chinese Societies

Stage	Society	Behavior	Motive or Reason
4	Mainland	Advocating capital punishment	Maintain law and order
		Abhorring corruption and robbery	Maintain law and order
	Hong Kong	Gambling in the legalized horse races rather than in the illegal casino	Obey the law
		Resisting socialism after 1997 Communist takeover	Maintain the present system
	Taiwan	Opposing independence from the mainland	Maintain the status quo
		Advocating gradual reform and opposing revolution	Avoid a breakdown in the system

Moral Judgment of the Educated and the Less Educated

To our second question, the groups in each society gave variant answers as follows.

Mainland:

1. There is not much difference between the educated (ED) and the less educated (LED) because both have been under the influence of the same cultural traditions and the same social environment.

2. The ED's modal (the most frequent) stage is 4 or 4/5 while the LED's modal stage is 3 or 2/3.

3. The ED move toward Stage 5 while the LED move toward Stage 4.

4. The ED are less influenced by traditional values and more modern in their thinking than the LED (e.g., more of the ED people believe to a greater extent in freedom, democracy, and equality than the LED).

***Hong Kong*:**

 1. The ED's modal stage is 3 or 4 while the LED's modal stage is 2 or 3.

 2. The ED are generally at Stage 3 but can go as high as Stage 6, while the LED are mostly at Stage 2 and can go no higher than Stage 4.

 3. The ED are higher in moral judgment but not in moral behavior.

 4. The ED's moral judgment is not necessarily higher than the LED's. Education is not the only condition that influences moral reasoning, the cultural values may affect moral judgment more profoundly than education. For example, the LED people of the older generation, with greater and deeper exposure to Confucian values than the ED people of the young generation who are exposed more to the profit-oriented commercial world, may be mostly at Stage 3 while the latter may be found most frequently at Stage 2.

***Taiwan*:**

 1. The ED's moral judgment should be higher than the LED's but not necessarily so.

 2. The ED's moral judgment is generally higher than the LED's.

 3. The ED's moral judgment can generally reach Stage 4 while the LED's can generally reach Stage 3.

 4. The modal stage of the ED is 3/4 while that of the LED is 2.

Comparison of the Three Social Classes

 To our third question, the answers also varied as follows.

***Mainland*:**

 1. The upper class (UC) may vary in moral judgment from Stage 2 to Stage 5. The middle class (MC) is mostly at Stage 4. The lower class (LC) is often at Stage 3 or 4.

 2. The better educated people of the three social classes are often higher in

moral judgment than the less educated.

3. Besides education, the moral atmosphere and economic development of the whole society are also important in their impact on moral development of people of all social classes.

Hong Kong:

1. The modal stage of moral judgment of the educated people in UC is 4, in MC is 3 or 4, in LC is 5 or 6 (few educated people are in LC, however).

2. The modal stage of moral judgment of the less educated people in UC is 2, in MC is 2 or 3, in LC is 1 or 2.

3. The modal moral judgment stages of the educated people of the three social classes are 5 (UC), 4 (MC), and 3 (LC), while those of the less educated are 4 (UC), 3 (MC), and 2 (LC).

4. In general, the LC's moral judgment is at Stage 2 or 3, the MC's is at Stage 3 or 4, and the UC's is at Stage 4 or 5.

Taiwan:

1. The modal moral judgment stage of the educated people in UC is 5 or 5/6, in MC is 4 or 4/5, and in LC is 3 or 3/4.

2. The modal moral judgment stage of the less educated people in UC is 4 or 3/4, in MC is 3 or 3/4, and in LC is 2 or 1/2.

Inconsistency between Moral Judgment and Moral Behavior

Most groups of informants observed that moral judgment in test situations (e.g., taking part in MJI or DIT) is generally made at a stage higher than the stage at which moral judgment is made on personal behavior in real-life situations. The moral judgment or reasoning is often higher stagewise when the situation or moral dilemma is hypothetical (like Kohlberg's hypothetical stories) or involves other people as actors than when the person making the judgment , especially in private, is the actor whose self-interest is involved. In other words, a person, especially of the educated upper class, usually reasons at a stage higher than the stage which he or she lives up to. The following were the answers to our fourth question. This question was designed to assess, though in a crude and indirect way, the degree of inconsistency between moral cognition and moral action (Blasi, 1980).

Mainland: UC > MC > LC or MC > UC > LC

The distance or degree of inconsistency between moral judgment (cognition) and moral behavior (action) of the upper class (UC) or middle class (MC) is larger than that of MC or UC, which, in turn, is larger than that of the lower class (LC). This is because the UC and MC people are generally better educated and more face-conscious or status-conscious than the LC people, so they talk at a higher stage of moral judgment than that they would actually think (or act) at or live up to.

Hong Kong: UC > MC > LC

The UC and MC people are generally better educated and more mature cognitively than the LC people. The former are, therefore, able to reason at a higher stage of moral judgment than the latter. To protect their personal image, the former, especially the UC people, often pretend to make a higher stage moral judgment in public but regress to a lower stage in private. On the other hand, the LC people are more consistent in their moral cognition and moral action, though both at relatively low stages.

The LC people are more straightforward, they act or live more often as they talk or make moral judgment, in public as well as in private, than the UC and MC people. They tend not to hide their real selves. In other words, Chinese in private have similar motives or reasons for their actions, regardless of their social class and educational level. In public, however, Chinese of higher social class and/or higher educational level tend to make moral judgment at a higher stage than their compatriots of lower social class and/or lower educational level.

Taiwan: UC > MC > LC

The interpretations were similar to those given above by the Hong Kong informants.

The Most Influential Factor on Moral Development

To our fifth question, the various responses are presented below. This is a broad question. We asked it because this is a question often talked about by Chinese in the three societies when they discuss influential factors of an individual's personality development, of which moral development is an integral part.

Mainland:

1. The greatest influence comes from family, mainly the parents. This is reflected by the adage, "Like parents, like children."

2. School influence is just as great as family influence on moral development.

3. Societal influence, including socioeconomic status (SES), is no less powerful than the influence of family and school.

4. Family is most influential before school age. School is most influential during school years. Society at large is most influential when a person is employed in the work world.

Hong Kong:

1. Each has its influence; but the greatest influence comes from the family, then the school. Society at large is not so influential as the family and the school.

2. For the educated people, the greatest influence comes from school. For the less educated people, the greatest influence comes from society at large. Family influence is profound but not as powerful as the influence of school and society for both educated and less educated people.

3. Societal influence, especially the influence of mass media and SES, is no

less profound and powerful than the influence of family and school. According to a recent survey, the average grade school pupil is exposed to TV three hours a day.

Taiwan:

1. The SES of the family exerts the greatest influence on a child's moral development because it affects child rearing practices and attitudes of the parents toward the child, especially during childhood. School influence, however, is central during adolescence.

2. Family, school, and society at large have equal influence on moral development, perhaps each exerting its influence during different periods of an individual's life. First comes the family, then the school, and finally the society at large.

3. The influence varies with an individual's social class and educational level. The educated UC and MC people are affected more by family and school than by society, the less educated UC and MC people more by family and society than by school. The LC people, mostly less educated, are also affected more by family and society than by school. In general, family has the most significant effect on moral development of most people in Chinese society.

Discussion

The present study used a qualitative method to investigate morality in three Chinese societies which have never been studied simultaneously this way before. It yielded findings some of which were new and others were either similar or different from the results of work by previous researchers. Instead of using Chinese students as subjects to study their morality, this study treated them as informants whose observations and perceptions of morality in the three Chinese societies provided data for a comparative analysis.

While all the six stages of moral development were observed as evidence of the cross-cultural universality of Kohlberg's theory, the modal (most common) stages of the three Chinese societies varied. The modal stages were Stage 4 for mainland China (ML), Stage 2 for Hong Kong (HK), and Stages 2 and 3/4 for Taiwan (TW). When taken as a whole, the three societies have two modal stages, namely, 2 and 4. This is understandable because Stage 2 may represent the moral judgment of the less educated Chinese whereas Stage 4 that of the educated Chinese. Most ML Chinese are less educated but their most frequent stage of moral judgment is Stage 4, which is similar to that found by Walker and Moran (1990) who used both hypothetical and real-life moral dilemmas for assessment.

TW has two modal stages (2 and 3/4)--Stage 2 probably represents the mode of the less educated while Stage 3/4 is the mode of the educated people, the latter being consistent with Lei's finding (Lei, 1980,1981; Lei & Cheng, 1984; cited in Snarey, 1985). The mode of HK is Stage 2, which, however, differs from Grimley's HK mode (Stage 4) (Grimley, 1973, 1974; cited in Snarey, 1985). Yet in Grimley's (1973, 1974) cross-cultural study of moral judgment, the HK sample was too small (n=12) to be representative.

That the modal stages of both HK and TW Chinese were lower than that of ML Chinese is probably because the mainlanders live in a collectivist society of socialism while their HK and TW counterparts are members of individualist societies of capitalism. This implies that education is not the only influential factor of moral development and the sociopolitical factor may be just as influential. Meanwhile, because the three societies share the same cultural traditions, they converge at Stage 3, the second most frequent stage found in each of them.

From the answers to our second question, it may be concluded that the modal moral judgment stages of the educated people in the three Chinese societies are 4 (ML), 3 (HK), and 3/4 (TW) and those of the less educated people are 3 (ML), 2

(HK), and 2 (TW). So in the answers to our first question, the modal stage of ML Chinese may actually refer to the educated people, that of HK Chinese to the less educated people, and those of TW to both the educated and less educated people, depending on what most of the informants (college and graduate students) had in mind in their relevant discussions.

In comparing the moral judgment of the three social classes, the best answers to our third question seem to be as follows: for the ML Chinese, the moral judgment of UC (upper class) varies from Stage 2 to Stage 5, that of MC (middle class) is often Stage 4, and that of LC (lower class) is usually Stage 3, regardless of educational level; the modal stages of the educated HK Chinese are 5 (UC), 4 (MC), 3 (LC) and those of the less educated HK Chinese are 4 (UC), 3 (MC), 2 (LC); and the modal stages of the educated TW Chinese are 5 (UC), 4 (MC), 3/4 (LC) and those of the less educated TW Chinese are 3/4 (UC), 3/4 (MC), 2 (LC). Our findings are consistent with those of Walker and Moran (1990) in that their moral leaders (equivalent to our UC people) and intellectuals (corresponding to our educated people) attained higher level of moral reasoning than their workers (equivalent to our LC people) and junior high school students (corresponding to our less educated people).

To our fourth question regarding the degree of inconsistency or discrepancy between moral judgment and moral behavior of the three social classes, the answer is UC > MC >LC in all the three Chinese societies. Because the UC and MC Chinese are generally better educated and more cognitively mature than the LC Chinese, the former often make moral judgment at a higher stage than the latter. The higher the social class to which the people belong, the more face-conscious or status-conscious they are. This is another reason why the people of the higher social class, especially the UC people, tend to make higher stage moral judgment than the people of the lower social class. But the higher the stage of moral judgment, the less able are the people to live up to it. So the degree of inconsistency between moral judgment and moral behavior is positively related to the people's social class: the higher the social class, the greater the inconsistency.

In the body of research reviewed by Blasi (1980), some findings suggest that the moral reasoning and moral behavior are unrelated while other studies demonstrate that they are statistically related. It may be said that the relations between cognition and action in the moral sphere are "less direct and more complex" than we expect (Blasi, 1980, p. 9) Perhaps the findings of the present study on the inconsistency between moral judgment and moral behavior can shed some light on the complex relations between the two aspects of moral functioning.

Rest (1979) also noted that the relation between verbally espoused moral statements and the way a person lives his life is an "exceedingly complex" issue (p. 169). He (Rest, 1979, p. 169) cited two conflicting ancient views on this matter. The Socratic view links ideology and behavior closely, but the New Testament views "knowledge of the good" as a very different matter from "choosing the good." Throughout the Gospels, it is a common observation that the spirit is willing but the flesh is weak, and that there are many who do not practice what they preach. This observation may explain, at least partially, why there exists a discrepancy between moral judgment and moral action, especially as the educated people of upper and middle classes are concerned.

Social influences on moral development include the influences of the family, school, and society at large. They primarily involve parents, teachers, peers, and life experiences of the individuals (Gibbs & Schnell, 1985; Leahy, 1981; Lonky, Kaus, & Roodin, 1984; Rest & Thoma, 1985; Saltzstein, 1976; Wilson, 1981). Yet what constitutes the greatest influence is, of course, a complicated question to answer.

Hence the responses of our informants to our fifth question were variant. The degree and depth of the influence probably vary with experiences of the individuals in the family, school, and society at large. Specifically, three factors determine the rate and direction of moral development: the discipline by parents and teachers; the moral atmosphere of the family, school, and society; and the role-taking opportunities as provided by socialization in the family, school, and other social settings (Kohlberg, 1976; Piaget, 1932; Saltzstein, 1976). No empirical evidence is available, however, as to which of the three factors in what specific setting is the most influential on an individual's moral development.

STUDY 2

INTERPERSONAL RELATIONSHIPS

Chinese are very concerned about interpersonal relationships. Traditionally, there have been five cardinal relationships: the ruler and the minister, the father and the son, the husband and the wife, the elder brother and the younger brother, and the friend and the friend. In Confucian teachings, the five relationships are established on the basis of mutual moral obligation (Chan, 1963). In modern China. these five relationships still exist in essence but are extended or modified to include other human relations. This chapter reports a study of interpersonal relationships found in contemporary China on the mainland.

Subjects were the same 120 interviewees (educated men and women of various ages) as described in Chapter One. Whenever appropriate, I asked my interviewees about their relationships with parents, siblings, teachers, schoolmates, friends, colleagues, spouses, children, students, and other people. I also asked them about the same kinds of relations experienced by the people they knew as they observed them.

The content of the interviewees' answers to my questions was analyzed and categorized. Ten interpersonal relationships were found. Some of them were more specific (e.g., parent-child relationship) and others were more general (e.g., intergenerational relationship). The details of the findings are presented below.

Parent-Child relationship

1. In most one-child families, parents prefer to have a son, especially in the countryside. If the parents are educated people, they will accept a daughter just as well. Many grandparents may not be as happy if the grandchild is a girl.

2. Parent-child relationship of different sexes is often more cordial than that of the same sex. For example, father-son relations are, in many cases, less warm than father-daughter relations.

3. In the family with more than one child, the first born, especially daughter, is the best assistant to parents, especially to mother. On the farm in the countryside, however, the eldest son is the best assistant to father.

4. If the parent is a school teacher, he or she is generally more gentle in dealing with students than with own children. This is probably because the parent is more self-controlled with students than with children.

5. While most parents protect and defend their children, some parents make derogatory remarks about their children (e.g., "She is stubborn." "He is stupid." "She doesn't study well.") before friends and relatives with a view to showing modesty or shaming the child. But most young parents of the one-child families treasure and pamper their only child.

6. When a parent dies and another parent remarries, parent-child relations often suffer because the child will feel alienated with the new step-parent.

7. The middle-aged and older generations observe filial duties more earnestly than the young generation. For example, they take better care of their aged parents.

8. Parents generally regard daughters as weaker sex needing more protection

than sons. They, therefore, place greater restrictions on social activities of the daughter.

9. Children often find mother more approachable than father. There is usually more communication between mother and child than between father and child.

10. Most sons seldom talk to father. If they do talk, the conversation seldom lasts more than ten minutes except on occasional matters of some importance.

11. During adolescence and early adulthood, the generation gap appears larger than in other periods of the child's life. There is, therefore, more disagreement between parents and child in attitudes and ways of doing things before the child is fully mature afterwards.

12. Children are trained to obey, and with or without intention, to depend on parents. Parents tend to dominate their children by making almost every decision for them in childhood, adolescence, and even in adulthood.

13. Most young adults in the city are still dependent on parents for living because of scanty income and housing shortage. Many of them live with and receive financial aid from parents. Their wedding expenses are often paid with money borrowed from parents' friends and relatives.

14. As a rule, when a son or daughter gets married, he or she wants no longer to live with parents unless the young couple are short of means to live by themselves or have to take care of parents.

15. Only occasionally in the countryside, we find two or more young couples (usually sons and their wives) in the same family living with parents. This is almost impossible in the city due to shortage of living space.

16. Shortage of housing or living space is a serious problem for the city young people but not for their country counterparts. Although most married young

people in the city would like to live without their parents, most of them are allotted no housing and cannot but live with their parents. The country people, however, usually have their houses either built by themselves or by their ancestors.

17. Although we often find a married son and his wife and only child live with his retired parents, the city parents are more or less depended on by their married son while the country parents are dependent on their married son for living. There are also some parents living with their married daughter and her husband and child (or children).

18. Retired intellectuals, workers, government and party cadres (officials) all have pension, an income usually larger in amount than that of their working children. They also have living quarters. They are, therefore, more inclined and able to take care of their grown-up children than the peasants who have no pension and, as a result, must be looked after by their adult children.

19. After marriage, the son's love of parents is inevitably distracted by his love of wife. In most cases, the married sons love their wives more than they love parents. The married daughter, however, is generally more attentive to parents than the married son.

20. Daughters-in-law today do not respect their parents-in-law as much as those of yesterday. On the other hand, parents nowadays are discreet in order not to offend their son's wife lest they may jeopardize their son's marriage.

21. Conflict between mother and son's wife is common. The son stands in between and finds it difficult to please both mother and wife. As the son's attention shifts from mother to wife, mother would rather have her married son live away but nearby. There is not, however, much conflict between father and daughter-in-law.

22. Most married children do not live with parents. They are, however, supposed to visit with parents once in a while usually during weekends or holidays,

and many of them do, usually bringing along some gifts for and staying to eat dinner with their parents.

Intergenerational Relationship

1. Deference for elders (parents, teachers, and other elder people) is a traditional Chinese virtue. This virtue used to be taught by parents but fewer and fewer parents are doing so today. This tradition is still observed but on the decline. It is better observed by the educated than the less educated, and by the older and middle-aged people than the young people.

2. It is still considered normal for the older people to criticize the young ones, but unusual or impolite for the latter to criticize the former.

3. The young people today are less polite and obedient to elders than the middle-aged and older people. For example, they often talk back to elders, while people seldom did so forty years ago.

4. There exist two types of intergenerational relationship: one is traditional, authoritarian and the other is modern, democratic. In the former, the elders act as authority figures and treat the young people as inferiors or subordinates. In such relations, there is neither mutual respect nor rational dialogue between generations. The elders, as a rule, demand absolute obedience of the young generation. In the modern, democratic type of intergenerational relationship, which is gradually becoming common, the elders act as equals or peers and treat the young people as friends. Generation gap is often large in the authoritarian intergenerational relations but small in the democratic relationship between generations.

5. The relationship between parents and child (son or daughter)-in-law is an important form of intergenerational relations. Conflict occurs more often between mother and daughter-in-law than between mother and son-in-law or between father and child (son or daughter)-in-law. The married child (son or daughter), depending

on his or her personality, may serve as a lubricant or an agitator in the relations between parent and child-in-law.

Teacher-Student Relationship

1. In general, students today are less respectful, polite, and obedient to teachers than they were before 1957 when a series of political campaigns started which lasted for about twenty years. The student-teacher relationship, however, has somewhat recovered since Chairman Mao died in 1976.

2. Teacher-student relationship in college and university is not as close as in senior high school. Yet high school teachers are more concerned about students' college entrance rate than any thing else. The teacher's status or reputation is a function of the number of his or her students passing the college entrance exam successfully.

3. To avoid conflict with students, the teacher usually entrusts disciplinary matters to the class cadres (student self-governing officers). This can also help the teacher get an objective view of the students and train the student cadres's leadership abilities.

4. From primary school to college, most teachers are only interested in the high-achieving students and ignore the average and under-achieving students or slow learners.

5. When economic conditions were worse before 1976 when Chairman Mao died, the only way for the underprivileged students to compete with peers was by means of academic achievement.

6. The class master or mistress has a closer relationship with students than other teachers because he or she is responsible for the success or failure of the class.

7. Some graduate classes at some universities are conducted in the house of the professor for the convenience of the teacher.

8. The college students today are younger and more numerous but less mature than those before 1949 when the Communists came in power. They are less polite and respectful to teachers, especially to the mediocre ones who don't have much "stuff" to offer. Over-achieving students are, however, more respectful to teachers than under-achieving students.

9. In order not to leave a bad impression and be disfavored, students are cautious when talking with teachers for fear of saying something wrong. They avoid the teacher for fear of exposing weaknesses. Occasionally, but not very often, however, some students, but not many, will make a home visit to their teacher to please and/or show respect for the teacher.

10. Occasionally, we find a college instructor really concerned about students' personal matters and voluntarily offering guidance. Students will go individually to see such a teacher in his or her house without having to make an appointment.

11. The reasons for the remoteness in teacher-student relations in college include: (1)teachers go home right after class, in many cases, to avoid wasting time on students; (2)there are more different classes taught by more different teachers in college than in elementary and secondary schools; (3)college students do not respect teachers as much as grade and high school students; (4)college students have more activities to attend to; (5)job opportunities are not determined by teachers; (6)there is less competition among college teachers for popularity on campus than in secondary schools, (7)college students are more independent than grade and high school students, (8)college teachers are uninterested in things concerning the students other than teaching the subject matter and covering ground.

12. There is more students' contact with teaching assistants than with teachers of higher rank in college. Teacher accessibility or frequency of contact with students is negatively related with the rank of the teacher.

Husband-Wife Relationship

1. In general, the relationship of husband and wife has been becoming increasingly equal. The young generation is more equal than the middle-aged generation which is in turn more equal than the older generation. One of the reasons for the increasing equality is that the number of people, especially men, receiving higher education has been increasing. Education improves people's cognition of the relationship between sexes in general and between spouses in particular. Another reason is that most women work, the husband and the wife are generally equal in socioeconomic status. Education and employment promote independence of women intellectually, economically, and socially.

2. In general, if both husband and wife are well-educated or have received higher education, the relationship is most equal. If both are uneducated, the relationship is most unequal. If the husband is well-educated and the wife is not, the relationship is more equal than that of both uneducated but less so than that of both well-educated. Few wives' education level is higher than that of the husband. The educated husband usually respects his wife more than the less educated husband.

3. The educated husband is more inclined than the less educated one to help his wife with housework. He is also more considerate and tolerant to wife than the less educated husband. A more important reason is that most young and middle-aged wives work and do not have the time to do housework well alone. So the husband has to share with wife the burden of housekeeping.

4. The educated husband and wife usually discuss important matters before making a decision and each has his or her own way or yields to each other on minor matters. The less educated husband, however, often dominates the family and seldom discusses with wife on any matter.

5. The husband-wife relations are generally good. The divorce rate is only

about 5%, much lower than that in Hong Kong and Taiwan. Divorce is considered shameful if not sinful. People, especially the educated, make every effort to avoid a divorce.

6. Divorce rate, though low, is on the increase under outside influence. The major causes of divorce are lack of harmony and extramarital affairs. The young people, susceptible to Western and other outside influences, are less inclined than the older and middle-aged people to regard divorce as a shame.

7. Relations are unstable for the young couples but stable for the older couples. In general, stability or harmony of marriage is a function of age of the couple.

8. Disagreement between husband and wife is unavoidable. Yet quarrels can be avoided if and when one spouse gets angry the other spouse stays quiet. With a greater sense of shame or love of face, the educated are more inclined to refrain from quarreling than the less educated.

9. In the city, both husbands and wives of the young and middle-aged generations are generally employed. This has a positive effect on women's rights and social status. In the rural areas where most people are less educated and work on farm, however, women's status is lower than their city sisters'.

10. Equality in husband-wife relations is a function of age (negatively related) and education (positively related). The young and educated couples are usually more equalitarian than the older and less educated couples.

11. Husband is still the head of a household. In general, the traditional labor division is still observed that the husband takes care of external affairs outside the house (e.g., dealing with outside people)while the wife looks after internal matters inside the house (e.g., child care and housekeeping). The division of labor, however, is not so clearcut as it used to be.

12. Many couples, especially wives, love their children more than spouses. This may or may not jeopardize the husband-wife relations, depending on the personality of the couple and how they both love their children.

13. Continuance of the family line is no longer an important reason for marriage. Instead, people marry for their own well-being rather than for their ancestors.

14. The traditional virtue of a widow to remain in widowhood for the rest of her life is no longer observed.

Heterosexual Relationship

1. Men and women are becoming increasingly equal. The educated men generally treat women more equally than the less educated men. Regardless of educational level, more women than before are seen to be more assertive than men. Docile and submissive women are becoming rare.

2. Affected by sex-conscious traditions, heterosexual friendship between students has been often jeered at in primary school, prohibited in secondary school, and discouraged in college. An important reason is that it will distract one from studying. Such traditions, however, have been somewhat loosened in recent years.

3. Several years ago, dating was uncommon in school and college, although more common than before. Even in college, only two or three out of ten students had ever dated, often in junior and senior years. Heterosexual contact, if any, normally occurred in groups for academic or extracurricular purposes. Students were not supposed, though no longer prohibited, to have friends of the opposite sex for fear of hindering academic achievement.

4. A few years ago, people would gossip if a boy and a girl in school or college were seen being together too often. The boy and the girl would be frowned upon if they left the impression of being too intimate. Chinese on the mainland were

more conservative than their counterparts in Hong Kong and Taiwan regarding heterosexual relations.

5. Not long ago, most high school and college students were naturally interested in the opposite sex but would not admit it. Many would like to have friends of the opposite sex but were fearful of violating the group norm. Some were hesitant to approach the opposite sex because of shyness or lack of confidence.

6. The scene has changed a great deal since around 1987, especially on college campus. Dating is now common in college, although less than two out of ten couples dated eventually get married. The change is mainly due to outside influences following the open-door policy.

7. Outside school and college, heterosexual relations are more open and free, particularly in the cities and among the new social class of well-to-do merchants. Premarital sex is becoming more common. Extramarital sex, nevertheless, is still strongly disdained by many people.

8. Premarital sex with a woman often entails the obligation to marry her. The man involved in the affair will be strongly condemned if he refuses to fulfill such an obligation.

9. Friendship between sexes is often associated with marriage; many people do not think it make sense to have friends of the opposite sex without anticipating marriage. It happens quite often that a married couple are not assigned jobs in the same city or town. That is one reason why quite a few college students hesitate to have friends of the opposite sex for fear of having to work in different places after graduation.

10. As a rule, a man takes the initiative to date a girl. Girls are not supposed to take the initiative in dating.

11. Girls normally expect to find mates who are stronger or superior in

training or talent. They also hope to share common interests with mates. Although many women would not mind having a mate weaker or inferior in training or talent so long as they can get along well, they are worried that such a man would avoid them for fear of being unable to handle them due to their superiority.

12. A traditional notion is that in mating the man should be superior or at least equal to the woman in some way (usually in training or socioeconomic status). So a man is normally unwilling to date or marry a woman superior to him in education or socioeconomic status.

13. It is regarded as immoral or irresponsible for a man to change dates frequently. For example, a man is not supposed to date several girls in a short period of time (e.g., in a week or two) or quit a girl he has dated many times (e.g., ten or more times). A person is. therefore, rather careful about deciding to make the first move--to date or accept a date for the first time.

14. Parents often guard their children against violating the societal norm. For example, no premarital sex is allowed. Doors and windows must be kept open when a boy and a girl are together alone in the house so that people won't talk. Parents realize that young people nowadays are less fearful than before to do what they want.

Sibling Relationship

1. Sibling relationship is generally good. Elder siblings are supposed to yield to and take good care of younger siblings, and younger siblings are expected to respect elder ones.

2. When elder siblings are working and younger ones are in school or college, the former often give some spending money to the latter.

3. In general, younger siblings are helped and influenced to a greater extent by the elder ones than vise versa. Quite often, the elder siblings act as parent surrogates to guide and look after the younger ones.

4. Jealousy and friction are sometimes observed among siblings as among peers and colleagues. Harmony and mutual dependence are emphasized in sibling relationship as in other interpersonal relationships. Siblings have a moral responsibility to love and help each other.

5. In many cases, relations are better between siblings of different sexes than between siblings of the same sex, i.e., better between sister and brother than between brothers and between sisters.

Relationship between Friends

1. Friendship depends on need (e.g., emotional need, social need, sexual need) and reciprocity (mutual need and mutual dependence or reciprocal interdependence).

2. Friendship developed in schools and colleges generally lasts longer than that developed in the work world. A person normally has one or several good friends made in school, usually during adolescence.

3. Similarity is an important factor in the development of friendship. Friends are, as a rule, similar in some respect (e.g., in age, interest, residence, status, or educational level).

4. Friendship ties are stronger among the less educated than the well educated people because the latter are too proud of themselves to show due respect for their peers. Some uneducated or less educated men tend to form cliques or gangs, members of which are sometimes irrationally loyal to each other even at the risk of life.

5. Friendship ties are also stronger in the young and older generations than in the middle-aged generation because most middle-aged people experienced the Cultural Revolution which produced mistrust among people that is not entirely extinguished yet. Self-disclosure is uncommon, even between friends, due to mutual

mistrust caused by political factors.

6. Mutual help among friends is common in the form of financial assistance or service. Quite often, people lend money to friends in need without interest charge or do something for friends without pay. This kind of free help is, however, on the decline as a result of capitalist influence.

Relationship between Students

1. Friendship between students of the same sex in schools and colleges generally exists on the basis of needs, interests, chance of contact, and matching of personality.

2. Relationship between students of the same sex is not as cordial as it was before the Cultural Revolution. Association among students from the same native place is more frequent than that among students from different localities.

3. Students of the same sex may be jealous of higher achievers and attribute peers' achievement to teachers' favoritism or peers' ingratiation (e.g., social calls on teachers, presenting gifts to teachers, seeking connections with teachers, for instance, by being from the same birth place).

4. Relations with classmates are generally better than with schoolmates from different classes.

5. Bullying lower-class students sometimes happens in elementary and secondary schools but seldom occurs in colleges and universities.

6. Girls are more jealous and suspicious than boys. So boys get along better in school and college. Girls experience greater but less overt interpersonal friction in college than in grade and high schools.

7. Since 1977 when the college entrance exam was restored after Chairman Mao's death, over-competition in academic achievement has been detrimental to peer relations in grade and high schools. In colleges and universities, competition for

admission to the graduate school is keen among upper-class students.

8. Over-achievers are often unwilling to help under-achievers for fear that the latter may surpass them in test performance. Rivals in academic competition, like those in other competitions in and out of school, are modest in the presence of their opponents but boastful in the absence of them.

9. Although relations among students are generally superficial, the real friendship that does develop in schools lasts longer than the friendship developed out of school.

10. Friendship developed in secondary schools or during adolescence is often more intimate and lasts longer than friendship developed latter.

Relationship between Colleagues

1. It is said that people fight people in 1960s, hate people in 1970s, and guard against people in 1980s. It is hoped that people will trust each other in 1990s. The best policy today is to work hard quietly and not to poke one's nose into another's affairs.

2. Covert conflict occurs between generations. In institutions of higher learning, for example, the young colleagues (assistants and lecturers) sometimes complain that the senior colleagues (associate and full professors) get higher pay but have lighter teaching load and look down on them.

3. Full and associate professors usually have assistants assigned to them. Generational conflict occurs if the assistant is not cooperative and willing to learn or does not respect his or her mentor. Most assistants respect only mentors strong in some specialty.

4. Successful colleagues (superior in ability, rank or scholarship) are often the targets of jealousy while inferior colleagues are the objects of disparagement.

5. The popularity of an educated person is determined not only by his or her

professional accomplishment but also by his or her way of dealing with colleagues.

6. People find it harder to get along with superiors than with peers and subordinates. So people have less contact with superiors or bosses. The frequency of social contact is negatively related with power distance between people.

7. Colleague relations were better before the Cultural Revolutions. Colleagues have been less sincere and trustful since then.

8. Older colleagues are often fastidious of the young ones. They can hardly tolerate any nonconformity in the young colleagues.

9. Quite a few colleagues tend to criticize others behind their back. Cliques are often found in an organization (e.g., in a college department).

10. Professional competition and interpersonal conflict in mainland China seem to be less severe than in Taiwan and Hong Kong because promotion is based more on seniority than on merit. People can just wait for his or her turn to be promoted. Besides, promotion is not necessarily accompanied by salary or wage increment.

11. Cooperation is a function of advantage to be gained. If the job is beneficial, colleagues will be cooperative, otherwise there will be sloth and deferment in the job to be done.

12. While some colleagues are really friendly and helpful and many are superficially so, friction, jealousy, and rivalry are common between colleagues.

Boss-Subordinate Relationship

1. `Since the Cultural Revolution the relationship between the boss and the subordinates has become more egalitarian than before. Vertical contact is, however, much less than horizontal interaction because people do not feel at ease with authority figures as with peers and inferiors. People are very cautious in dealing with their boss for fear of leaving a bad impression.

2. Although the government encourages people to offer suggestions or make recommendations to the boss for common good, very few people dare to express their opinions to the boss for fear of offending him or her.

3. There are more young people who are daring to speak out to their boss than the older and middle-aged colleagues. Most young people as well as older and middle-aged colleagues, however, are careful not to displease their boss.

4. Occasionally, we find an able, efficient, and fearless young man who does his job without always asking for the permission of his boss before or reporting to his boss after the job is done. He does what he thinks is right at the right moment.

5. It sometimes happens that a boss places his confidants or obedient friends and relatives in the important positions under him so as to facilitate his control of the unit or organization he heads.

Discussion

Chinese culture assumes and values reciprocal interdependence among individuals (Markus & Kitayama, 1991). Good human relations has long been a central aim of Chinese education. According to the Chinese classics *Four Books*, the ancient emperor Shun, who was idealized by Confucius, appointed a minister of education to teach people human relations with special emphasis on five cardinal relations: the relationship between ruler and minister, father and son, husband and wife, elder brother and younger brother, and that between friends (Chan, 1963). As a result, the Chinese children have through the centuries been taught to behave as good boys and nice girls in harmonious relations with an immediate group of significant people. Even today, Chinese children are taught by their parents and teachers to be *guai* (good or nice) in Hong Kong and Taiwan as well as in mainland China. This corresponds exactly, in Kohlbergian terms, to Stage 3 (the good boy/nice girl orientation) of moral development, which is a frequent stage of moral judgment shared by the three Chinese societies as found in Study 1.

The ten relationships found in this study and the aforementioned five cardinal relations are primarily personal or private relationships with somebody in the in-group or an immediate group of significant people. Of the five cardinal relationships three exist between family members (those between father and son, husband and wife, elder and younger brothers). It is evident that the Chinese have long been socialized to value in-group, private or personal relations (those between individuals close to each other, especially between family members) rather than out-group or public relations (those between individuals or groups unknown to or unfamiliar with each other). Loyalty and filial piety have thus become the two central values or virtues embodied in the five principal relations. The Walker and Moran's (1991) study of moral reasoning in Communist China also revealed that about 40% of the recent real-life moral dilemmas (20 out of 52) recalled by the Chinese subjects from their own experiences involved some form of personal relationships with others (spouse, friend, parent, neighbor, colleague, teacher). These private or personal relationships can be made public or impersonal, however, through *jen* (pronounced *zun* in Chinese). *Jen* is the cornerstone of Confucianism (Chan, 1963; Mei, 1967). It means universal love for everybody as in Mencius' saying, "The man of *jen* loves others." This Confucian ideal of human relations is, however, not substantially actualized in daily life of the Chinese people since egocentrism, disrespect, jealousy, mistrust, and discrimination are common in interpersonal relationships as illustrated in the preceding section.

While the Chinese people's moral judgment is at Kohlberg's Stage 3 with an emphasis on maintaining good relations with significant others, their moral behavior or action, in general, stays at Kohlberg's Stage 2 with an instrumental-relativist orientation. This is most evidently manifested in the attachment between people, such as between friends, between relatives, and between student and teacher. Attachment between people is a function of personal needs or interests. When the need or interest diminishes, so does the attachment. Almost all interpersonal relationships are contingent upon personal needs. The need may be obligatory, financial, professional, political, religious, intellectual, social, emotional, or sexual. Interpersonal relationships are often utilized or even manipulated to serve the needs or interests of the individuals involved.

A 1990 survey on sexual relations found a noteworthy change in "sex culture" in mainland China (Shanghai Sex Sociology Study Center, 1992). For instance, 78% of college students would approve premarital sex and 58% of them could tolerate extramarital sex. This is a far cry from the attitudes held by the Chinese college students a few years earlier. This attitude change reflects a shift in their moral judgment about heterosexual relationship from Stage 3 or 4 to Stage 2 wherein the satisfaction of personal needs (sexual and related needs in this case) takes precedence of good interpersonal relations (Stage 3 morality) or law and order (Stage 4 morality). This Stage 2 moral judgment corresponds to the moral action at the same stage of an increasing number of Chinese people who actually engage in premarital and/or extramarital sex.

A relevant term often heard in Chinese is *guanshi* (connection or relationship). People try to find or build up *guanshi* for any goal they wish to attain. In a *guanshi* usually two parties are involved. According to Hwang's model of resource distribution (Bond & Hwang, 1986; Hwang, 1987), the two parties to a dyadic interaction in any *guanshi* or interpersonal relationship are conceptualized as petitioner and resource allocator. Either party may control some kind of resource desired by the other party, and therefore may play the role of petitioner in one instance and resource allocator in another. The resources for interpersonal exchange may include affection, face, money, power, goods, sex, information, service, status, or anything that may be desired by one party and allocated by the other party. If no need or desire for any resource exists in one party or no resource can be allocated by the other party, the bond between the two parties usually loosens and the dyadic interaction often comes to a standstill.

In a similar vein, Markus and Kitayama (1991) suggest that the Chinese construal of the self is interdependent. The reciprocal interdependence with others is the sign of the interdependent self. In most cases, the responsive and cooperative actions of the Chinese are exercised only when there is a reasonable assurance of others' commitment to continue to engage in reciprocal interaction and mutual support. Although some Chinese will do something in favor of others (e.g., render a service, give a donation, send a gift, make a visit, or invite to a dinner) merely out of altruism, sympathy, care, love, respect, empathic concern, or social responsibility, most Chinese on most occasions will not do so without expecting immediate advantage or future payoff. Many will do so for the purpose of building up some *guanshi* with somebody to attain a certain goal or meet a certain need.

The interpersonal relationships of a narcissistic person are characterized by exploitativeness (Raskin & Terry, 1988; Raskin & Shaw, 1988). The Chinese people are narcissistic. Their reliance on *guanshi* or personal connection with others in interpersonal relationships for goal attainment or need satisfaction, a Stage 2 morality with an instrumental-relativist orientation, is probably an outcome of *rule of man* rather than rule of law in traditional China. It is a particularistic morality rather than a universalistic ethic (King, 1991). It is deplored by modern Chinese, especially the intellectuals (Chu & Ju, 1990; King, 1991). It seems that only when rule of law becomes a firmly established practice in Chinese society, will the morality in daily life of the masses be elevated to Kohlberg's Stage 4 with a law and order orientation.

There may be cultural variation in the definition of moral maturity (Dien, 1982; Ma, 1988a), such as that defined by the postconventional level of Kohlberg's theory. Kohlberg's first three or four stages are quite applicable to Chinese culture, but his Stage 5 and 6, as shown in Study 1 above, do not apply equally well.

STUDY 3
SUPPORTIVE RELATIONSHIPS

Some researchers (e.g., Schaefer, Coyne, & Lazarus, 1982) have assumed that there are several types of social support, such as emotional support (understanding) and informational support (advice), and have devised measures that include subscales for the various types of support. Other researchers (e.g., Procidano & Heller, 1983), however, have devised unidimensional measures. Sternberg and Grajek (1984) factor analyzed adults' responses to several measures in close relationships. Their analyses yielded a large general factor which they labeled Interpersonal Communication, Sharing, and Support. Argyle and Furnham (1983) studied sources of satisfaction and conflict in nine relationships (spouse, friend, sibling, parent, neighbor, etc.). They found three factors (Instrumental Reward, Emotional Support, and Shared Interests) for sources of satisfaction and two factors (Emotional Conflict and Criticism) for sources of conflict.

Human relationships often function as social support for children and adults faced with stressful life events. The social supports available to children and adolescents, however, have been investigated less often than those available to adults (Berndt & Perry, 1986). The present study was designed to examine Chinese adults's remembrance of the availability of supportive relationships during adolescence when they were faced with stressful events. In a questionnaire (MTPI), 2640 adults sampled from four Chinese populations (mainland China, Taiwan, Hong Kong, and the United States) were asked whom they usually discussed with during adolescent years (age 12-19) when they had personal problems or worries. The purpose was to detect what interpersonal relationships provided the Chinese subjects as adolescents with the social support they needed.

As described in Chapter One, the subjects were 2640 educated adults sampled from four Chinese populations: mainland China (662 men and 263 women), Taiwan (398 men and 253 women), Hong Kong (442 men and 345 women), and the United States (178 men and 99 women). Some subjects were not included in the analysis because of missing data on the relevant items.

In Part I of the questionnaire MTPI (see Chapter One), there is a question asking the subject whom he/she usually discussed with during adolescence (age 12-19) when confronted with personal problems or worries: nobody, father, mother, elder brother, elder sister, teacher, schoolmate, friend, or other people. The respondent has to recall and choose from the nine categories of people. He/she has to specify if the last category (other people) is chosen.

The analysis of the responses to the MTPI question was first performed by dividing the subjects in terms of sex and age (30 and below vs. 31 and above) into 16 groups (four groups in each of the four samples). As no significant difference was found between the age groups in response, so we divided the subjects by sex and sample into 8 groups and computed the frequency of their responses as presented in Table 1. Because the frequency for the category "other people" was negligible, it was omitted from the table.

Table 1

People Talked to When Faced with Personal Problems during Adolescence as Recalled by Four Samples of Chinese

Relationship/ People talked to		Mainland		Taiwan		Hong Kong		United States		Total	
		M	F	M	F	M	F	M	F	M	F
0/Nobody	n	169	57	74	45	154	72	42	15	439	186
	%	26.7	23.8	20	19	38	23.9	26.3	19.7	28	22.2
	Rank	1	1	3	2	1	2	1	3	1	2
1/Father	n	75	19	40	21	16	10	17	3	148	53
	%	11.8	7.9	10.8	8.9	4	3.3	10.6	3.9	9.4	6.2
	Rank	5	5	4	5	6	6	5	6	5	6
2/Mother	n	85	54	82	45	39	33	27	14	233	146
	%	13.4	22.6	22.1	19	9.6	11	16.9	18.4	14.8	17.1
	Rank	4	2	2	2	4	3	3	4	3	3
3/Elder brother	n	24	5	19	8	18	8	6	2	67	23
	%	3.8	2.1	5.1	3.4	4.4	2.7	3.8	2.6	4.3	2.7
	Rank	7	8	5	6	5	7	8	7	6	7
4/Elder sister	n	26	14	16	25	9	28	8	6	59	73
	%	4.1	5.9	4.3	10.5	2.2	9.3	3.8	7.9	3.8	8.6
	Rank	6	6	6	3	7	5	6	5	7	5

Table 1 (Continued)
People Talked to When Faced with Personal Problems during Adolescence as Recalled by Four Samples of Chinese

Relationship/People talked to		Mainland		Taiwan		Hong Kong		United States		Total	
		M	F	M	F	M	F	M	F	M	F
5/Teacher	n	26	6	7	3	5	3	7	1	45	13
	%	4.1	2.5	1.9	1.3	1.2	1	4.4	1.3	2.9	1.5
	Rank	6	7	7	7	8	8	7	8	8	8
6/School-mate	n	142	49	93	68	111	115	28	19	374	251
	%	22.4	20.5	25.1	28.7	27.4	38.2	17.5	25	23.8	29.4
	Rank	2	3	1	1	2	1	2	1	2	1
7/Friend	n	87	35	40	22	53	32	25	16	205	105
	%	13.7	14.6	10.8	9.3	13.1	10.6	15.6	21.1	13	12.3
	Rank	3	4	4	4	3	4	4	2	4	4
Total	n	634	239	371	237	405	301	160	76	1570	853

As Table 1 shows, the rank order of each relationship is similar among the eight groups. A few differences, however, between sexes, between relationships, and even between samples or populations, are noticeable. On the average, more men (28%) than women (22.2%) during adolescence talked to nobody when faced with personal problems or worries. Schoolmates (usually classmates, including friends in school) ranks first for women (29.4%) and second for men (23.8%) in mean frequency as persons talked to in case of troubles. If we combine the two relationships schoolmate and friend (primarily friend outside school), then peer (presumably of the same sex, encompassing both schoolmate and friend) becomes by far the most frequent relationship providing social support for both men (36.8%) and women (41.7%) as adolescents.

Next to peer comes mother as the most frequent supportive relationship, ranking the third for both sexes. Teacher is the least frequent supportive relationship, ranking the last (8th) for both sexes. Though infrequently, more men than women as adolescents talked to father (9.4% vs. 6.2%),and elder brother (4.3% vs. 2.7%) while more women than men during adolescence talked to elder sister (8.6% vs. 3.8%). On the other hand, more women than men during adolescence talked to mother (17.1% vs. 14.8%) and schoolmate (29.4% vs. 23.8%) while about the same percentage of men (13%) and women (12.3%) during adolescence talked to friend.

There were several findings about the difference among the four populations. One of them reveals that Hong Kong is a peculiar Chinese society. Some of its peculiarities are (in comparison with other three Chinese populations): (1)More Hong Kong men (38%) during adolescence do not seek social support from other people. (2)Fewer men (13.6%) and women (14.3%) during adolescence seek support from parents (father and mother combined). (3)More men (40.5%) and women (48.8%) as adolescents communicate with peers at times of stress.

Another important difference among populations concerns Taiwan. As Table 1 shows, Taiwan is the lowest in percentage of men (20%) and women (19%) as adolescents who do not talk to anybody about their problems but the highest in percentage of men who turn to parents (32.9% for father and mother combined) for support. The second highest percentage of subjects during adolescence seeking support from parents is found in mainland Chinese women (30.5% for father and mother combined). The two highest groups in percentage who communicate with peers (schoolmate plus friend) are women in Hong Kong (48.8%) and the United States (45.1%).

In other relationships, the groups or populations are not very different; some are very similar, such as mainland (26.7%) and the United States (26.3%) men, Taiwan (19%) and the United States (19.7%) women, mainland (23.8%) and Hong Kong (23.9%) women, all in Relationship 0 (nobody); and mainland (11.8%), Taiwan (10.8%), and the United States (10.6%) men in Relationship 1 (father). The implications or meanings of all the important differences and similarities will be discussed in the following section.

Discussion

One of the findings of the present study was that more Chinese adolescents turn to peers than to other people for social support. This finding is consistent with the common observation that "peer interaction seems to hit a peak of importance" during adolescence (Ingersoll, 1989, p.25). As adolescents spend about half of their waking time with peers in and out of school (Larson, 1979, 1983), it is natural that they often turn to peers at times of stress. The finding may also be accounted for by the fact that adolescents gain more satisfaction (e.g., emotional support) and suffer less conflict (e.g., criticism) (Argyle & Furnham, 1983) from peers than from other people.

Since peers in the case of the present study were primarily friends in and out of school, the aforementioned finding reflects intimate self-disclosure as a critical feature of friendship (Berndt, 1982). Disclosing intimate thoughts and feelings to another person is also viewed as a defining characteristic of an emotionally supportive relationship (Kessler, Price, & Wortman, 1985). One implication of the finding for Chinese morality is that adolescents' moral judgment and moral behavior are influenced by peers, especially friends, to a greater extent than by other people through frequent interaction and role taking.

In family relationships, more Chinese adolescents, as expected, seek emotional or social support from mother than from father and siblings. Somewhat unexpectedly, however, more adolescent sons than daughters come to father for support and vice versa to mother. This finding is inconsistent with the psychoanalytic theory of Oedipus and Electra complex. It is understandable that more Chinese men and women as adolescents seek social support from siblings of the same sex than from those of the opposite sex.

Considering the time (about one quarter of waking hours) spent in school (Larson, 1979) and even more time (over 40 hours a week in Taiwan's secondary schools) spent in Chinese schools, it was unexpected that less than 3% of Chinese men or women as adolescents talked to their teachers about their personal problems or worries. One of the reasons may be that most Chinese teachers look lofty, authoritarian, and awe-inspiring, and thus keep the students away from them.

The finding that a large percentage of Chinese adolescents prefer to keep their stressful thoughts and feelings to themselves is probably a reflection of introversion, a salient personality trait of the Chinese people, especially men. In all, more men (28%) than women (22.2%) talk to nobody (Relationship 0)at times of stress. This finding also indicates relative lack of interpersonal communication in Chinese society, particularly between people differing in age, sex, status, authority, and/or power. Its implication for morality is negative because insufficient communication between people leads to shortage of role-taking opportunities needed for moral development (Kohlberg, 1976). Because "role taking goes on in all social interaction and communication situations," (Kohlberg, 1976, p. 49) to shut oneself off from social interaction and interpersonal communication will certainly impede one's moral development.

The peculiar findings about Hong Kong imply that Hong Kong Chinese, especially men, are more independent than Chinese in other three societies. They are more independent because they depend less on parents for support in case of stress. They would rather remain silent or go to peers than turn to parents. This is partially due to their parents' less availability because most of their parents immigrated to Hong Kong as refugees from the mainland around 1949 and had to work hard for living during those difficult years (roughly from 1949 to 1970). The rule of law by the British government in this colony may have also contributed to the independency training of Hong Kong Chinese, so they are less dependent on the connections or relationships with other people than their compatriots on the mainland and Taiwan where rule of man often overrides rule of law.

Our United States sample may be too small to be representative of the Chinese population in American society. The sample is more like our Taiwan or mainland sample than our Hong Kong sample because the sample comprises subjects who came to the United States for further education as adults, mostly from Taiwan. More like the mainland and the United States sample than the Hong Kong sample, our Taiwan sample seems to be quite representative of Taiwan Chinese who have been more deeply influenced by traditions of old China where parent-child ties were extremely strong. So they, especially men, are more attached to and more dependent on their parents as reflected by the sample's lowest percentage in Relationship 0 (nobody) for both men (20%) and women (19%) and by the male group's highest percentage (32.9%) in Relationship 1 (father 10.8%) and 2 (mother 22.1%) combined.

Next to Taiwan male group, mainland women as adolescents are also more attached to and more dependent on their parents, especially mother, than other groups as indicated by their combined percentage (30.5%) for Relationship 1 (7.9%) and 2 (22.6%). As indicated by their combined percentage for Relationship 6 and 7, Hong Kong (48.8%) and the United States (46.1%) women have higher frequency of peer interaction than other six groups in the four samples. This may reflect their relative extraversion as a personality trait. The implications of these findings for moral development may be that Taiwan men and mainland women tend to be influenced by their parents and peers to a similar extent during adolescence while all other groups of Chinese men and women may be influenced in their moral development by their peers to a greater degree than by other people, at least during adolescent years.

✦ ✦ ✦

CHAPTER EIGHT

CONCLUSIONS

To begin with, a word about research methods is in order. As mentioned in Chapter 1, the 21 studies reported in this book constituted the research project I launched more than ten years ago in Hong Kong. It is the first project on the Chinese people in four populations--- mainland China (ML), Taiwan (TW), Hong Kong (HK), and the United States (US). An adequate study of personality in the context of culture requires an approach that is both nomothetic (involving a large sample) and idiographic (involving individual cases) (Westen, 1985). There is a need to use multiple methods. Campbell (1986) suggested that a multimethod approach is essential because traditional positivism often leads to dead ends. The methods used in the present project included questionnaire survey, case study, biographical interview, and participant/naturalistic observation. The data collected by one method complemented those obtained by other methods. Prior work on Chinese personality usually used questionnaires with high school or college students as subjects (Yang, 1986, 1996). The present project employed a multimethod approach that is both nomothetic and idiographic with educated adults as subjects mostly 20 to 65 years old. Data on less educated Chinese were derived from the educated subjects' reports about the people they contacted. My daily observation in naturalistic settings also involved people in almost every walk of life.

With the research methods used in mind, a summary of the major findings of the studies reported in Chapter 2 through Chapter 7 will be provided and the implications of the findings will be discussed in this final chapter.

MAJOR FINDINGS

Parenting Patterns and the Child's Personality

In Chapter 2 the relationship of parenting patterns to the child's personality development was fully explored. The emphasis was on the effect of parental behavior or child-rearing practices on the child rather than the reciprocal influence in parent-child interaction because the unidirectional model (the parent affects the child) is more applicable to the parent-directed Chinese families than the bidirectional perspective (parent and child influence each other). Three studies were reported in Chapter 2. Study 1 confirmed the unidirectional model with data provided by 159 educated men and women as informants in mainland China. In Study 2 data collected from 109 educated men and women as interviewees were used to define the two most familiar terms characterizing parental behavior or attitudes in Chinese society---*yan* and *chi*. *Yan* refers to strict, controlling, awe-inspiring, punitive, and authoritarian. *Chi* refers to tender, warm, approachable, lenient, and permissive. Rather than the behavior of the father or mother as the single socializer in most prior studies, seven *joint* (combined) parenting patterns or types of socialization by *both* parents were identified: father *yan* and mother *chi* (FYMC), father *chi* and mother *yan* (FCMY), both parents *yan* (FYMY), and both parents *chi* (FCMC), both parents just right (FRMR), father as principal socializer (FAPS), and mother as principal socializer (MAPS). Cases were presented to illustrate the child's personality under possible impact of each of the seven socialization types or parenting patterns.

Study 3 used data derived from a questionnaire (MTPI) administered to 2640 educated Chinese in mainland China (ML), Taiwan (TW), Hong Kong (HK), and the

United States (US). The purpose of the study was to explore further the impact of *yan* and *chi* of both parents in the four joint or combined parenting patterns---FYMC, FCMY, FYMY, and FCMC. It was found that *yan* is correlated with parental control or discipline, exercise of authority, and anger or bad temper and that *chi* is associated with parental love, care, contacting or communicating with the child, and granting the child autonomy or independence. The questionnaire survey revealed that in Chinese families FYMC is the most prevailing pattern of joint parenting (49% for sons and 32% for daughters), FCMY (14% for sons and 22% for daughters) is not as common as FCMC (25% for sons and 33% for daughters), and FYMY (12% for sons and 13% for daughters) is the least common pattern. Relevant variables (the child's age, sex, birth order, number of siblings, personality traits, and childhood life settings) as related to the four joint parenting patterns were also examined. An important trend was that the number of the traditional FYMC families is decreasing whereas that of the FCMC families is on the increase in both ML and TW. This trend reflects increasing tenderness and permissiveness of the parents, especially the father, toward children, especially daughters, in the two major Chinese societies. As Study 3 suggested, TW and ML subjects are more similar to each other than to HK subjects in their perceptions of parenting, and TW and ML parents treat sons and daughters more differently or less equally than HK parents.

As the ML parents are allowed to have only one child and most TW parents do not want more than two children, the resultant permissiveness may lead to extreme FCMC (overpermissive or indulgent parenting) rather than FRMR (authoritative parenting). Preference for the son (a Chinese tradition) and some fathers' favoritism toward the daughter may result in either overpermissive or authoritarian parenting toward either the son or daughter, which is detrimental to personality development of children of both sexes. Meanwhile, increasing divorce rate has made many children parentless (or living with a single parent, usually the mother) or without proper parenting, which is extremely pernicious to the child's development.

The three studies in Chapter 2 demonstrated that the right kind and degree of *yan* and *chi* are most salutary to the healthy personality development of all children. The FYMC pattern is not too bad if the father refrains from using too much power assertion or too severe physical punishment. In general, FCMY is better than FYMC in producing a healthy personality of the child. Proper (but not extreme) FCMC or FRMR is probably the most desirable parenting pattern for the child's optimal personality development.

Family Harmony, Education, and Personality

Study 1 in Chapter 3 investigated a rarely studied but very important variable---family harmony---for it is closely related to both parenting and the child's personality. This study used the same instrument (MTPI) and the same subjects (2640 men and women of various ages in four Chinese populations) as in some other studies reported in this book. It was found that parental anger and moralization are negatively related to family harmony whereas the parent's loving the child, talking to the child, discussing with the child, and being pleasant to approach are all positively related to family harmony. The father's attitudes or behaviors were found to be even more influential than the mother's so far as family harmony is concerned. Statistical analyses revealed significant correlations between the nine personality factors of the subjects as adult children, family harmony and the three factors of parenting (warmth, control, and indulgence). For example, the adult child's extraversion, self-discipline, and other-orientation are positively correlated with family harmony, father's warmth, and mother's warmth. Neuroticism is positively correlated with father's control, mother's control, father's indulgence, and mother's indulgence. Authoritarianism and neuroticism are negatively correlated with family harmony, father's warmth, and mother's warmth.

Study 2 was based on the data collected from reports as assignments submitted by 95 students in 17 discussion groups at two ML universities where I taught as visiting professor. The students discussed Chinese education as they had undergone and observed according to the questions I assigned for two class periods (100 minutes). Analysis of the data resulted in a fairly complete picture of Chinese education with most practices also found in Taiwan and Hong Kong where I did a similar study. The prevailing practices in the three Chinese societies include (1)overemphasis on academic achievement as assessed by frequent tests, (2)teaching to the test (teaching is test-directed), (3)neglect of education for the whole person, (4)intense competition for college admission, (5)lax requirements for college graduation, (6)overuse of lecture in teaching, (7)learning by rote, (8)shortage of qualified teachers in many schools, and (9)discrimination against slow learners and underachievers in elementary and secondary schools.

Study 3 reported a case of education reform in Taiwan. The data were obtained from participant observation. While there are problems at all levels of education, only one fundamental reform has been proposed by the Nationalist government since its retreat to the island in 1949. The reform endeavor is the voluntary promotion plan (VPP), meant to be a preparation for extension of the current 9-year compulsory education to 12 years. An important change introduced is the abolition of the highly competitive and anxiety-arousing senior high school joint (unified) entrance examination (SHSJEE). Since most parents are reluctant to have their children admitted to vocational (considered second-rate) and private (considered low in quality) high schools, the competition in the SHSJEE for admission to the academic public high schools, especially the prestigious ones, is extremely keen. Instead of the SHSJEE, the VPP assigns junior high school (JHS) graduates for promotion to the senior high schools, academic or vocational, on a "voluntary" rather than compulsory basis according to the scores they earned in the three JHS years in all subjects, activities, conduct, and attendance. Because the VPP treats all students, classes and schools in an equal manner and stresses well-rounded development of the students, no ability grouping is allowed and the class norm is used for assessment of performance in the five domains of education and development---intellectual, social, moral, physical, and aesthetic.

The VPP is considered less competitive and more healthy for adolescent development than the SHSJEE. Unfortunately, a powerful minority of lay people led by the parents (mostly science professors around 40 to 45 years of age) of high-achieving students (mostly 10 to 15 years old) strongly oppose the reform. They argue that the SHSJEE is a much more equitable system to select JHS graduates for admission to senior high schools. Consequently, the VPP is demoted to a trial basis on a negligible scale instead of nation-wide implementation. The failure of the reform endeavor has thus exposed not only educational inequality but social injustice in a Chinese society as testified by these facts: (1)parents of elite students dominate the educational scene, (2)the opponents of the reform (including teachers in cram schools) have only their own interests in mind, (3)the students who dislike the SHSJEE are neglected, (4)only the elite or high-achieving students are accommodated in schools, (5)people mistake test scores as the only indicator of quality of education, (6)the professional educators (professors of education and educational administrators) are too conservative and self-protective to speak up and defend the reform.

The case study of education reform also mirrored three types of human conflict---political (power struggle between political leaders), philosophical (battle between divergent schools of educational philosophy), and social (clash between different interest groups)---which are common features in Chinese culture. The dismissal of a competent, popular and reform-minded minister of education further reflects Chinese politics in an authority-directed culture in which the will of the common people is neglected in decision making. It is incongruous with Taiwan's democratization.

Personality of Chinese in Four Populations

Four studies were reported in Chapter 4. They dealt with personality types and traits of Chinese in ML, TW, HK, and US. The data were derived from questionnaire survey, biographical interview, and participant observation. Thirteen personality types with component traits were found for ML Chinese in Study 1. Personality traits of three ML generations (older, middle-aged, and young) were identified. The sociopolitical environment that contributed to the age differences and variation of personality was discussed and will not be repeated here. The personality of the Chinese in general and that of the educated in particular fluctuated with the political situations created by Mao Zedong and Deng Xiaoping. The older and middle-aged generations are, however, more stable in thoughts, feelings, and actions than the young generation who are more sensitive and responsive to the unpredictable political situation and outside influence, and, therefore, more subject to change.

I speculate that the future of mainland China may follow one of two courses as the old leaders pass control to a younger generation. One course is that the new leaders will continue to support free enterprise for economic growth under an authoritarian government. The other course will be a gradual democratization granting greater freedom to the people who are more or less inspired with Taiwan's direct election of a president in March, 1996. Because following an old course is much easier than a new one, the first prediction is more probable than the second one, at least for the foreseeable future. This implies that the peaceful reunification of the two Chinas (Communist and Nationalist) will remain as difficult to achieve for some time as it is today.

Nine types of personality with component traits were identified for the TW Chinese in Study 2. The personality of overseas (HK and US) Chinese and Chinese in general were dealt with in Study 3. It was found that ML, TW, HK, and US Chinese share most of the personality types. The six   most common types are the self-protective, conservative, scholar (intellectual), radical, egoistic, and manager (commercial). While many ML, TW, and HK Chinese long for the opportunity to emigrate to the United States, the cases cited in Study 3 showed that most US Chinese have a feeling of marginality in their host country. Due to the unstable circumstances in their homelands, however, the US Chinese prefer to remain in the United States because of its better living and working conditions, and its more humanistic education for their children. As for the Chinese in general, Study 3 found four major personality traits, namely, extreme narcissism, high achievement motivation, authoritarianism, and introversion. Their minor traits include perseverance, dependence, dominance, emotionality, aggressiveness, double-facedness, snobbery, and extrapunitiveness.

An important finding of Study 3 was that the Chinese are generally authority-directed. A person *in authority* is at once treated as *an authority.* Whoever possesses authority or higher authority based on position, status, power, tradition, knowledge, and/or wealth commands greater respect than one with no or less authority. The former, therefore, has greater social power than the latter. The topmost authority in Chinese society is the highest political leader, like the emperor in ancient China, Mao Zedong and Deng Xiaoping in Communist China, and Chiang Kai-shek and Lee Teng-hui in Nationalist China. Authority-directed seems to be a better term to characterize Chinese culture and personality than situation-centered (Hsu, 1981), social-oriented (Yang, 1981), tradition-, inner-, or other-directed (Riesman, 1961), and collectivist or individualist (Triandis, McCusker, & Hui, 1990).

Life Span Personality Development

Chapter 5 reported two studies. Study 1 presented 28 (14 male and 14 female) brief HK cases with data derived from graduate students' case reports. Study 2 presented 6 detailed ML cases with data obtained from biographical interview. The two studies tested the validity of Erikson's theory of 8-stage life span development of personality. Study 1 detected some sex differences. At Stage 4 (age 6-12) more boys experience negative development and have a deeper sense of inferiority than girls probably due to greater pressure on boys than on girls from parents and teachers for academic achievement. More women than men have to delay their identity resolution; they have to deal with the intimacy issue (Stage 6 issue) before the identity issue (Stage 5 issue). Both boys and girls usually need a moratorium in adolescence (Stage 5) to integrate their identity elements ascribed to the childhood stages. Many men and women, therefore, are unable to conquer their identity crisis until well after adolescence. For the development of intimacy, my HK data showed that marriage does not guarantee intimacy. Some men and women can achieve intimacy without marriage. The findings suggest two things: First, overemphasis on academic achievement imperils personality development, especially for boys. Second, adolescents need special guidance and counseling regarding identity crisis with emphasis on moratorium and intimacy issues.

The 28 cases in Study 1 covered the first six stages of development for all the subjects were under the age of 40. Of the six ML cases in Study 2, four subjects were over 60 years of age and reached Erikson's last stage (Stage 8). The six ML cases illustrated a variety of personality development. Case 1 (a 27-year-old woman) exemplified a compromised identity before intimacy. Case 2 (a 29-year-old man) achieved intimacy and identity simultaneously. Case 3 (a 91-year-old man) enjoyed generativity far beyond the age proposed by Erikson. Case 4 (a 66-year-old man) experienced a rebellious identity and overdue intimacy. Case 5 (a 64-year-old woman) had identity achievement but no intimacy. Case 6 (a 66-year-old woman) overcame the identity crisis in an unusually hard way. Although the two studies evidenced a general support for Erikson's theory of epigenetic development of personality, some age and sex differences in development were found. Perhaps Erikson's theory needs some overhaul or a new and more flexible theory of life-span personality development is needed.

Values and Their Correlates

There were six studies presented in Chapter 6, all related to Chinese values and personality. Content analysis of interview data gathered from 120 educated ML men and women found 69 cultural values in Study 1. The 69 Chinese values were categorized by the ten universal value types proposed by Schwartz (1992), which revealed that the more salient Chinese value types are power, security, conformity, benevolence, tradition, and achievement while the less salient value types are hedonism, stimulation, self-direction, and universalism. Power as the most salient value type is obviously related to authority-directedness of Chinese culture and personality because power is characterized by status, prestige, authority, wealth, control or dominance over other people and resources (Schwartz, 1992). Values mirror personality. The value of power seems to be closely related to narcissism. The prime value placed on power implicates that power struggle is unavoidable in Chinese politics, which makes authority-directedness necessary and authentic democracy almost impracticable in Chinese culture. Even the popular election of a head of state in Taiwan for the first time in more than 4,000 years of Chinese civilization does not guarantee authentic democracy.

In Study 2, factor analysis of data on 122 personality trait items in an indigenous questionnaire (MTPI) yielded nine personality factors or dimensions in bipolar form. They are Introversion--Extraversion (E), Negligence--Self-Discipline (D), Democratism--Authoritarianism (A), Dominance--Submission (S), Adventurism--Cautiousness (C), Self-Orientation--Other-Orientation (O), Dependency--Independency (I), Traditionalism--Modernism (M), and Healthiness--Neuroticism (N). For convenience, we may simply use the second term on the right-hand side in the bipolar form and its initial to designate a factor or dimension, such as Extraversion (E) instead of Introversion--Extraversion (E). The questionnaire data were collected from four Chinese samples---ML, TW, HK, and US---totaling 2640 subjects. As the subjects perceived themselves, there are both commonalities and differences in personality among samples, between sexes, and among age groups. An important finding was that the youngest group (age 19-30) of both sexes in the four samples are all less self-disciplined, submissive, and other-oriented but more modern than the older groups. This implies that the Chinese of future generations in general will be less traditional, conservative, realistic, cooperative, conscientious, self-effacing and self-controlled but more liberal, dominant, rebellious and self-interested.

Study 3 used the same instrument and subjects as in Study 2, but the statistical analysis was applied to the 122 personality traits (e.g., responsible, forgiving, works quietly) as designated by the 122 trait items in the questionnaire instead of the nine personality factors or dimensions. As a result, salient traits (e.g., realistic, sincere, opposes premarital sex) for various age groups of both sexes of the four samples were identified. Making use of interview data collected from the same 120 ML subjects as in Study 1, Study 4 investigated the ambitions and aspirations of the Chinese people. It was found that many Chinese aspire that, for example, "China will improve economically and politically," "people will be less selfish," "I will have a successful career," and "I will have a happy family and a good spouse."

With the same method and subjects as Study 4, Study 5 dealt with personality and value change. Cases were cited for illustration in both Study 4 and 5. Study 5 demonstrated that causes of change in values and personality are generally personal (e.g., health), interpersonal (e.g., marriage), educational (e.g., academic pressure), occupational (e.g., work experience), intellectual (e.g., changed cognition), and political (e.g., change in political environment). Study 6 investigated mate preferences by interviewing college students in ML and TW. The preferred mate characterisitics, as ambitions and aspirations in Study 4, reflect cultural values. Some of the preferred mate characteristics (e.g., education, health, occupation, good looks, good character) have their equivalents in the findings of Study 1 through 4. All the six studies in Chapter 6 examined directly or indirectly Chinese values and personality traits with an emphasis on the relationship between them. Since personality depicts the people and values reflect the culture, Chapter 6 should enable the reader to gain a better insight into the Chinese people and culture.

Morality and Interpersonal Relationships

There were three studies reported in Chapter 7 on morality and interpersonal relationships. Morality is highly valued in Chinese philosophy (particularly Confucianism) and Chinese education. Yet it has never been empirically studied in Chinese society until inspired by Kohlberg's theory of moral psychology in recent years. Study 1 dealt with moral judgment and moral behavior primarily of Chinese adults as related to educational level and social class. It had 247 ML, TW, and HK university students as informants who discussed in small groups at their respective institutions the questions on Chinese morality I assigned in a psychology course I taught. The contents of the reports submitted by 45 discussion groups were analyzed. The results indicated that the most prevailing stages of moral judgment in the three Chinese societies are Stage 3 and 4 (ML), 2 and 3/4 (TW), and 2 and 3 (HK). There are two modal stages of moral judgment---Stage 2 and 4, presumably characterizing the less educated and the well-educated Chinese respectively. Inconsistency between moral judgment (cognition) and moral behavior (action) was also observed. As a rule, moral judgment is stage-wise higher than moral behavior. The distance or degree of inconsistency between the two is generally the largest among the upper-class people and smallest among the lower-class people. Although the first four stages of moral development postulated by Kohlberg apply quite well so far as Chinese adults are concerned, we are not sure about the last two stages (Stage 5 and 6).

Interpersonal relationship is important in Chinese morality. Study 2 derived ten interpersonal relationships from interview data with 120 ML Chinese of both sexes and various ages as interviewees. The ten relationships as the interviewees experienced and observed them were described. They are parent-child, teacher-student, husband-wife, boss-subordinate, intergenerational, heterosexual, and the relationship between siblings, friends, students, and colleagues. These ten modern relationships, like the five cardinal relations in ancient China (ruler-minister, father-son, husband-wife, elder brother-younger brother, and friend-friend), are primarily private or personal relations with somebody in the in-group or with some significant person. In Chinese morality, maintenance of good relations with people in the five ancient relations or in the ten modern relationships is emphasized. This corresponds with Kohlberg's Stage 3 morality. Considering the findings of both Study 1 and 2, the moral judgment or behavior of most Chinese, regardless of age, sex and education, ranges from Stage 2 to Stage 4.

Study 3 in Chapter 7 reported the data derived from the responses of 2640 Chinese subjects to a question in the MTPI concerning their supportive relationships during adolescent years (age 12-19). It was found that the peer (friend and schoolmate) is by far the most prevailing supportive relationship providing social support for adolescents (37% for boys and 42% for girls). Next to peers comes the mother (15%

for boys and 17% for girls). More male (9%) than female (6%) subjects during adolescence seek support from father. Teacher (3% for males and 2% for females) is the least sought supportive relationship, ranking the last below other six relationships (schoolmate, mother, friend, father, elder sister, and elder brother in descending order). About as many Chinese during adolescence talk to nobody (28% for males and 22% for females) when faced with personal problems as those who talk to schoolmates (24% for males and 29% for females).

A Central Focus

As the foregoing summary of findings displays, this chapter, or rather, this book covers multiple topics. The central focus is, however, on Chinese personality or national character in general and personality of educated Chinese in particular. This focus is manifested in some important aspects of Chinese culture---family, school, values, morality, and interpersonal relationships. It is around this central focus that this book has been written. In Chapter 2 , we saw parent-child interaction and how various parenting patterns affect the child's personality development. Chapter 3 explored the relationship among family harmony, parenting, and the child's personality. It also presented a close-up of education in China and a case of education reform in Taiwan that mirror Chinese personality.

Chapter 4 portrayed personality types and traits of Chinese in four populations---mainland China, Taiwan, Hong Kong and the United States. Chapter 5 illustrated life-span personality development by individual cases in two Chinese societies---Hong Kong and the mainland. In Chapter 6, a nine-factor structure of Chinese personality was proposed, 69 Chinese values reflecting Chinese personality were identified and categorized, and other topics related to Chinese personality and values were discussed. In Chapter 7 Chinese personality as reflected in morality and interpersonal relationships was depicted. While a broad insight into Chinese character can be gained by reading this final chapter, an in-depth understanding of the Chinese people will be acquired by reading the whole book.

IMPLICATIONS

The findings of the 21 studies have a wide range of implications, particularly for international understanding, cultural ideology, national development, social change, child-rearing and educational practices, and future research on personality and culture. Some of the implications were already mentioned in the preceding section. As we note from the 21 studies, many of the findings are consistent with the results of previous researches by Westerners (mostly Americans), which implies that the Chinese people are more similar to than different from Westerners (particularly Americans). I have also closely observed the American people for nearly 40 years as student, friend, colleague, and researcher. It seems to me that the Chinese American anthropologist Francis Hsu (1981) has overstated the differences between Americans and Chinese because he saw the differences as "a matter of kind" (p. 137) while I see the differences as a matter of *degree*. For example, most of the personality types and traits found in Chinese culture (see Chapter 4) may also be observed in American culture although there may be more Chinese than Americans in certain types (e.g., the conservative type) and with certain traits (e.g., authoritarianism). If Americans are characterized by mistrust and psychological insecurity as Hsu (1981) observed them, even more so are the Chinese as I have observed them, though for different reasons (such as political persecution, peer competition and jealousy, punishment for disobedience at home and low achievement in school).

Markus and Kitayama's (1991) characterization of the differences between Western and Asian views of the self applies more to Americans and Japanese than to Chinese. The Japanese are more cooperative than the Chinese and less narcissistic than the Americans (DeVos, 1985). Narcissism is a trait shared by both Americans and

Chinese, but the Chinese are more narcissistic than the Americans as I have observed it. A narcissistic remark was made recently by Present Lee Teng-hui. He said, "Taiwan is a small place, but it is *great* in many ways. We are building a *Great Taiwan*." Nationalism in China has been an extension of narcissism at the national level. Underneath narcissism, however, the Chinese have a feeling of inferiority and/or envy in the face of Westerners, particularly Americans.

Riesman (1961) argued that the Americans are other-directed. So are the Chinese, I would say. But the Chinese are other-directed in the sense that they are more authority-directed than peer-directed while the Americans are more peer-directed than authority-directed. Hsu (1981) saw the beginning of the contrasts between Americans and Chinese in the fact that American children, relative to Chinese children, are allowed much greater independence by their parents. My interpretation is that Chinese parents are the first authority figures encountered by their children in an authority-directed culture whereas American parents treat their children as peers in a peer-directed culture. The Chinese have been socialized since childhood to respect authority. For them the acceptance of authority is a key to finding personal security (Pye, 1985).

If we say that American culture is characterized by individualism and Chinese culture by collectivism, it does not mean that individualism exists only in America and collectivism exists only in China; it actually means that American culture is more individualist and less collectivist than Chinese culture. To paraphrase Markus and Kitayama (1991, p. 247), even within highly individualist American culture, many people are still much less self-reliant, self-contained, or self-sufficient than the prevailing cultural ideology suggests that they should be. Sampson's (1989) argument on the reality of globalization and a shrinking world will force a rethinking of the differences between cultures. Perhaps our findings will not only help the non-Chinese understand the Chinese, but also serve as a looking glass for both the Chinese and the non-Chinese to see themselves more clearly.

If we say that all Chinese are ugly as Po-yang (1986) described them, it is of course untrue. Perhaps in general, women are less ugly than men. Chinese women in the four societies under study are more other-oriented than men (see Study 4 in Chapter 4). Like their Western counterparts (Brabeck, 1983), Chinese women's care for and sensitivity to the needs of others are the traits that have defined the "goodness" of women. It seems that the ugliness of Chinese is associated with wealth, authority and power which are indirectly associated with gender and education. There are, however, good people everywhere in Chinese society regardless of gender and educational level. Yet these good people are not organized to serve the common good; their goodness has little impact on society at large. An exceptional case is the self-educated Taiwanese nun Cheng Yen. She founded the Tzu Chi Foundation and organized the Buddhist Compassion Relief with thousands of male and female followers in Taiwan and overseas. She helps the needy at home and abroad.

As mentioned in Chapter 4 (see Study 3), the educated Chinese have a potential trait---a sense of mission. This personality trait is only occasionally displayed in mass behavior. A historic example was the May 4th Movement led by students and intellectuals in 1919. It amounted to "a vast modernization movement to build a new China" (Chow, 1960, p. 1). It stressed Western ideas of science and democracy and attacked traditional Chinese values. Recent examples were the Tiananmen Square demonstration calling for democracy on June 4, 1989 in Peking and the two presidential square demonstrations demanding law and order on May 4 and 18, 1997 in Taipei. The May 4th Movement and recent demonstrations in Peking and Taipei manifested the dissatisfaction of the people in general and intellectuals in particular with their government and demanded intellectual, social and/or political reforms. They also demonstrated the seemingly paradoxical personality of the Chinese that they may occasionally defy or rebel against authority even though they have been socialized to respect and obey authority in an authority-directed culture.

Personality of the people plays a decisive role in national development. The significant differences between nations in people's personality or national character make a great difference in determining the destiny of a nation. As I read the Chinese history, I am inclined to believe that heightened achievement motivation, superior intelligence and normal or moderate narcissism of the Chinese, coupled with favorable sociopolitical conditions at intervals (such as internal peace and supportive government policy), have contributed to the creation of one of the world's oldest civilizations and to the recent economic growth in Hong Kong, Taiwan, and mainland China. To emulate Western democracies, Taiwan held the first popular election of a chief executive in Chinese history on March 23, 1996.

The extreme or pathological narcissism of the Chinese (see Study 3 in Chapter 4) and their excessive valuing of power (see General Discussion in Chapter 6), on the other hand, jeopardizes integrity and solidarity. That, along with other factors, seems to have led to centuries of corruption, dictatorship, power struggle, and civil war. Extreme narcissism and power as the most salient value, along with other negative traits of the Chinese (see Chapter 4) may account for the fact that, though having a mean (average) IQ higher than that of white Americans (Herrnstein & Murray, 1994), the Chinese today lag far behind the Americans in many aspects of national strength (e.g., science, education, democracy, and national defense). My reasoning may lack substantial evidence. It at least provides some useful hypotheses for further research.

While I dare not claim that I am able to explain cultural, societal or political outcomes entirely from the personality of individual Chinese, it is evident that the personalities and ideologies of some powerful figures in Chinese history, from

Confucius to Mao Zedong and Deng Xiaoping, did function in considerable measure to shape China's culture, society and/or politics (Kissinger, 1997; Nathan & Shi, 1996; Pye, 1985; Solomon, 1971). The types and traits of personality shared by individuals as a group, particularly the prevailing types (e.g., the conservative type or group) and traits (e.g., authoritarianism), I would speculate, tend to have a direct impact on a nation's political, economic, and social development. My speculation is consistent with Nathan and Shi's view (1993, 1996), for example, that the conservative mainland Chinese, especially the less educated, may have helped the Communist regime to survive. Conservatism is a personality trait of Chinese in general regardless of educational level (see Study 3 in Chapter 4).

As a result of person-situation interaction (Mischel, 1976), the situation or environment in turn also exerts an influence on the individuals. For instance, it has been widely publicized that in the aftermath of premature democratization quite a number of people in Taiwan are less self-disciplined, as reflected in the chaotic legislative body and the rising crime rate, than their compatriots in America, Hong Kong, and mainland China. As a longtime observer of my compatriots and their culture in Taiwan, I designate Taiwan's democracy as premature because it is culturally, psychologically and educationally unprepared. Culturally, Taiwan as a Chinese society is still authority-directed and power-oriented. Psychologically, the personality of most people in Taiwan is predominantly egocentric and conservative. Educationally, Taiwan's schools have never adequately prepared its citizens for democracy as a way of life or as a system of genuine pluralism, active participation and fair competition.

Worth noting is extreme nationalism as an extension of extreme narcissism in mainland China. Nationalism in China was defensive in nature during the period from the Opium War (1840-1842) against the British till the Resistance War (1937-1945) against the Japanese. It has gradually become aggressive in nature since the Communists seized power on the mainland and the Nationalists retreated to Taiwan in 1949. Taiwan, however, does not share such an aggressive nationalism with the mainland. According to Princeton University historian Professor Y. S. Yu (1996), nationalism in the People's Republic of China differs from nationalism as espoused by the founding father Dr. Sun Yat-sen of the Republic of China in his Three Principles of the People --- Nationalism, Democracy, and Economy. Dr. Sun's nationalism is cooperative in nature, advocating cooperation among the races within the country and among the peoples of the world (Shih, 1997). Nationalism, somewhat extreme but self-productive rather than aggressive, is utilized, nevertheless, by some Taiwanese for the cause of independence from the mainland. Its aim is to conquer the crisis of identity and achieve the status of a nation-state in the international community.

Unlike intelligence which is shaped more by heredity than environment, personality is shaped more by environment than heredity. Culture plays a central role in personality development. Parenting, schooling, and values all have a powerful impact on personality development as demonstrated by our relevant studies (see Chapters 2, 3, 5, 6). Even though there is a trend of change, the prevailing pattern of parenting remains to be FYMC---- a *yan* (strict, controlling, awe-inspiring, punitive, and authoritarian) father and a *chi* (tender, warm, approachable, lenient, and permissive) mother. This parenting pattern also prevailed in 19th-century Western societies but has since been democratized. FYMC in its extreme form tends to produce a very narcissistic personality, especially in the male child. A striking example is Mao Zedong, the late chairman of the Chinese Communist Party. Mao was an extreme narcissist (Li, 1994). He had a very *yan* father and a very *chi* mother (Pye, 1976). There were many emperors more or less like Mao in Chinese history. There are also many common people more or less narcissistic like Mao in Chinese society today.

I have no evidence that the parents' IQ is an important source of the differences in parenting styles in Chinese culture like Western culture as suggested in *The Bell Curve* (Herrnstein & Murray, 1994). I have observed, however, that like the working-class rather than middle-class parents in Western culture as proposed by Melvin Kohn (1959, cited in Herrnstein & Murray, 1994), the Chinese parents, regardless of cognitive ability, educational level, and socioeconomic status, are most concerned about qualities in their children that ensure respectability. The Chinese parents, especially the father, in FYMC and FYMY families tend to be authoritarian and use physical punishment impulsively.

Education in Chinese culture is a means to the end of attaining status, fame, authority, and wealth. But the need for achievement is met in schools primarily by academic achievement as assessed by tests and examinations emphasizing memorization and standard (uniform) answers to test questions. Creativity and divergent thinking are discouraged. Even though Taiwan is experimenting on democracy, learning for democracy (such as peer discussion of public and moral issues) is lacking in schools. Students in both mainland China and Taiwan face excruciating competition through entrance examinations in their quest for places in high schools and universities, especially the prestigious ones. The misuse of test scores to jeopardize educational equity is more serious in mainland China, Taiwan and Hong Kong (see Study 2 and 3 in Chapter 3) than that in the United States as discussed by Darling-Hammond (1994).

In a recent issue, *Time* (October 9, 1995) reported the need for emotional education to enhance emotional intelligence or EQ, which is considered more important for a person's success in life than IQ (Goleman, 1995). Over a decade ago,

I emphasized the significance of emotional education for the Chinese people (Lew, 1982). The Chinese people are high in IQ but relatively low in EQ. I would like to junk the CUJEE (see Study 3 in Chapter 3), which is far more detrimental to emotional intelligence than the American SAT. Professor Stevenson urges the Americans to learn from Chinese education because his comparative study showed that Chinese 1st, 5th and 11th graders greatly surpassed their American counterparts in mathematics achievement (Stevenson & Stigler. 1992; Stevenson, Chen, & Lee, 1993). But his tested samples, like those in recent international comparisons of science and mathematics achievement, were not equivalent (Berliner, 1993; Bracey, 1992). Contrary to Stevenson, I think, as many other Chinese parents and teachers do, that the Chinese have a lot to learn from American education because American schools and universities, though not flawless, have produced far more talents (such as Nobelists) than their Chinese counterparts have ever produced.

In Chinese culture interpersonal relationship is highly valued. Human relations are manipulated by the Chinese to satisfy personal needs or short-term self-interest. Long-term self-interest which may lead to altruism (because actions that promote the welfare of others may also serve an individual's long-term welfare) is overlooked by most Chinese. Success in politics and business depends on tactful manipulation of *guanxi* (connections), especially with people in authority, which often involves gifts and dinner parties, and sometimes bribe and sex . Chinese morality is thus often instrumental-relativist oriented (see Chapter 7). Although Chinese culture is considered more collectivist than individualist, the concern of the Chinese people for collectivist interest seldom extends beyond their in-group or significant others. Rising individualism causes decline of traditional Confucian values, notably filial piety. While modern Chinese, especially males, are no less dependent than their forebears on parents, they are not so filial as their forebears to parents. Not as many married children as before are willing to live with and take care of their aged parents. As a result, nuclear families are prevalent. Under Western influence, an increasing number of young people prefer to cohabit or stay childless after marriage. Homosexuals are also claiming legitimacy in Taiwan.

Chinese culture and personality are both changing. Wealth increasingly becomes the paramount value for Chinese, including intellectuals who in Confucian tradition used to disregard wealth (see Chapter 4 and 6). This is true in Hong Kong and Taiwan, even in mainland China as a result of recent economic growth. In Taiwan for example, almost all legislators and high-ranking government officials are wealthy people. On the mainland, even intellectuals and military personnel engage in commercial activities to make money.

Some elements of the culture (e.g., authority-directedness) and some traits of the personality (e.g., narcissism), however, remain unchanged. The political leaders on either side of the Taiwan Strait are narcissistic, power-oriented and authority-directed. They think they are doing the right thing and have the power or authority to demand the other side to succumb. The Communist leaders of the People's Republic of China (PRC) claim the sovereignty over Taiwan which the PRC (founded in 1949) has never governed. The Republic of China (ROC) has existed since 1911, first on the mainland (1911-1949) and then on Taiwan (1949-present). The Nationalist leaders of the ROC, on he other hand, demand the PRC to give up its one-party rule as a requisite for reunification because the Chinese in Taiwan are reluctant to unite with the mainland under Communism. Democracy, as Nathan and Shi (1996) found in a national survey, is understood by most mainland Chinese not as a system of pluralism and participation, but as a term for the good polity whereas Taiwan's democracy is of the Western style in an authoritarian culture. The disparity in political culture of the two Chinas makes their immediate peaceful reunification impossible.

Hong Kong has been a free and rich international city. Its sovereignty reverted to China on July 1, 1997. One may wonder what is going to be the fate of Hong Kong after the end of 156 years (1841-1997) of British colonial rule. If the rule of law continues to work in this "Special Administrative Region" of China, we may say, as it did in the colonial days, this Chinese society will remain clean, decent, and prosperous. The future will prove whether Hong Kong Chinese as their own masters will be different from the mainland Chinese and whether their character and strength will not be eroded by corruption and connections that contaminate China's politics and business practices.

Although the importance of family and education continues to be recognized, Chinese parenting and schooling have failed to make children as happy, creative, and spontaneous as American children. As a rule in the family, the father is too authoritarian and the mother is too overprotective. Teaching in school is usually equated with indoctrinating, lecturing and testing. Learning is not by doing or acting (Dewey, 1916). It is generally by memorizing, reciting and at best by knowing, disregarding whether the knowledge acquired can be translated into action and practice.

Because the family and the school are the two basic environments where individual personality and national character are shaped, it may be proposed that, while upholding such traditional values as family harmony and educational accomplishment, the rigid, passive and authoritarian child-rearing and educational practices be reformed in order to develop a viable culture and national character capable of authentic democracy and rule of law at home and cooperative and peaceful coexistence with other nations of the world. Yet it depends on whether the leaders in the highest political authority of the nation have the foresight and altruism needed to carry out such a cultural reform in China (including the mainland and Taiwan).

There is a question that puzzles people who seek to understand China. The question is: Why is it that with such a long history, such a high intelligence, such a strong motivation for achievement, and such a deep love of face, China as a nation is not as advanced, developed, and solidified as, or even more so than, Japan and the United States? It is hoped that this book can help the reader answer that perplexing question.

✦ ✦ ✦

APPENDICES

Appendix 1

The Multi-Trait Personality Inventory (MTPI)

This is a questionnaire intended to study personality and its possible relationship to childhood experience. Your cooperation will be greatly appreciated.

I. Please fill out the appropriate blanks by a tick (✓) or the right answer when necessary.

Name (optional): _____, Male _____, Female _____, Married _____, Never married _____,

Once married _____, Birth place: _____, Place of current residence: _____, Age: _____,

Occupation: _____, Education or highest degree: _____, Field of study: _____, Religion: _____,

Number of siblings: _____ elder brother(s), _____ elder sister(s), _____ younger brother(s), _____

younger sister(s).

Now please recall your past experience before the age of twelve(unless otherwise specified) by completing the following:

1. My family had two _____, three _____, four _____, five _____ generations living together.

2. I lived most of the time on a farm _____, in a small town _____, in a city _____.

3. In my family the person with the greatest authority was my grandfather _____, grandmother _____, father _____,

   mother _____, elder brother _____, elder sister _____, other person (please specify): _____.

4. The person who loved me most was (please specify): _____.

5. The person with whom I had the most contact was (please specify): _____.

6. The person who disciplined me most was my father _____, mother _____, other person (please specify): _____

   .

7. The person I feared most was my father _____, mother _____, other person (please specify): _____.

8. The person I liked most was (please specify): _____.

9. During adolescent years (age 12 - 19) I never/seldom discussed my problems or worries with anybody _____;

   often discussed with my father _____, mother _____, elder brother _____, elder sister _____, teacher _____,

   schoolmate _____, friend _____, other person (please specify) : _____.

10. The combined pattern of my parents's behavior toward me was father strict-mother lenient _____, father lenient-

    mother strict _____, both strict _____, both lenient _____.

11. I thought my father was too strict _____, rather strict _____, too lenient _____, rather lenient _____, just about right _____.

12. I thought my mother was too strict _____, rather strict _____, too lenient _____, rather lenient _____, just about right _____.

13. I often _____, sometimes _____, seldom _____, never _____ saw my father become angry.

14. I often _____, sometimes _____, seldom _____, never _____ saw my mother become angry.

15. Relationships in my family were very _____, fairly _____ harmonious; rather _____, very _____ inharmonious.

16. My parents' or their substitutes' attitudes and child-rearing practices were as follows (please circle the appropriate number in each case, such as 1 2 3 4): 1 = never/least, 4 = very often/most.

	Father	Mother	Substitute(please specify: _____)
(1) overprotects me	1 2 3 4	1 2 3 4	1 2 3 4
(2) allows me autonomy	1 2 3 4	1 2 3 4	1 2 3 4
(3) too permissive/spoils me	1 2 3 4	1 2 3 4	1 2 3 4
(4) too restrictive/controls me	1 2 3 4	1 2 3 4	1 2 3 4
(5) loves me	1 2 3 4	1 2 3 4	1 2 3 4
(6) talks to me	1 2 3 4	1 2 3 4	1 2 3 4
(7) discusses with me	1 2 3 4	1 2 3 4	1 2 3 4
(8) moralizes to me	1 2 3 4	1 2 3 4	1 2 3 4
(9) doesn't like me	1 2 3 4	1 2 3 4	1 2 3 4
(10) keeps me in awe	1 2 3 4	1 2 3 4	1 2 3 4
(11) pleasant to approach	1 2 3 4	1 2 3 4	1 2 3 4

II. The following items on a 6-point scale are randomly arranged and some of them are related or similar. Each item has two poles representing two opposite personality traits. Each item requires two responses: one about yourself(self-perception) and the other about educated Chinese in general you know well (perception of other Chinese with a higher education you often see). Please circle an appropriate number for each response; such as 1 2 3 4 5 6 . In Item 1, for example, 1 = most introverted, 6 = most extraverted.

Bipolar description	Perception of Yourself	Perception of others
1. Introverted -- Extraverted	1 2 3 4 5 6	1 2 3 4 5 6
2. Subjective -- Objective	1 2 3 4 5 6	1 2 3 4 5 6
3. Talkative -- Quiet	1 2 3 4 5 6	1 2 3 4 5 6
4. Bold in speaking out -- Cautious about speaking out	1 2 3 4 5 6	1 2 3 4 5 6
5. Rigid -- Flexible	1 2 3 4 5 6	1 2 3 4 5 6
6. Hypocritical -- Sincere	1 2 3 4 5 6	1 2 3 4 5 6
7. Bold -- Shy	1 2 3 4 5 6	1 2 3 4 5 6
8. Dictatorial -- Democratic	1 2 3 4 5 6	1 2 3 4 5 6
9. Optimistic -- Pessimistic	1 2 3 4 5 6	1 2 3 4 5 6
10. Radical -- Conservative	1 2 3 4 5 6	1 2 3 4 5 6
11. Plays it safe in word and deed -- Straightforward in word and deed	1 2 3 4 5 6	1 2 3 4 5 6
12. Self-motivated -- Passive	1 2 3 4 5 6	1 2 3 4 5 6
13. Prefers a life of action -- Prefers a quiet life	1 2 3 4 5 6	1 2 3 4 5 6
14. Generous -- Stingy	1 2 3 4 5 6	1 2 3 4 5 6
15. Impulsive -- Calm	1 2 3 4 5 6	1 2 3 4 5 6
16. Adventurous -- Cautious	1 2 3 4 5 6	1 2 3 4 5 6
17. Frank -- Reserved	1 2 3 4 5 6	1 2 3 4 5 6
18. Bold in taking action -- Afraid of taking action	1 2 3 4 5 6	1 2 3 4 5 6
19. Strict -- Lenient	1 2 3 4 5 6	1 2 3 4 5 6
20. Humble -- Arrogant	1 2 3 4 5 6	1 2 3 4 5 6
21. Prefers things foreign -- Prefers things native	1 2 3 4 5 6	1 2 3 4 5 6
22. Is a person of word -- Is a person of deed	1 2 3 4 5 6	1 2 3 4 5 6
23. Critical -- Tolerant	1 2 3 4 5 6	1 2 3 4 5 6
24. Extreme -- Moderate	1 2 3 4 5 6	1 2 3 4 5 6

	Scale A						Scale B					
25. Person-oriented -- Issue-oriented	1	2	3	4	5	6	1	2	3	4	5	6
26. Sentimental -- Rational	1	2	3	4	5	6	1	2	3	4	5	6
27. Patient -- Impatient	1	2	3	4	5	6	1	2	3	4	5	6
28. Traditional -- Innovative	1	2	3	4	5	6	1	2	3	4	5	6
29. Gregarious -- Solitary	1	2	3	4	5	6	1	2	3	4	5	6
30. Interested in money -- Uninterested in money	1	2	3	4	5	6	1	2	3	4	5	6
31. Obliging -- Obstinate	1	2	3	4	5	6	1	2	3	4	5	6
32. Jolly and humorous -- Sober and inhibited	1	2	3	4	5	6	1	2	3	4	5	6
33. Amiable -- Aloof	1	2	3	4	5	6	1	2	3	4	5	6
34. Polite -- Informal	1	2	3	4	5	6	1	2	3	4	5	6
35. Energetic -- Languid	1	2	3	4	5	6	1	2	3	4	5	6
36. Principled -- Opportunistic	1	2	3	4	5	6	1	2	3	4	5	6
37. Low in need for achievement -- High in need for achievement	1	2	3	4	5	6	1	2	3	4	5	6
38. Suffers from insomnia -- Sleeps well	1	2	3	4	5	6	1	2	3	4	5	6
39. Sane -- Neurotic	1	2	3	4	5	6	1	2	3	4	5	6
40. Unrealistic -- Realistic	1	2	3	4	5	6	1	2	3	4	5	6
41. Dependent -- Independent	1	2	3	4	5	6	1	2	3	4	5	6
42. Has a good memory -- Often forgets	1	2	3	4	5	6	1	2	3	4	5	6
43. Clumsy in speech -- Eloquent	1	2	3	4	5	6	1	2	3	4	5	6
44. Popular -- Unpopular	1	2	3	4	5	6	1	2	3	4	5	6
45. Respects authority -- Defies authority	1	2	3	4	5	6	1	2	3	4	5	6
46. Conforming -- Individualistic	1	2	3	4	5	6	1	2	3	4	5	6
47. Ill-tempered -- Good-tempered	1	2	3	4	5	6	1	2	3	4	5	6
48. Jealous of colleagues -- Helpful to colleagues	1	2	3	4	5	6	1	2	3	4	5	6
49. Enjoys exercise -- Dislikes exercise	1	2	3	4	5	6	1	2	3	4	5	6

If you feel bored, please take a break. Your patience is appreciated.

Item	Scale 1	Scale 2
50. Obedient -- Rebellious	1 2 3 4 5 6	1 2 3 4 5 6
51. Responsible -- Irresponsible	1 2 3 4 5 6	1 2 3 4 5 6
52. Least self-confident -- Most self-confident	1 2 3 4 5 6	1 2 3 4 5 6
53. Protects self cautiously -- Champions justice bravely	1 2 3 4 5 6	1 2 3 4 5 6
54. Adheres to what is right -- Says what others say	1 2 3 4 5 6	1 2 3 4 5 6
55. Thoughtful to others -- Interested in self only	1 2 3 4 5 6	1 2 3 4 5 6
56. Despises others -- Respects others	1 2 3 4 5 6	1 2 3 4 5 6
57. Has a feeling of superiority -- Does not feel superior	1 2 3 4 5 6	1 2 3 4 5 6
58. Overconcerned about face -- Unconcerned about face	1 2 3 4 5 6	1 2 3 4 5 6
59. Snobbish -- Unsnobbish	1 2 3 4 5 6	1 2 3 4 5 6
60. Has a strong desire for power -- Has no desire for power	1 2 3 4 5 6	1 2 3 4 5 6
61. Has a feeling of inferiority -- Does not feel inferior	1 2 3 4 5 6	1 2 3 4 5 6
62. Works quietly -- Talks without working	1 2 3 4 5 6	1 2 3 4 5 6
63. Often brags -- Never brags	1 2 3 4 5 6	1 2 3 4 5 6
64. Talks rapidly -- Talks slowly	1 2 3 4 5 6	1 2 3 4 5 6
65. Concentrates on work -- Has many things in mind	1 2 3 4 5 6	1 2 3 4 5 6
66. Consistent in word and deed -- Inconsistent in word and deed	1 2 3 4 5 6	1 2 3 4 5 6
67. Trustful -- Suspicious	1 2 3 4 5 6	1 2 3 4 5 6
68. Imaginative -- Unimaginative	1 2 3 4 5 6	1 2 3 4 5 6
69. Self-controlled -- Easily tempted	1 2 3 4 5 6	1 2 3 4 5 6
70. Shrewd and sophisticated -- Simple and naive	1 2 3 4 5 6	1 2 3 4 5 6
71. Escapes reality -- Faces reality	1 2 3 4 5 6	1 2 3 4 5 6
72. Acts alone -- Follows the crowd	1 2 3 4 5 6	1 2 3 4 5 6
73. Cooperative -- Competitive	1 2 3 4 5 6	1 2 3 4 5 6
74. Deeply believes in the existence of a god or gods -- Does not believe in the existence of any god	1 2 3 4 5 6	1 2 3 4 5 6
75. Has many friends -- has few friends	1 2 3 4 5 6	1 2 3 4 5 6
76. Worried about falling behind others -- Disinclined to compete	1 2 3 4 5 6	1 2 3 4 5 6

		1	2	3	4	5	6		1	2	3	4	5	6
77.	Demanding -- Forgiving	1	2	3	4	5	6		1	2	3	4	5	6
78.	Ostentatious -- Self-effacing	1	2	3	4	5	6		1	2	3	4	5	6
79.	Considers self first -- Considers group first	1	2	3	4	5	6		1	2	3	4	5	6
80.	Satisfied with status quo -- Inclined to reform	1	2	3	4	5	6		1	2	3	4	5	6
81.	Most adaptable -- Least adaptable	1	2	3	4	5	6		1	2	3	4	5	6
82.	Uncommunicative -- Unrestrained in talk and laughter	1	2	3	4	5	6		1	2	3	4	5	6
83.	Physically healthy -- Physically feeble	1	2	3	4	5	6		1	2	3	4	5	6
84.	Has too high ideals -- Has no ideals	1	2	3	4	5	6		1	2	3	4	5	6
85.	Has too many cares -- Does not care about anything	1	2	3	4	5	6		1	2	3	4	5	6
86.	Often gives in -- Never gives in	1	2	3	4	5	6		1	2	3	4	5	6
87.	Values virginity -- Advocates free love	1	2	3	4	5	6		1	2	3	4	5	6
88.	Deeply believes in fate -- Does not believe in fate at all	1	2	3	4	5	6		1	2	3	4	5	6
89.	Faithful in love -- Unfaithful in love	1	2	3	4	5	6		1	2	3	4	5	6
90.	Favors people from native place -- Has no preference for people from native place	1	2	3	4	5	6		1	2	3	4	5	6
91.	Dominant -- Submissive	1	2	3	4	5	6		1	2	3	4	5	6
92.	Inclined to moralize -- Inclined to listen	1	2	3	4	5	6		1	2	3	4	5	6
93.	Has leadership ability -- Has no leadership ability	1	2	3	4	5	6		1	2	3	4	5	6
94.	Has self-knowledge -- Has no self-knowledge	1	2	3	4	5	6		1	2	3	4	5	6
95.	Sociable -- Unsociable	1	2	3	4	5	6		1	2	3	4	5	6
96.	Often blames others -- Often blames self	1	2	3	4	5	6		1	2	3	4	5	6
97.	Anxious and nervous -- Imperturbable	1	2	3	4	5	6		1	2	3	4	5	6
98.	Speculative -- Empirical	1	2	3	4	5	6		1	2	3	4	5	6
99.	Planful -- Unplanful	1	2	3	4	5	6		1	2	3	4	5	6

Item		1	2	3	4	5	6		1	2	3	4	5	6
100.	Materialistic -- Spiritual	1	2	3	4	5	6		1	2	3	4	5	6
101.	Willing to be led by a leader -- Unwilling to be led by others	1	2	3	4	5	6		1	2	3	4	5	6
102.	Has a changeable mood -- Has a stable mood	1	2	3	4	5	6		1	2	3	4	5	6
103.	Quick to admit errors -- Inclined to defend own errors	1	2	3	4	5	6		1	2	3	4	5	6
104.	Inclined to try new things -- Inclined to keep old habits	1	2	3	4	5	6		1	2	3	4	5	6
105.	Interested in politics -- Uninterested in politics	1	2	3	4	5	6		1	2	3	4	5	6
106.	Eager to be praised -- Self-sufficient	1	2	3	4	5	6		1	2	3	4	5	6
107.	Afraid to express own opinions -- Bold in expressing own opinions	1	2	3	4	5	6		1	2	3	4	5	6
108.	Often worries about health -- Never worries about health	1	2	3	4	5	6		1	2	3	4	5	6
109.	Often self-examining -- Never self-examining	1	2	3	4	5	6		1	2	3	4	5	6
110.	Accepts new things easily -- Accepts new things with difficulty	1	2	3	4	5	6		1	2	3	4	5	6
111.	Active in social contact -- Passive in social contact	1	2	3	4	5	6		1	2	3	4	5	6
112.	Interested in opposite sex -- Uninterested in opposite sex	1	2	3	4	5	6		1	2	3	4	5	6
113.	Approves of premarital sex -- Opposes premarital sex	1	2	3	4	5	6		1	2	3	4	5	6
114.	Tolerant of different opinions -- Intolerant of different opinions	1	2	3	4	5	6		1	2	3	4	5	6
115.	Overestimates self -- Underestimates self	1	2	3	4	5	6		1	2	3	4	5	6
116.	Prefers group activities -- Prefers individual activities	1	2	3	4	5	6		1	2	3	4	5	6
117.	Easily moved to tears by touching stories -- Never moved to tears	1	2	3	4	5	6		1	2	3	4	5	6
118.	Depressed at frustration -- Unruffled at frustration	1	2	3	4	5	6		1	2	3	4	5	6
119.	Advocates restrictive child training -- Advocates permissive child training	1	2	3	4	5	6		1	2	3	4	5	6
120.	Always looks at problems from own point of view -- Often looks at problems from others' point of view	1	2	3	4	5	6		1	2	3	4	5	6
121.	Uneasy with authority figure -- Easy with authority figure	1	2	3	4	5	6		1	2	3	4	5	6
122.	Wants to do 3 times as much as is able to do -- wants to do only 1/3 as much as is able to do	1	2	3	4	5	6		1	2	3	4	5	6

III. If **we** try to classify the educated Chinese according to their personality types, into how many types would you classify them? Please describe each type briefly in the space below.

Date of completion: _____.

Thank you very much for your cooperation.

Appendix 2

Some Statistical Information concerning the MTPI

A. The items statistically related to each of the nine personality factors (9 PFs)

PF Bipolar description of 9 PFs	Items related to each factor (as numbered in the MTPI)
E: Introversion -- Extraversion	16 items: 1, -3, 5, -7, -13, -29, -32, -33, 43, -44, -75, 82, -93, -95, 107, -111
D: Negligence -- Self-discipline	16 items: 22, -34, -36, 37, 40, -51, -54, -62, -65, -66, -69, -87, -89, -94, -99, -109
A: Democratism -- Authoritarianism	14 items: -2, -8, 20, 31, -56, -57, -63, 67, -77, -92, -96, 103, 114, -120
S: Dominance -- Submission	10 items: -45, -46, -50, 72, -73, -86, 91, -101, -116, -119
C: Adventurism -- Cautiousness	13 items: 4, 10, -11, 12, 15, 16, 17, 18, 19, 23, 24, 64, -85
O: Self-Orientation -- Other-Orientation	13 items: 6, 21, 30, 48, 53, -55, 59, 60, 79, 100, 112, 113, 115
I: Dependency -- Independency	14 items: 25, 26, 41, 52, 61, -70, 71, 74, 88, 90, 98, 102, 117, 118
M: Traditionalism -- Modernism	12 items: 28, 58, -68, -76, -78, 80, -84, -104, -105, -106, -110, -122
N: Healthiness -- Neuroticism	14 items: 9, 14, 27, 35, -38, 39, 42, -47, 49, 81, 83, -97, -108, -121

B. Correlation matrix of the 9 PFs

	E	D	A	S	C	O	I	M	N
E	1.00	.19*	-.04	-.01	-.51*	.02	.25*	.50*	-.51*
D		1.00	-.45*	.11*	.02	.53*	.40*	.16*	-.42*
A			1.00	-.24*	-.24*	-.57*	-.30*	.14*	.28*
S				1.00	.28*	.12*	-.20*	-.24*	.03
C					1.00	.01	-.09*	-.46*	.16*
O						1.00	.27*	-.13*	-.21*
I							1.00	.21*	.53*
M								1.00	-.28*
N									1.00

Note. *$p < .001$. Our factor analysis is oblique rather than orthogonal, so the relationship between factors can be shown.

C. Reliability and sample items of the 9 PFs in the MTPI

PF		Item no.	Sample Item Bipolar description	Factor loading
E	.87	111	Active in social contact -- Passive in social contact	-.48
D	.84	69	Self-controlled -- Easily tempted	-.50
A	.79	114	Tolerant of different opinions -- Intolerant of different opinions	.58
S	.68	72	Acts alone -- Follows the crowd	.54
C	.80	18	Bold in taking action -- Afraid of taking action	.53
O	.77	48	Jealous of colleagues -- Helpful to colleagues	.41
I	.74	25	Person-oriented -- Issue-oriented	.42
M	.70	104	Inclined to try new things -- Inclined to keep old habits	-.52
N	.76	38	Suffers from insomnia -- Sleeps well	-.45

Appendix 3

Validity Coefficients of MTPI's 9 PFs with Cattell's 16 PFs as Criterion

MTPI's 9 PFs	A	B	C	E	F	G	H	I	L	M	N	O	Q1	Q2	Q3	Q4
												Cattell's 16 PFs				
E	.35						.39					-.30		-.41		
D		.29	.37	.65	.47								.21		.43	-.23
A		-.25	.27	-.32							.21		-.24		-.33	.24
S			-.37				-.26							.26		
C	-.26		-.41	-.27		.22	-.27	.31	-.22							
O		.21	-.27					-.34				-.43	.31		.31	-.48
I		.39														
M	.28		.36	.43			.42							-.24	-.28	
N		-.50										.53				.53

Note. Only r's with $p < .001$ are shown. The popular description of Cattell's 16 PFs is as follows:

A = reserved--outgoing, B = stupid--intelligent, C = emotional--stable, E = humble--assertive, F = somber--lighthearted, G = expedient--conscientious, H = shy--venturesome, I = tough-minded--tender-minded, L = trusting--suspicious, M = practical--imaginative, N = forthright--shrewd, O = placid--apprehensive, Q1 = conservative--liberal, Q2 = group-dependent--self-sufficient, Q3 = undisciplined--self-controlled, Q4 = relaxed--tense.

REFERENCES

Adams, G. R., & Jones, R. M. (1983). "Female adolescents identity development: Age comparisons and perceived child-rearing experience." *Developmental Psychology*, 19, pp. 249-256.

Allison, S.T., Messick, D. M., & Goethals, G. R. (1987). *On being better but not smarter than others: The Muhammad Ali effect*. Unpublished manuscript, University of California, Santa Barbara.

Allport, G. W., & Odbert, H. S. (1936). "Trait-names: A psycho-lexical study." *Psychological Monographs*, 47(1).

American Psychiatric Association. (1980). *Diagnostic and statistical manual of mental disorders* (3rd ed.). Washington DC: Author.

Argyle, M.,& Furnham, A. (1983). "Sources of satisfaction and conflict in long-term relationships." *Journal of Marriage and the Family*, 45, pp. 481-493.

Atkinson, J. W. (1977). "Motivation for achievement." In T. Blass(Ed.), *Personality variables in social behavior* (pp. 25-108). Hillsdale, NJ: Erlbaum.

Atkinson, P., Delamont, S., & Hammersley, M. (1988). "Qualitative research traditions: A British response to Jacob." *Review of Educational Research*, 58, pp. 231-250.

Baltes, P. B., & Schaie, W.K. (Eds.) (1973). *Life-span development psychology: Personality socialization*. New York: Academic Press.

Bateson, P. (1983). *Mate choice*. Cambridge: Cambridge University Press.

Baumrind, D. (1971). "Current patterns of parental authority." *Developmental Psychology Monographs*, 4 (1, Pt. 2).

Bee, H. L, & Mitchell, S. K. (1980). *The developing person: A life-span approach.* San Francisco: Harper & Row.

Beggan, J. K., Messick, D. M., & Allison, S. T. (1988). "Social values and egocentric bias: Two tests of the might over morality hypothesis." *Journal of Personality and Social Psychology*, 55, pp. 606-611.

Bell, R. (1968). "A reinterpretation of direction of effects in studies of socialization." *Psychological Review*, 75, pp. 81-95.

Benedict, R. (1946). *The chrysanthemum and the sword.* Boston: Houghton Mifflin.

Berliner, D. C. (1993). "International comparisons of student achievement: A false guide for reform." *National Forum*, LXXIII, Fall, pp. 25-29.

Berndt, T. J. (1982). "The features and effects of friendships in early adolescence." *Child Development*, 53, pp. 1447-1460.

Berndt, T. J., Cheung, P. C., Lau, S., Hau, K. T., & Lew, W. J. F. (1993). "Perceptions of parenting in mainland China, Taiwan, and Hong Kong: Sex differences and societal differences." *Developmental Psychology*, 29, pp. 156-164.

Berndt, T. J., & Perry, T. B. (1986). "Children's perceptions of friendships as supportive relationships." *Developmental Psychology*, 22, pp. 640-648.

Berry, J. W. (1969). "On cross-cultural comparability." *International Journal of Psychology*, 4, pp. 119-128.

Birren, J. E., & Hedlund, B. (1987). "Contributions of autobiography to developmental psychology." In N. Eisenberg (Ed.), *Contemporary topics in developmental psychology* (pp. 394-415). New York: Wiley.

Birren, J. E., Kinney, D. K., Schaie, K. W., & Woodruff, D. S. (1981). *Developmental psychology: A life-span approach.* Boston: Houghton Mifflin.

Blasi, A. (1980). "Bridging moral cognition and moral action: A critical review of the literature." *Psychological Bulletin*, 88, July, pp. 1-45.

Block, J. (1971). *Lives through time.* Berkeley, CA: Bankroft.

Block, J. H. (1984). *Sex role identity and ego development.* San Francisco: Jossey-Bass.

Bond, M. H. (1988). "Finding universal dimensions of individual variation in multicultural studies of values: The Rokeach and Chinese value surveys." *Journal of Personality and Social Psychology*, 55, pp. 1009-1015.

Bond, M. H. (1986). *The psychology of the Chinese people.* Hong Kong: Oxford University Press.

Bond, M. H., & Hwang, K. K. (1986). "The social psychology of Chinese people." In M. H. Bond(Ed.), *The psychology of the Chinese people* (pp. 213-266). Hong Kong: Oxford University Press.

Borkenau, P. (1990). "Traits as ideal-based and goal-derived social categories." *Journal of Personality and Social Psychology*, 58, pp. 381-396.

Brabeck, M. (1983). "Moral judgment: Theory and research on differences between males and females." *Developmental Review*, 3, pp. 274-291.

Bracey, G. W. (1992). "The second Bracey report on the condition of public education." *Phi Delta Kappan*, October, pp. 104-117.

Braithwaite, V. A., & Law, H. G. (1985). "Structure of human values: Testing the adequacy of the Rokeach Value Survey." *Journal of Personality and Social Psychology*, 49, pp. 250-263.

Brislin, R. W. (1980). "Translation and content analysis of oral and written materials." In H. C. Triandis & J. W. Berry (Eds.), *Handbook of cross-cultural psychology*, vol. 2, methodology (pp. 389-444). Boston: Allyn & Bacon.

Brody, L. R. (1985). "Gender differences in emotional development: A review of theories and research." *Journal of Personality*, 53, pp. 102-149.

Brunk, M. A., & Henggeler, S. W. (1984). "Child influences on adult controls: An experimental investigation." *Developmental Psychology*, 20, pp. 1074-1081.

Buss, D. M., & 49 coauthors(1990). "International preferences in selecting mates: A study of 37 cultures." *Journal of Cross-Cultural Psychology*,21, pp. 5-47.

Cairns, R. B. (1979). *Social development: The origins and plasticity of interchanges.* San Francisco: W. H. Freeman.

Campbell, D. T. (1986). "Science's social system of validity -enhancing collective belief change and the problems of the social sciences." In D. W. Fiske & R. A. Shweder (Eds.), *Metatheory in social science* (pp. 108-135). Chicago: University of Chicago Press.

Cattell, R. B. (1966). "The scree test for the number of factors." *Multivariate Behavioral Research*, 1(2), pp. 245-276.

Cattell, R. B., Eber, H. W., & Tatsuoka, M. M. (1970). *Handbook for the Sixteen Personality Factor Questionnaire.* Champaign, IL: Institute for Personality and Ability Testing.

Chan, W. T. (1963). *A source book in Chinese philosophy.* Princeton, NJ: Princeton University Press.

Chen, S. C. (1994). "Research trends in mainland Chinese comparative education." *Comparative Education Review*, 38, pp. 233-252.

Chen, T. H. E. (1981). *Chinese education since 1949: Academic and revolutionary models.* New York: Pergamon.

Cherry, F., & Byrne, D. (1977). "Authoritarianism." In T. Blass (Ed.), *Personality variables in social behavior.* Hillsdale, NJ: Lawrence Erlbaum.

Cheung, P. C., & Lau, S. (1985). "Self-esteem: Its relationship to the family and school social environments among Chinese adolescents." *Youth and Society*, 16, pp. 438-456.

Chinese Culture Connection (1987). "Chinese values and the search for culture-free dimensions of culture." *Journal of Cross-Cultural Psychology*, 18, pp. 143-164.

Chou, E. (1980). *Mao Tse-Tung: The man and the myth*. New York: Stein & Day.

Chow, T. T. (1960). *The May Fourth Movement: Intellectual revolution in modern China*. Stanford, CA: Stanford University Press.

Chu, G. C., & Ju, Y. (1990). *The great wall in ruins: Cultural change in China*. Honolulu: East-West Center.

Coates, S. (1974). "Sex differences in field dependence among preschool children." In R. Friedman, R. Reichert, & R. Vande Weile (Eds.), *Sex differences in behavior* (pp. 259-274). New York: Wiley.

Colby, A., Kohlberg, L., Gibbs, J., & Lieberman, M. (1983). "A longitudinal study of moral judgment." *Monographs of the Society of Research in Child Development*, 48 (1-2).

Conger, J. J. (1973). *Adolescence and youth: Psychological development in a changing world*. New York: Harper & Row.

Costa, P. T., Jr., & McCrae, R. R. (1988). "Personality in adulthood: A six-year longitudinal study of self-reports and spouse ratings on the NEO Personality Inventory." *Journal of Personality and Social Psychology*, 54, pp. 853-863.

Croll, E., Davin, D., & Kane, P. (Eds.) (1985). *China's one child family policy*. London: Macmillan.

Cronbach, L. J. (1970). *Essentials of psychological testing*, 3rd ed. New York: Harper & Row.

Cronbach, L. J. (1977). *Educational psychology*, 3rd ed. New York: Harcourt.

Daniels, D., & Plomin, R. (1985). "Differential experience of siblings in the same family." *Developmental Psychology*, 21, pp. 747-760.

Darling-Hammond, L. (1994). "Performance-based assessment and educational equity." *Harvard Educational Review*, 64, pp. 5-30.

Davin, D. (1990). "The early childhood education of the only child generation in urban areas of mainland China." In B. J. Lin &L. M. Fan (Eds.), *Education in Mainland China: Review and Evaluation* (pp. 315-336). Taipei, TW: Institute of International Relations, National Chengchi University.

DeVos, G. (1985). "Dimensions of the self in Japanese culture." In A. J. Marsella, G. DeVos, & F. L. K. Hsu(Eds.), *Culture and self: Asian and Western perspectives* (pp. 141-184). New York: Tavistock.

Dewey, J. (1916). *Democracy and education.* New York: Macmillan.

Dien, D. S. F. (1982). "A Chinese perspective on Kohlberg's theory of moral development." *Developmental Review*, 2, pp. 331-341.

Dishion, T. J., Patterson, G. R., Stoolmiller,M., & Skinner,M.L. (1991). "Family, school, and behavioral antecedents to early adolescent involvement with antisocial peers." *Developmental Psychology*, 27, pp. 172-180.

Erikson, E. H. (1963). *Childhood and society*, 2nd ed. New York: Norton.

Erikson, E. H. (1968). Identity: *Youth and crisis.* New York: Norton.

Erikson, E. H. (1974). *Dimensions of a new identity : The 1973 Jefferson lectures in the humanities.* New York: Norton.

Estrada, P., Arsenio, W. F., Hess, R. D., & Holloway, S. D. (1987). "Affective quality of the mother-child relationship: Longitudinal consequences for children's school-relevant cognitive functioning." *Developmental Psychology,* 23, pp. 210-215.

Evans, R. (1967). *Dialogue with Erik Erikson.* New York: Harper & Row.

Eysenck, H. J. (1967). *The biological basis of personality.* Springfield, IL: Charles C. Thomas.

Eysenck, H. J., & Eysenck, S. B. G. (1975). *Manual of the Eysenck Personality Questionnaire*. London: Hodder & Stoughton.

Fan, L. M. (1990). "Secondary education in mainland China." In B. J. Lin & L. M. Fan (Eds.), *Education in mainland China* (pp. 111-129). Taipei, TW: Institute of International Relations, National Chengchi University.

Fernandez, R. (1975). *The promise of sociology*. New York: Praeger.

Feshbach, S. & Weiner, B. (1982). *Personality*. Lexington, MA: Heath.

Finnis, J. M. (1990). "Authority." In J. Raz (Ed.), *Authority* (pp. 174-202). Oxford: Basil Blackwell.

Franz, C. E., & White, K.M. (1985). "Individuation and Attachment in personality development: Extending Erikson's theory." *Journal of Personality*, 53, pp. 226-256.

Friedman, R. B. (1990). "On the concept of authority in political philosophy." In J. Razz (Ed.), *Authority* (pp. 56-91). Oxford: Basil Blackwell.

Gage, N. L. (1978). *The scientific basis of the art of teaching*. New York: Teachers College Press, Columbia University.

Gibbs, J. C., & Schnell, S. V. (1985). "Moral development "versus" socialization." *American Psychologist*, 40, pp. 1071-1080.

Gilligan, C. (1977). "In a different voice: Women's conceptions of the self and of morality." *Harvard Educational Review*, 47, pp. 481-517.

Gilligan, C. (1979). "Woman's place in man's life cycle." *Harvard Educational Review*, 49, pp. 431-446.

Gilligan, C. (1982). *In a different voice*. Cambridge, MA: Harvard University Press.

Goldman, M., Cheek, T., & Hamvin, C. L. (Eds.) (1987). *China's intellectuals and the state: In search of a new relationship*. Cambridge, MA: Harvard University Press.

Goleman, D. (1995). *Emotional intelligence.* New York: Bantam Books.

Good, T. L., & Weinstein, R. S. (1986). "Schools make a difference." *American Psychologist,* October, pp. 1090-1097.

Goodlad, J. A. (1979). "Can our schools get better?" *Phi Delta Kappan,* 60, pp. 342-347.

Gough, H. G., & Heilbrun, A. B., Jr. (1965).*The Adjective Check List manual.* Palo Alto, CA: Consulting Psychologists Press.

Grieder, J. B. (1981). *Intellectuals and the state in modern China: A narrative history.* New York: Free Press.

Grimley, L. (1973). *A cross-cultural study of moral development.* Unpublished doctoral dissertation, Kent State University. Kent. OH.

Grimley, L. (1974). "Moral development in different nations." *School Psychology Digest,* 3, pp. 43-51.

Guo, S. (Ed.) (1989). *New China's education in the last forty years.* Fuchow: Fukien Education Press. (in Chinese)

Harding, H. (1993). "The concept of "Greater China": Themes, Variations and Reservations." *China Quarterly,* December, pp. 660-686.

Hau, K.T., & Lew, W. J. F. (1989). "Moral development of Chinese students in Hong Kong." *International Journal of Psychology,* 24, pp. 561-569.

Haviland, J. M. (1984). "Thinking and feeling in Woolf's writing: From Childhood to adulthood." In C. E. Izard,, J. Kagan, & R. B. Zajonc (Eds.), *Emotions, cognition, and behavior* (pp. 515-546). New York: Cambridge University Press.

Hayhoe, R. (1985). *Contemporary China's education.* London: Croom House.

Helson, R., Mitchell, V., & Hart, B. (1985). "Lives of women who became autonomous." *Journal of Personality,* 53, pp. 257- 285.

Herrmann, T., & Stapf, A. (1977). "Personality and culture: The family. In Cattell R. B., & Dreger, R. M. (Eds.), *Handbook of modern personality theory* (pp. 477-495.). New York: Wiley.

Herrnstein, R. J., & Murray, C. (1994). *The bell curve: Intelligence and class structure in American life*. New York: Free Press.

Ho, D. Y. F. (1976). "On the concept of face." *American Journal of Sociology*, 81, pp. 867-884.

Ho, D. Y. F.(1980). "Face and stereotyped notions about Chinese face behavior." *Philippine Journal of Psychology*, 13, pp. 20-33.

Ho, D. Y. F. (1981). "Traditional patterns of socialization in Chinese society." *Acta Psycholgica Taiwanica*, 23, pp. 81-95.

Ho, D. Y. F. (1986). "Chinese patterns of socialization: A critical review." In M. H. Bond (Ed.), *The psychology of the Chinese people* (pp. 1-37). Hong Kong: Oxford University Press.

Ho, D. Y. F. (1989). "Continuity and variation in Chinese patterns of socialization." *Journal of Marriage and the Family*, 51, pp. 149-163.

Ho, D. Y. F., & Kang, T.K. (1984). "Intergenerational comparisons of child-rearing attitudes and practices in Hong Kong." *Developmental Psychology*, 20, pp. 1004-1016.

Hoffman, L. W. (1991). "The influence of the family environment on personality: Accounting for sibling differences." *Psychological Bulletin*, 110, pp. 187-203.

Hofstede, G. (1980). *Culture's consequences: International differences in work-related values*. Newbury Park, CA: Sage.

Homer, P. M., & Kahle, L. R. (1988). "A structural equation test of the value-attitude-behavior hierarchy." *Journal of Personality and Social Psychology*, 54, pp. 638-646.

Hsieh, Y. W. (1967). "Filial piety and Chinese society." In C. A. Moore (Ed.), *The Chinese mind: Essentials of Chinese philosophy and culture* (pp. 167-187). Honolulu: East-West Center Press.

Hsu, F. L. K. (1981). *Americans and Chinese: Passage to differences.* Honolulu: University of Hawaii Press.

Hsu, F. L. K. (1985). "The Chinese family: Relations, Problems, and therapy." In W. S. Tseng & D. Y. H. Wu (Eds.), *Chinese culture and mental health* (pp. 95-112). San Diego, CA: Academic Press.

Huang, S. H. (1993). *VPP students in Taipei: Stress, coping behavior, mental and physical health, and class climate.* Unpublished Master's thesis, Graduate School of Education, National Chengchi University. Taipei, Taiwan. (in Chinese)

Hurlock, E. B. (1964). *Child development*, 4th ed. New York: McGraw-Hill.

Hurlock, E. B. (1967). *Adolescent development*, 3rd ed. New York: McGraw-Hill.

Hwang, K. K. (1987). "Face and favor: The Chinese power game." *American Journal of Sociology*, 92, pp. 944-974.

Ingersoll, G. M. (1989). *Adolescents*, 2nd ed. Englewood Cliffs, NJ: Prentice Hall.

Jacob, E. (1987). "Traditions of qualitative research : A review." *Review of Educational Research*, 57, pp. 1-50.

Jacob, E. (1988). "Clarifying qualitative research: A focus on traditions." *Educational Researcher*, 17, pp. 16-24.

Jiao, S. L., Ji, G. P., Jing, Q. C. (1986). "Comparative study of behavioral qualities of only children and sibling children." *Child Development*, 57, pp. 357-361.

Kagan, J. (1978). "The child in the family." In A. S. Rossi, J. Kagan & T. K. Hareven (Eds.), *The family* (pp. 33-56). New York: Norton.

Kahle, L. R. (Ed.). (1983). *Social values and social change: Adaptation to life in America.* New York: Praeger.

Kenny, D. A. (1975). "Cross-lagged panel correlation: A test for spuriousness." *Psychological Bulletin*, 82, 887-903.

Kessler, R. C., Price, R. H., & Wortman, C. B. (1985). "Social factors in psychopathology: Stress, social support, and coping processes." *Annual Review of Psychology*, 36, pp. 531-572.

King, A. Y. C. (1991). "Kuan-hsi and network building: A sociological interpretation." *Daedalus*, Spring, pp. 63-84.

Kissinger, H. A. (1997). "The philosopher and the pragmatist." *Newsweek*, March 3, pp. 28-33.

Kleiman, S. L., Handal, P. J., & Enos, D. (1989). "Relationship between perceived family climate and adolescent adjustment." *Journal of Clinical Child Psychology*, 18, pp. 351-359.

Kluckhohn, C. (1951). "Values and value orientations in the theory of action." In T. Parsons & E. S. Shilds (Eds.), *Toward a general theory of action* (pp. 388-433). Cambridge, MA: Harvard University Press.

Kohlberg, L. (1969). "Stage and sequence: The cognitive-developmental approach to socialization." In D. A. Goslin (Ed.), *Handbook of socialization theory and research* (pp. 347-480). Chicago: Rand McNally.

Kohlberg, L. (1976). "Moral stages and moralization: The cognitive-developmental approach." In T. Lickona (Ed.), *Moral development and behavior: Theory, research, and social issues* (pp. 31-53). New York: Holt.

Kohlberg, L. (1981). *Essays in moral development, vol. I, The philosophy of moral development.* New York: Harper & Row.

Kohlberg, L. (1984). *Essays in moral development, vol. II, The psychology of moral development.* New York: Harper & Row.

Kohn, M. L. (1959). "Social class and parental values." *American Journal of Sociology*, 64, pp. 337-351.

Kurdek, L. A., & Fine, M. A. (1993). "The relation between family structure and young adolescents' appraisals of family climate and parenting behavior." *Journal of Family Issues*, 14, pp. 279-290.

Lamb, M. E. (1978). *Social and personality development.* New York: Knopf.

Lamb, M. E. (1981). "Fathers and child development: An integrative overview." In M. E. Lamb (Ed.), *The role of the father in child development* (2nd ed., pp. 1-70). New York: Wiley.

Lamb, M. E., & Bornstein, M. H. (1986). *Development in infancy* (2nd ed.) New York: Random House.

Lamborn, S.D., Mounts, N. S., Steinberg, S., & Dornbusch, S. M. (1991). "Patterns of competence and adjustment among adolescents from authoritative, authoritarian, indulgent,and neglectful families." *Child Development*, 62, pp. 1049-1065.

Larson, R. W. (1979). *The significance of solitude in adolescents lives.* Unpublished doctoral dissertation, University of Chicago.

Larson, R. W. (1983). "Adolescents daily experience with family and friends: Contrasting opportunity systems." *Journal of Marriage and the Family*, 45, pp. 739-750.

Lasswell, H., & Kaplan, A. (1965). *Power and society.* New Haven, CT: Yale University Press.

Lasswell, H., Lerner, D., & Montgomery, J. D. (Eds). (1976). *Values and development: Appraising Asian experience.* Cambridge, MA: MIT Press.

Lau, S., & Cheung, P. C. (1987). "Relations between Chinese adolescents' perception of parental control and organization and their perception of parental warmth." *Developmental Psychology*, 23, pp. 726-729.

Lau, S., Lew, W. J. F., Hau, K. T., Cheung, P. C., & Berndt, T. J. (1990). "Relations among perceived parental control, warmth, indulgence, and family harmony of Chinese in mainland China." *Developmental Psychology*, 26, pp. 674-677.

La Voie, J. C. (1976). "Ego identity formation in middle adolescence." *Journal of Youth and Adolescence*, 5, pp. 371-385.

Leahy, R. L. (1981). "Parental practices and the development of moral judgment and self-image disparity during adolescence." *Developmental Psychology*, 17, pp. 580-594.

Lefrancois, G. R. (1990). *The lifespan*, 3rd ed. Belmont, CA: Wadsworth.

Lei, T. (1980). *An empirical study of Kohlberg's theory and scoring system of moral development in Chinese society.* Unpublished bachelor's thesis. National Taiwan University, Taipei.

Lei, T. (1981). *The development of moral, political, and legal reasoning in Chinese societies.* Unpublished master's thesis. University of Minnesota, Minneapolis.

Lei, T. (1984). "A longitudinal study of moral judgment development in Taiwan: An interim report." In *The Sixth Interrnational Symposium on Asian Studies* (pp. 235-255). Hong Kong: International Center for Asian Studies.

Lei, T., & Cheng, S. W. (1984). *An empirical study of Kohlberg's theory and scoring system of moral judgment in Chinese society.* Unpublished manuscript, Harvard University, Center for Moral Education, Cambridge, MA.

Levinson, D. J., Darrow, C. N., Klein, E. B., Levinson, M. H., & McKee, B. (1978). *The seasons of a man's life.* New York: Knopf.

Lew, W. J. F. (1982). *Developmental psychology and education: Development and education of the whole person.* 6th printing, 1995. Taipei, TW: Taiwan Commercial Press. (in Chinese)

Lew, W. J. F. (1994). *Education and society.* Taipei, TW: Yuan Liu Publications, Inc. (in Chinese)

Li, Z. S. (1994). *The private life of Chairman Mao.* New York: Random House.

Lightfoot, S. L. (1983). *The good high school: Portrait of character and culture.* New York: Basic Books.

Lin, B. J., & Fan, L. M. (Eds.) (1990). *Education in mainland China*. Taipei, TW: Institute of International Relations, National Chengchi University.

Lin, Y. T. (1939). *My Country and My People*, revised ed. London: Heinemann.

Liu, A. P. L. (1990). "Aspects of Beijing's crisis management:The Tiananmen Square demonstration." *Asian Survey*, XXX, May, pp. 505-521.

Liu, C. (Ed.) (1973). *The way of the teacher*. Taipei, TW: Chung-hua Book Co. (in Chinese)

Lo, L. N. K. (1991). "State patronage of intellectuals in Chinese higher education." *Comparative Education Review*, 35, pp. 690-720.

Lonky, E., Kaus, C. R., & Roodin, P. A. (1984). "Life experience and mode of coping: Relation to moral judgment in adulthood." *Developmental Psychology*, 20, pp. 1159-1167.

Lytton, H., & Romney, D. M. (1991). "Parents' differential socialization of boys and girls: A Meta-analysis." *Psychological Bulletin*, 109, pp. 267-296.

Ma, H. K. (1988a). "The Chinese perspectives on moral judgment development." *International Journal of Psychology*, 23, pp. 201-227.

Ma, H. K. (1988b). "Objective moral judgment in Hong Kong, mainland China, and England." *Journal of Cross-Cultural Psychology*, 19, pp. 78-95.

Maccoby, E.E., & Martin, J. A. (1983)." Socialization in the context of the family: Parent-child interaction." In P. H. Mussen(Ed.), *Handbook of child psychology* (4th ed.) : Vol. 4. *Socialization, personality, and social development* (pp. 1-101). New York: Wiley.

Marcia, J. E. (1980). "Identity in adolescence." In J. Adelson (Ed.), *Handbook of adolescent psychology* (pp. 159-187). Toronto: Wiley.

Markus, H. R., & Kitayama, S. (1991). "Culture and self: Implications for cognition, emotion, and motivation." *Psychological Review*, 98, pp. 224-253.

Maslow, A. H. (1968). *Toward a psychology of being*, 2nd. ed. New York: Van Nostrand.

Maxwell, J.A. (1992). "Understanding and validity in qualitative research." *Harvard Educational Review*, 62, pp. 279-300.

McAdams, D. P. (1992). "The five-factor model in personality: A critical appraisal." *Journal of Personality*, 60, pp. 329-361.

McAdams, D. A., & St. Aubin, E. D. (1992). "A theory of generativity and its assessment through self-report, behavioral acts, and narrative themes in autobiography." *Journal of Personality and Social Psychology*, 62, pp. 1003-1015.

McClelland, D. C. (1961). *The achieving society*. Princeton, NJ: Van Nostrand.

McClelland, D. C., Atkinson, J. W., Clark, R. A., & Lowell, E. L. (1953). *The achievement motive*. New York: Appleton.

McCrae, R. R., & Costa, P. T., Jr. (1987). "Validation of the five-factor model of personality across instruments and observers." *Journal of Personality and Social Psychology*, 52, pp. 81-90.

Mead, M. (1953). "National character." In A. L. Kroeber (Ed.), *Anthropology today* (pp. 642-667).Chicago: University of Chicago Press.

Mei, Y. P. (1967). "The basis of social, ethical, and spiritual values in Chinese philosophy." In C. A. Moore (Ed.), *The Chinese mind: Essentials of Chinese philosophy and culture* (pp. 149-166). Honolulu: East-West Center Press.

Mershon, B., & Gorsuch, R. L. (1988). "Number of factors in the personality sphere: Does increase in factors increase predictability of real-life criteria?" *Journal of Personality and Social Psychology*, 55, pp. 675-680.

Messick, D. M., Bloom, S., Boldizar, J. P., & Samuelson, C. D. (1985). "Why we are fairer than others." *Journal of Experimental Social Psychology*, 21, pp. 480-500.

Ministry of Education(1997). *The final report of the evaluation committee on the junior high school graduates' voluntary promotion plan.* Taipei: Ministry of Education (in Chinese).

Mink, I. T., & Nihira, K. (1986). "Family life-styles and child behaviors: A study of direction of effects." *Developmental Psychology*, 22, pp. 610-616.

Mischel, W. (1976). *Introduction to personality*, 2nd ed. New York: Holt.

Mohan, M., & Hull, R. E. (Eds.) (1975). *Teaching effectiveness: Its meaning,assessment, and improvement.* Englewood Cliffs, NJ: Educational Technology.

Morey, A. I., & Zhou, N. Z. (1990). "Higher education in mainland China: An overview." In B. J. Lin & L. M. Fan (Eds.), *Education in mainland China* (pp. 67-91). Taipei, TW: Institute of International Relations, National Chengchi University.

Myers, D. G., & Ridl, J. (1979). "Can we all be better than average?" *Psychology Today*, 13, pp. 89-92.

Nathan, A. J., & Shi, T. (1993). "Cultural requisites for democracy in China: Findings from a survey." *Daedalus*, 122(Spring), pp. 95-123.

Nathan, A. J., & Shi, T. (1996). "Left and right with Chinese characteristics: Issues and alignments in Deng Xiaoping's China." *World Politics*, 48(July), pp. 522-550.

Nicholls, J. G., Cheung, P. C., Lauer, J., & Patashnick, M. (1989). "Individual differences in academic motivation: Perceived ability, goals, beliefs, and values." *Learning and Individual Differences*, 1, pp. 63-84.

Noller, P., Law, H., & Comrey, A. L. (1987). "Cattell, Comrey, and Eysenck personality factors compared: More evidence for the five robust factors?" *Journal of Personality and Social Psychology*, 53, pp. 775-782.

Ochse, R., & Plug, C. (1986). "Cross-cultural investigation of the validity of Erikson's theory of personality development." *Journal of Personality and Social Psychology*, 50, pp. 1240-1252.

O'Connell, A. N. (1976). "The relationship between life style and identity synthesis and resynthesis in traditional, neo-traditional, and non-traditional women." *Journal of Personality*, 44, pp. 675-688.

Owen, S. V., Blount, H. P., & Moscow, H. (1981). *Educational Psychology: An introduction*. Boston: Little Brown.

Pervin, L. A. (1985). "Personality: Current controversies, issues, and directions." *Annual Review of Psychology*, 36, pp. 83-114.

Piaget, J. (1932). *The moral judgment of the child*. London: Kegan Paul.

Plomin, R., McClearn, G. E., Pedersen, N. L., Nesselroade, J. R., & Bergeman, C.S. (1988). "Genetic influence on childhood family environment perceived retrospectively from the last half of the life span." *Developmental Psychology*, 24, pp. 738-745.

Po-yang (pen name) (1986). *The ugly Chinese*, 8th printing. Taipei, TW: Lin Pai Press. (in Chinese)

Procidano, M. E., & Heller, K. (1983). "Measures of perceived social support from friends and from family: Three validation studies." *American Journal of Community Psychology*, 11, pp. 1-24.

Pulkkinen, L. (1996). "Female and male personality styles: A typological and developmental analysis." *Journal of Personality and Social Psychology*, 70, pp. 1288-1306.

Pye, L. W. (1976). *Mao Tse-tung: The man in the leader*. New York: Basic Books.

Pye, L. W. (1985). *Asian power and politics: The cultural dimensions of authority*. Cambridge, MA: Belknap Press of Harvard University Press.

Pye, L. W. (1988). *The mandarin and the cadre: China's political cultures*. Ann Arbor: Center for Chinese studies, The University of Michigan.

Pye, L. W. (1990). "Tiananmen and Chinese political culture." *Asian Survey*, XXX, April, pp. 331-347.

Raskin, R., & Shaw, R. (1988). "Narcissism and the use of personal pronouns." *Journal of Personality*, 56, pp. 393-405.

Raskin, R., & Terry, H. (1988). "A principal-components analysis of the Narcissistic Personality Inventory and further evidence of its construct validity." *Journal of Personality and Social Psychology*, 54, pp. 890-902.

Rest, J. (1975). "Longitudinal study of the Defining Issues Test: A strategy for analyzing developmental change." *Developmental Psychology*, 11, pp. 738-748.

Rest, J. R. (1976). "New approaches in the assessment of moral judgment." In T. Lickona (Ed.), *Moral development and behavior: Theory, research, and social issues* (pp. 198-218). New York: Holt.

Rest, J. R. (1979). *Development in judging moral issues.* Minneapolis: University of Minnesota Press.

Rest, J.R., & Thoma, S. J. (1985). "Relation of moral judgment development to formal education." *Developmental Psychology*, 21, pp. 709-714.

Riesman, D. (1961). *The lonely crowd* (abridged ed. with a 1969 preface). 33rd printing, 1978. New Haven, CT: Yale University Press.

Roberts, G. C., Block, J. H., & Block, J. (1984). "Continuity and change in parents' child-rearing practices." *Child Development*, 55, pp. 586-597.

Rokeach, M. (1973). *The nature of human values.* New York: Free Press.

Rowe, D. C. (1981). "Environmental and genetic influences on dimensions of perceived parenting: A twin study." *Developmental Psychology*, 17, pp. 203-208.

Rowe, D. C., & Plomin, R. (1981). "The importance of nonshared (E_1) environmental influences in behavioral development." *Developmental Psychology*, 17, pp. 517-531.

Saltzstein, H. D. (1976). "Social influence and moral development: A perspective on the role of parents and peers." In T. Lickona (Ed.), *Moral development and behavior: Theory, research, and social issues* (pp. 253-265). New York: Holt.

Sampson, E. E. (1989). "The challenge of social change for psychology: Globalization and psychology's theory of the person." *American Psychologist*, 44, pp. 914-921.

Sanford, N. (1982). "Social psychology: Its place in personology." *American Psychology*, 37, pp. 896-903.

Schaefer, C., Coyne, J.C., & Lazarus, R. S.(1982). "The health-related functions of social support." *Journal of Behavioral Medicine*, 4, pp. 381-406.

Schaefer, E. S. (1959). "A circumplex model for maternal behavior." *Journal of Abnormal and Social Psychology*, 59, pp. 226-235.

Schiedel, D. G., & Marcia, J. E. (1985). "Ego identity, intimacy, sex role orientation, and gender." *Developmental Psychology*, 21, pp. 149-160.

Schwarcz, V. (1986-87). "Behind a partially open door: Chinese intellectuals and the post-Mao reform process." *Pacific Affairs*, 59, pp. 577-604.

Schwartz, S. H. (1992). "Universals in the content and structure of values: Theoretical advances and empirical tests in 20 countries." In M. Zanna (Ed.), *Advances in experimental social psychology* (Vol. 25) (pp. 1-65). New York: Academic Press.

Shambaugh, D. (1993). Introduction: The emergence of "Greater China." *China Quarterly*, December, pp. 653-659.

Shanghai Sex-Sociology Study Center. (1992). "The problem of sex among today's Chinese--- nationwide survey of "sex culture." *Chinese Education: A Journal of translation*, 25, Spring, pp. 56-67.

Shih, C. H. (1997). *The impact of Sun Yat-sen's nationalism on China's modernization.* Taipei, TW: Chang Lao-shih Press.

Shulman, S., & Prechter, E. (1989). "Adolescent perception of family climate and adaptation to residential schooling." *Journal of Youth and Adolescence*, 18, pp. 439-449.

Siegel,I. (Ed.) (1985). *Parental belief systems: The psychological consequences for children*. Hillsdale, NJ: Erlbaum.

Simon, D. F., & Kau, M. Y. M. (Eds.) (1992). *Taiwan: Beyond the economic miracle*. Armonk, NY: Sharpe.

Sinha, D., & Kao, H.S. R. (Eds.) (1988). *Social values and development: Asian perspectives*. Newbury Park, CA: Sage.

Snarey, J. R. (1985). "Cross-cultural universality of social-moral development: A critical review of Kohlbergian research." *Psychological Bulletin*, 97, pp. 202-232.

Solomon, R. H. (1971). *Mao's revolution and the Chinese political culture*. Berkeley: University of California Press.

Song, W. Z. (1985). "A preliminary study of the character traits of the Chinese. In W. S. Tseng & D. Y. H. Wu (Eds.), *Chinese culture and mental health* (pp. 47-55). San Diego, CA: Academic Press.

Spranger, E. (1923). *Kultur und erziehung*. Leipzig: Quelle & Meyer.

Sprecher, S., Sullivan, Q., & Hatfield, W. (1994). "Mate selection preferences: Gender differences examined in a national sample." *Journal of Personality and Social Psychology*, 66, pp. 1074-1080.

Staub, E. (Ed.) (1980). *Personality: Basic aspects and current research*. Englewood Cliffs, NJ: Prentice-Hall.

Sternberg, R. J., & Grajek, S. (1984). "The nature of love." *Journal of Personality and Social Psychology*, 47, pp. 312-329.

Stevenson, H.W. (1992). "Learning from Asian schools." *Scientific American*, December, pp. 70-76.

Stevenson, H. W., Chen, C. S., & Lee, S. Y. (1993). "Mathematics achievement of Chinese, Japanese,and American children: Ten years later." *Science, 253*, January, pp. 53-58.

Stevenson, H. W., & Stigler, J. W. (1992). *The learning gap.* New York: Summit Books.

Stewart, A. J., & Lykes, M. B. (1985). "Conceptualizing gender in personality theory and research." *Journal of Personality*, 53, pp. 93-101.

Stigler, J. W., Lee, S.Y., & Stevenson, H. W. (1987). "Mathematics classroom in Japan, Taiwan, and the United States." *Child Development*, 58, pp. 1272-1285.

Sun, L. K. (1985). *The deep structure of Chinese culture.* Hong Kong: Ji Shien Press. (in Chinese)

Tien, H.M. (1989). *The great transition: Political and social change in the Republic of China.* Stanford, CA: Hoover Institution Press, Stanford University.

Tolson, T. F. J., & Wilson, M. N. (1990). "The impact of two- and three-generational black family structure on perceived family climate." *Child Development*, 61, pp. 416-428.

Triandis, H. C., McCusker, C., & Hui, C. H. (1990). "Multimethod probes of individualism and collectivism." *Journal of Personality and Social Psychology*, 59, pp. 1006-1020.

Tu, W. M. (1991). "Cultural China: The periphery as the center." *Daedalus*, Spring, pp. 1-32.

Twenty-first Century Foundation. (1991). *A value survey report.* Taipei, TW: Twenty-first Century Foundation. (in Chinese).

Veroff, J., Reuman, D., & Feld, S. (1984). "Motives in American men and women across the adult life span." *Developmental Psychology*, 20, pp. 1142-1158.

Walker, L.J., & Moran, T. J. (1991). "Moral reasoning in a Communist Chinese society." *Journal of Moral Education*, 20, pp. 139-155.

Walters, J., & Walters, L. H. (1980). "Parent-child relationships: A review, 1970-1979." *Journal of Marriage and the Family*, 42, pp. 807-822.

Wang, G. W. (1991). "Among non-Chinese." *Daedalus*, Spring, pp. 135-157.

Werner, P. D., & Pervin, L.A. (1986). "The content of personality inventory items." *Journal of Personality and Social Psychology*, 51, pp. 622-628.

Westen, D. (1985). *Self and society: Narcissism, collectivism, and the development of morals*. Cambridge: Cambridge University Press.

White, L. T., III. (1988). "Do open doors open minds? Reforms and intellectuals." Paper presented at the *Seventeenth Sino-American Conference on Mainland China, June 5-11, Institute of International Relations*, National Chengchi University, Taipei, Taiwan, the Republic of China.

Wilson, R. W. (1981). "Moral behavior in Chinese society: A theoretical perspective." In R. W. Wilson, S. L. Greenblatt, & A. A. Wilson (Eds.), *Moral behavior in Chinese society* (pp. 1-20). New York: Praeger.

Witkin, H. & Goodenough, D.(1977). "Field dependence and interpersonal behavior." *Psychological Bulletin*, 84, pp. 661-689.

Woolfolk, A. E., & Nicolich, L. M. (1980). *Educational psychology for teachers*. Englewood Cliffs, NJ: Prentice-Hall.

Yang, K. S. (1981). "Social orientation and individual modernity among Chinese students in Taiwan." *Journal of Social Psychology*, 113, pp. 159-170.

Yang, K.S. (1986). "Chinese personality and its change." In M. H. Bond (Ed.), *The psychology of the Chinese people* (pp. 106-170). Hong Kong: Oxford University Press.

Yang, K. S. (1996). "Psychological transformation of the Chinese people as a result of societal modernization." In M. H. Bond (Ed.), *The handbook of Chinese psychology* (pp. 479-498). Hong Kong: Oxford University Press.

Yang, K. S., & Bond, M. H. (1990). "Exploring implicit personality theories with indigenous or imported constructs: The Chinese case." *Journal of Personality and Social Psychology*, 58, pp. 1087-1095.

Yin, Q. P., & White, G. (1994). "The marketisation of Chinese higher education: A critical assessment." *Comparative Education*, 30, pp. 217-237.

York, K. L., & John,O. P. (1992). "The four faces of Eve: A typological analysis of women's personality at midlife." *Journal of Personality and Social Psychology*, 63, pp. 494-508.

Youniss, J., & Smollar, J. (1985). *Adolescent relations with mothers, fathers, and friends*. Chicago: University of Chicago Press.

Yu, Y. S. (1996). "Popular election under missiles: Democracy vs. nationalism." *China Times*, March 29, p. 11. (in Chinese)

Zavalloni, M. (1980). "Values." In H. C. Triandis & R. W. Brislin (Eds.), *Handbook of cross-cultural psychology*, Vol. 5, *Social psychology* (pp. 73-120). Boston: Allyn & Bacon.

Zuroff, D. C. (1986). "Was Gordon Allport a trait theorist?" *Journal of Personality and Social Psychology*, 51, pp. 993-1000.

✦ ✦ ✦

SUBJECT INDEX

A

Academic degree or diploma, 220
Achievement, xiii, xviii, 12, 13, 19, 24,
  27, 47-49, 53, 67, 74, 75, 77, 84, 91,
  93, 96, 97, 109, 111, 113, 135, 136,
  166, 167, 171, 172, 174, 178, 180, 181,
  188, 192, 198, 199, 202, 210, 211, 217,
  219, 220, 229, 250, 258, 259, 287, 291,
  294, 295, 315, 318-320, 325, 328, 331,
  332, 335
  academic, 19, 67, 74, 75, 77, 84, 91,
    93, 96, 109, 166, 171, 172, 178, 181,
    188, 211, 217, 219, 220, 287, 291,
    295, 315, 319, 331
  motivation, xiii, xviii, 12, 111, 135,
    136, 138, 267, 318, 328, 335
  need for, 24, 47-49, 113, 135, 166,
    167, 229, 331
  surpassing others in, 211, 250
Adventurism, 7, 321
Agreeableness, 7, 215, 251, 260
Aggressiveness, xiv, 137, 318
Altruism, 138, 217, 252, 300, 332, 334
Americans and Chinese, xvii, 75, 131,
  133, 325, 326
Ambitions and aspirations, 9, 208, 234,
  261, 321, 322
Authoritarianism, 7, 60, 63, 68, 136,
  139, 147, 149, 211, 215, 223, 227, 228,
  314, 318, 321, 325, 329
Authority, xiii, xiv, 1-3, 17, 20, 26, 28,
  33, 34, 42, 47, 66, 68, 81, 85, 93-96,
  101-105, 112-114, 119, 120, 136-140,
  210, 211, 214, 218, 219, 253, 258, 259,
  261, 267, 285, 297, 307, 313, 317, 318,
  320, 326-329, 331-334
Authority-directed, 2, 85, 93, 94,
  138-140, 259, 318, 326, 328, 329, 333

B

Beauty in woman, 221, 254
Behavior, xii, xiv, 3, 9, 11-16, 18-23, 25,
  26, 29, 33, 35, 40, 41, 50, 51, 53, 59,
  123, 137, 139, 157, 214, 216, 265,
  267-273, 275, 280, 299, 307, 312, 322,
  323, 327
Being a good wife and mother, 120,
  133, 218, 244, 253
Being respected by others, 210, 261
Being useful to society, 211
Benevolence, xiv, 258, 259, 320
Big Five, 6, 7, 260
Breakthrough in career, 212, 237, 250,
  261

C

Cautiousness, 7, 60, 147, 149, 164, 223,
  227, 228, 230, 321
Central focus, 324
Change, 9, 38, 43, 68, 81, 94, 101, 102,
  113, 114, 116, 121, 137, 157, 168, 178,
  183, 198, 201, 209, 224, 236-240, 262,
  268, 291, 292, 299, 307, 315, 317, 322, 325,
  330
  personality and value, 9, 102, 121, 209,
    237, 238, 330
Character, xii, xiii, xv, xviii, 3, 8, 29, 31,
  107, 187, 212, 219, 220, 243, 245, 248,
  253, 262, 322, 324, 328, 334
Cheng Yen, 327
Chi, 21-25, 29, 30, 33-35, 38, 40, 41, 47,

373

✦   ✦   ✦

NAME INDEX

A

Adams, G. R., 175, 349
Allison, S. T., 151, 349, 350
Allport, G. M., 349, 371
American Psychiatric Association, 125, 349
Argyle, M., 301, 306, 349
Arsenio, W. F., 12, 354
Atkinson, J. W., 135, 349, 363
Atkinson, P., 349

B

Baltes, P. B., 155, 349
Bateson, P., 241, 349
Baumrind, D., 49, 51, 57, 63, 350
Bee, H. L., 156, 266, 350
Beggan, J. K., 151, 350
Bell, R., 11, 331 350, 357
Benedict, R., 207, 350
Bergeman, C. S., 11, 54, 365
Berliner, D. C., 332, 350
Berndt, T. J., xx, 2, 21, 50, 53, 55, 56, 302, 307, 350, 360
Berry, J. W., 5, 350, 351
Birren, J. E., 350
Blasi, A., 275, 280, 351
Block, J., 16, 50, 151, 351, 366
Bloom, S., 150, 363
Blount, H. P., 156, 365
Boldizar, J. P., 150, 363
Bond, M. H., xx, 5-7, 208, 249, 255, 256, 300, 351, 357, 370, 371
Borkenau, P., 150, 260, 351
Brabeck, M., 142, 150, 327, 351
Bracey, G. W., 332, 351
Braithwaite, V. A., 208, 259, 351

Brislin, R. W., 6, 21, 65, 351, 371
Brody, L. R., 142, 351
Brunk, M. A., 11, 352
Buss, D. M., 241, 243, 245-249, 352
Byrne, D., 136, 352

C

Cairns, R. B., 352
Campbell, D. T., 311, 352
Cattell, R. B., 6, 352, 357
Chan, W. T., xi, 135, 281, 298, 352
Chen, C. S., 64, 75, 332, 352, 355, 369
Chen, S. C., 64, 352
Chen, T. H. E., 75, 352
Cherry, F., 136, 352
Cheung, P. C., xx, 21, 50, 51, 55, 56, 350, 352, 360, 364
Chinese Culture Connection, 208, 249, 256, 353
Chou, E., xx, 116, 353
Chow, T. T., 115, 327, 353
Chu, G. C., 301, 353
Clark, R. A., 363
Coates, S., 142, 353
Colby, A., 353
Comrey, A. L., 6, 364
Conger, J. J., 15, 175, 353
Costa, P. T., Jr., 6, 238, 353, 363
Coyne, J. C., 301, 367
Croll, E., 16, 353
Cronbach, L. J., 59, 353

D

Daniels, D., 11, 31, 353
Darling-Hammond, L., 331, 354
Davin, D., 12, 16, 42, 64, 353, 354

✦   ✦   ✦

CHINESE STUDIES